The Craft and Context of Translation

THE CRAFT AND CONTEXT OF TRANSLATION

A Critical Symposium

EDITED BY

WILLIAM ARROWSMITH

AND

ROGER SHATTUCK

Anchor Books
Doubleday & Company, Inc.
Garden City, New York

The Craft and Context of Translation was originally published by the University of Texas Press. The Anchor Books edition is published by arrangement with the editors.

Postscript to a translation of *The Odyssey* by Robert Fitzgerald is in two parts. Part I was originally published in *Yearbook of Comparative and General Literature*, Number 11, 1962, Copyright © 1962 by The Comparative Literature Committee of Indiana University. Part II first appeared in the Anchor edition of *The Odyssey*, published January 1963, Copyright © 1963 by Robert Fitzgerald.

Anchor Books Edition: 1964

Library of Congress Catalog Card Number 64-16244

We gratefully acknowledge permission to quote from the following works:

Columbia University Press—"Tale of Igor's Campaign," translated by Roman Jakobson, from *Slavic Languages: A Condensed Survey* (1955). Reprinted by permission of Columbia University Press.

Grove Press, Inc.—Excerpt from "Heliodora," translated by Hilda Doolittle, from *Selected Poems of Hilda Doolittle*. Copyright © 1957 by Norman Holmes Pearson, and excerpt from "Iphigeneia in Aulis," translated by Hilda Doolittle, from *Collected Poems of Hilda Doolittle*. Copyright 1925 by Norman Holmes Pearson. Reprinted by permission of Norman Holmes Pearson and Grove Press, Inc.

Harcourt, Brace & World, Inc.—Excerpt from "Oedipus Rex," translated by Dudley Fitts and Robert Fitzgerald, from *Oedipus Rex: An English Version* (1955). Excerpt from *Oedipus at Colonnus*, translated by Robert Fitzgerald (1941). Excerpt from Aristophanes, *The Birds*. Copyright © 1957, translated by Dudley Fitts. Reprinted by permission of Harcourt, Brace & World, Inc.

Alfred A. Knopf, Inc.—Excerpt from "An Elegy" (Kiang Kang-Hu), translated by Witter Bynner, from *The Jade Mountain* by Witter Bynner. Copyright 1929 by Alfred A. Knopf, Inc. Reprinted by permission of Alfred A. Knopf, Inc.

Michigan State University Press—Excerpt from "Hippolytus," translated by Rex Warner, from *Three Greek Tragedies*. Reprinted by permission of The Michigan State University Press.

New Directions—Excerpt from Li Po, *"The River Merchant's Wife: A Letter,"* translated by Ezra Pound. Copyright 1926, 1954 by Ezra Pound. Reprinted by permission of New Directions.

Ivan Obolensky, Inc.—Excerpt from Homer's *Iliad* (Book XXI), translated by Christopher Logue, in *Songs* by Christopher Logue. Copyright © 1960 by McDowell, Obolensky, Inc. Reprinted by permission of Ivan Obolensky, Inc.

Penguin Books Ltd.—Excerpt from "Hippolytus," translated by Philip Vellacott, from *Three Plays* (Penguin Classics, 1953). Reprinted by permission of Penguin Books Ltd.

The Society of Authors—Excerpt from Dante's *Inferno* (Book V), translated by Laurence Binyon. Reprinted by permission of The Society of Authors.

University of Michigan—Excerpt from Aristophanes' *The Birds*, translated by William Arrowsmith. Copyright © 1961 by The University of Michigan Press. Excerpt from Aristophanes' *The Acharnians*, translated by Douglass Parker (1961). Reprinted by permission of The University of Michigan Press.

Introduction

Ten of the essays in this book were originally delivered at a Symposium on Translation held at the University of Texas in November, 1959. If this symposium had any predominant purpose, it was to bring together a group of professional translators sharing a stake in their craft but each committed to a different language or with a different purchase on the problem. With such a group we hoped both to obviate sterile polemic about principles and to get the kind of fruitful disagreement that sometimes comes from the serious shoptalk of craftsmen working at diverse but related jobs. On the ground that nothing is less valuable or interesting than theorizing about principles in the absence of examples, we asked each speaker to let his generalizations flower among his particulars or not at all. For the sake of good conversation and self-confidence, we deliberately excluded from the panel all machine translators, logicians, meta-linguists, and literal-minded scholars. Our conference was a closed shop of practicing literary craftsmen, or very nearly so.

Finally, in order to set the essays of the symposium proper into a general framework and to make the book more useful, we decided to commission a second group of papers—those forming the second section of the book. These were all to be devoted to the social, political, economic, and cultural context in which the translator's craft is practiced: translation from the viewpoint of the professional 'trade' translator and the editor; the relation between translation and the operatic libretto; the tangle of copyright laws which hedge translation, and so on. For reasons of time and space only a small number of the contextual aspects could be adequately discussed. And though we have tried to select aspects that seemed crucial or representative, several important matters were slighted or neglected. Three problems, it seems to us, deserve further discussion: first, the difficult question of subsidization and adoption of official or quasi-official controls in translation; second, the disturbing disappearance of translation as a technique of language-instruction in our schools and universities; and third, the deep, but insufficiently appreciated, relevance of historical considerations to contemporary 'principles' of translation and to the debate between 'fidelity' and 'freedom.' An introductory note cannot compensate for inadequate treatment of these matters, but the nature of the problem can at least be defined and clarified.

Translation takes place within a social and political context, a fact whose large implications are only now, in time of overwhelming cultural Cold War, becoming fully apparent. What are the practical implications of this fact? On the face of it, the business of translation is considerably like the knotty economic question of exports and imports. An active culture flourishes on a loose balance of payments. Yet, as in economics, an essentially political problem now presents itself (and Mr. Werner Winter in his essay on 'Translation as Political Action' implicitly raises it): Will that balance best establish itself by the free interplay of individual authors, translators, publishers, and readers in an open market, or should a central agency co-ordinate and direct these various elements? Can anything be done to raise the quality of commercial translation and the status of the commercial translator? Political traditions in the West commit us to a policy of modified *laisser faire,* but obviously we have a mixed culture as we have a mixed economy, incorporating pressures and regulators whose operation we are reluctant to recognize. The government, business, industry, universities, and foundations already underwrite limited areas of cultural exchange and translation, and in the future this commitment will almost certainly be extended. All that can finally be said about the situation is that it needs constant attention from alert minds. Any radical change in the haphazard and wasteful process by which, say, a Flemish novel or a Chinese poem reaches publication in New York would probably do considerable damage. A Department of Culture in Washington, a Central Committee of Editors, or a Translators' Union with a closed shop has no place in our way of doing things. Still, the arts and the practical circumstances of translation have run into a period of confusion in the midst of significant revival.

Confusion is both economically and culturally expensive. For this reason some modification of prevailing market conditions is highly desirable and perhaps inevitable. The problems of commercial translation are, of course, extremely complex. But it is ironical that, in a period in which literary translation has notably revived and Cold War politics more and more require ambitious translation projects, there should have been a sharp and tangible deterioration in the quality of commercial translation. This, as Denver Lindley points out ('The Editor's Problem'), is the direct consequence of a market 'squeeze': confronted with rising costs, the necessity of competing on the domestic market, paying foreign rights and a translator's fee. But the pathetic smallness of the translator's fee—approximately $400 for a book—handicaps the foreign book even more fatally by furnishing it with a poor or inadequate translation. True, many translators do their work as a labor of love; but many do not, and the number of books wholly translated by dictaphone—that is, with dictaphone style and grace—is noticeably and understandably on the rise. Publishers, in short, tend to get what they pay for—which is not much. The translator's prestige, of course, corresponds to his pay. It is low, much too low, in part because the supply of translators in some fields outruns demand, in part because far too few publishers have been concerned enough to demand really skilled, professional translators. Thus among the general public and publishers alike, hacks can pass for translators because of the common belief that translation is nothing more than hackwork anyway. It is doubtless with a view to eradicating this belief that the P.E.N. Committee on Translation is now attempting to ensure that the translator receives proper credit for his work, and its campaign is a welcome sign that the literary community recognizes the problem. But the prejudice is a deep one, and will not easily be altered by superficial measures. Indeed, until publishers pay their translators better than their secretaries, and until good and well-known writers again undertake part-time translation for pay (as they now undertake part-time teaching), there is little likelihood of any substantial improvement in the translator's income and condition.

One innovation does suggest itself, and that is a program—whether sponsored by the government or a foundation is immaterial—whereby able young writers and poets would be offered fellowships for promising projects in translation. Just as the Ford Foundation presently offers fellowships designed to place poets and writers in meaningful contact with the physical theater, so writers might, given suitable encouragement, be induced to try their hands at translation, thereby shedding new luster on an ancient profession and bringing it fresh skills of approach and perception. Certainly there is nothing novel in proposing that writers should also be part-time translators; from Dryden and Pope onward writers have been our major translators, and both English literature and the writer have in most cases benefited from the arrangement. (Indeed, one of the major reasons for the rise of the pedantic scholarly 'transcription' was the abandonment of translation by the writer at the close of the nineteenth century). Why, one wants to know, should such a resource be written off, or ceded to the universities? Corresponding to such a program, there might well be established a center which could operate as a clearing house for information, distribute expert recommendations to publishers about books that should be translated, and offer a form of loan toward translation of works whose qualities would not be persuasive to editors until available in English. A series of such measure could gradually improve the translator's status. Still more important, the advantages they might bring our culture as a whole, both as a positive aid in Cold War politics and as a defense against cultural provincialism, make such a scheme worth serious and imaginative consideration.

A second matter. None of the essays included here touches on one aspect of translation we believe to be of prime importance: its place in education. Traditionally the training of the mind in Europe has rested on the study of mathematics, history, and languages. Languages were learned together, not in isolation, and the basic exercises of translation kept eyes and ears attuned to subtleties in both the native and the foreign idiom. Probably the most systematic practice arose in France with the *version latine*; this translation from Latin into French was read just as much for the elegance of the French as for the accuracy of the transposition of thought. In other words the study of Latin was a means of learning both Latin and French. The 'old-fashioned' methods of teaching French and German in English-speaking countries often served the same purposes, even though the student was supposed to know his own language already.

Psychology and structural linguistics, as applied to language programs for missionaries and military personnel, have undermined that tradition, with the result that the study of modern languages today, in Europe as well as the United States, has begun to change its emphasis radically. Two things have happened. First, one learns a new language insofar as possible by itself, without relying on one's native tongue, in a process of accumulating repeated speech patterns as a child does. And second, in order to facilitate this very basic and elemental process of learning, the samples of language learned are kept as simple as possible—usually patterns having to do with everyday events like eating, meeting and greeting, buying and traveling, and the classroom. Texts are written specially to conform to these two conditions; literature comes later—so much that many students never encounter it. And, obviously, translation is either totally excluded as a dangerous heresy or kept to a strict minimum as a device to verify at intervals that a student understands the noises he is parroting.

Now, there is a certain gratification, even for the most cultivated of minds, in being able to follow a taped conversation between two 'native' speakers, and to give a barber proper instructions in a foreign country, and to know how to ask directions when one is lost without creating an international incident. Somewhere along the way these things must be learned, and probably taught. But must the price paid for this up-to-date language instruction be the sacrifice of all the benefits of the old system? Language teachers in the United States protest when they have to teach English to their students. Yet that is exactly one of the things they should be doing. And they protest when the text in the reader is too difficult, too literary, too subtle for an elementary student, though he may be in a 'university.' Everything goes by the board to make way for fluency in the spoken language. The careful translation of a literary text comes, if ever, in a 'literature course' where a student is already supposed to know the second language well. The language laboratory, which has become to the humanities program of many universities what the defense budget has become to the federal government, does offer enormous opportunities for learning the spoken language. But the language lab has grown so rapidly into an end in itself that the professional organization of modern language teachers has been obliged to recognize a dissident group trying to adapt laboratory methods to the teaching of literature. For that is what has been lost. Is it some kind of misplaced democratic ideal that has filled our language texts with vernacular idioms, incorrect forms, banal anecdotes based on vocabulary counts, and vulgarisms? Poems, fables, and proverbs have been, not bowdlerized, but simply eliminated in favor of synthetic texts written by 'experts.' Listen to Thoreau on the subject, in the chapter of *Walden* entitled 'Reading':

> Books must be read as deliberately as they were written. It is not enough even to be able to speak the language of that nation by which they were written, for there is a memorable interval between the spoken and the written language, the language heard and the language read. The one is commonly transitory—a sound, a tongue, a dialect merely, almost brutish, and we learn it unconsciously, like the brutes, of our mothers. The other is the maturity and experience of that: if that is our mother tongue, this is our father tongue, a reserved and select expression, too significant to be heard by the ear, for which we must be born again in

> order to speak. The crowds of men who merely spoke the Greek and Latin tongues in the Middle Ages were not entitled by the accident of birth to read the works of genius written in those languages, for these were not written in that Greek or Latin they knew, but in the select language of literature.

Interpreters, travelers, diplomats, and businessmen may have to learn a new mother tongue, but what business do our universities have teaching it to the exclusion of the father tongue? Mature students need and deserve both. Translation is one of the most ancient disciplines whose practice demands at least that the text dealt with be more than a succession of inanities and that teacher and student alike engage constantly in perfecting their command of two languages, their own and another.

The irony of all this, of course, is that we are in the midst of a great revival of translation. Not only are all kinds of ancient and classic texts being translated anew into English (and the same goes for several other languages), but modern works are shunted from one language to another with dazzling, though often misdirected, speed. Meanwhile, students in Europe as well as in the United States are being subjected to an insane process of learning an artificial language of phonetics before learning a real foreign language. If the order of things for infants is from speech to reading and writing, we adults do not all have to become as little children in order to learn a new tongue. Yet with the best intentions in the world, and with demonstrable success in its restricted goals, this is what we are being sold. The new theories of language instruction have a good deal to offer in the way of self-instruction and intensive learning of speech patterns. But they slight the supreme flower of language: *literature*. And they contrive to make translation look like worthless drudgery.

It would be enormously helpful if there existed a literate and comprehensive history of translation—a work that should ideally demonstrate true mastery of technics, linguistics, history of ideas, social history, and literary values. Even the most cursory reflection on such works as the Latin Vulgate, or Locke in French, or the English Bible makes it clear that translation is an activity ranging from individual discipline at one end of the scale to cultural conquest and appropriation at the other. The implications of this simple fact are not always recognized. An excellent case, for instance, might be made for treating Plautus, Vergil, Dante, Chaucer, and Montaigne as translators of genius; in the same way Latin literature as a whole could profitably and meaningfully be studied as translators' literature. A recent editorial in the *Times Literary Supplement* states the case in the bluntest terms: 'Two of the greatest developments in modern history are directly traceable to translations, the Reformation and the Renaissance: the one to the Bible and the other to the Greek and Latin classics.' Is it too much to hope, in an age when literary criticism and the history of ideas have become academic heavy industries, that serious study of translation as a cultural activity of moment might attract scholars? But as things stand now, intelligent comments on translation—a pamphlet by J. M. Cohen, a book in French by Georges Mounin, a duplicated report of a P.E.N. conference in Rome, some of the papers in Professor Brower's *On Translation*—tend to be unavailable or scattered, tucked away in odd corners, and their arguments diffused. The crucial, comprehensive volume of pioneering scholarship has yet to be written.

What might such a work teach us? For one thing, it would set contemporary practice, along with its unstated premises, in an illuminating historical perspective. Thus it could obviate the sterile polemics and verbal arguments about 'principles' that now disfigure and vex discussion. Translation, after all, is a general rubric for a wide range of very different activities, at once an art, a science, and a skill. Identifiable 'genres' come easily to mind: the literal 'trot' (or 'transposition,' as Mr. Carne-Ross calls it); the scholarly-genteel or belletristic translation; the 'free' version; the 'adaptation'; the 're-creation'; the 'imitation' (in Robert Lowell's sense); and so on. Each of these different 'genres' reflects a basic difference in function; each is good or bad according to its mode, and it is as idle to blame, say, a free version for not being literal (and vice versa) as it is to blame chalk for not being cheese. But if everyone recognizes the distinctions in principle, very few in fact observe them. A critic may in all other respects be an eminently fair-minded man, but confront him with a translation that violates his 'principles,' and he turns fanatically monist, sternly legislating his view as the only right one and condemning those who fail his expectations as willfully perverse or stupid. Indeed, so little agreement is there these days on translation, and so little is the distinction of 'genres' understood, that almost any article, any review, on the subject is apt to be a piece of barely disguised special pleading, insistently urging that a particular 'genre' be officially canonized. What is therefore desperately needed is patient, persuasive elaboration of the principles appropriate to different 'genres' as each one has found historical expression, as well as an awareness of their differing functions and their respective virtues and limitations. Lacking such a study, we are condemned to go on pointlessly and passionately demanding that a given translation perform functions it was never designed to perform.

Our notions of translation are, in short, profoundly uneducated; they lack historical perspective. Thus arguments about principles become verbal because the principles in question reflect, not facts, but disguised definitions, framed with only the slightest reference to actual historical practice. Because we regard our principles as *self-evident* and are unaware of the prejudices underlying them, we tend to assume, quite unwarrantably, that historical practice must support our case. Put it this way. For more than a century now there has been something like a dominant (but by no means absolute, and now increasingly threatened) consensus that the proper business of translation is to give us the original. By this is meant the making of a version which clings as closely as possible to the original without fatally endangering English style and syntax—a version, that is, whose primary virtue is fidelity and which regards elegance and grace as desirable, but, when they conflict with fidelity, dispensable. On the face of it this view is supported by two cogent considerations. First, it seems to enjoy the sanction of common sense, to appear self-evident (what on earth is translation *for*, we tend to think, if not to give us the original?). Second, it is a reasonable description of the actual possibilities in translating from one European language to another, since between languages which share a common culture, fidelity is both possible and easy. Against the first point it can be argued that common sense is a dubious ally, since it readily—and wrongly—assumes that between original work and translation the relationship is that which it posits between reality and art: photographic likeness. Against the second point it is enough to observe that, as cultural and temporal differences grow (as in the case of classical and oriental literature), the prospects for fidelity become increasingly bleak. What both arguments obscure is that the view of translation in question is precisely a theory and nothing more: a theory of specific purpose and therefore marked limitations, and finally no more self-evident than any other theory or 'genre.'

We should recognize, that is, that this dominant theory is neither particularly commonsensical (despite its appeal to the ordinary man's notion of translation—as literal copy), nor even old. It is in point of fact extremely recent, and its principles are radically opposed to the practice of previous ages, especially the great flowerings of translation in Renaissance Europe and Augustan Rome. In genre, it is unmistakably an academic theory of translation and ought, for clarity's sake, to be recognized as such. Its chief practitioners have always been scholars rather than literary men; it has consistently reflected the scholarly insistence upon loyalty to truth, accuracy, and fidelity; and it is actually little more than scholarly *arete* and attitudes adapted into a theory of translation. Originally intended to perform a modest scholarly task—the *haute vulgarisation* of ancient and foreign texts for a rising bourgeoisie, a task increasingly felt to be beyond the competence of the literary amateur—it gradually extended its claims until it came to be nearly synonymous with translation itself. And as the power and prestige of the scholar grew, the literary man more and more lost his traditional monopoly of translation. This is particularly true of the classics, but modern languages have suffered increasingly as writers and translators have been drawn into a university environment and lost their free-lance status. Victorian translation, for instance, is unique in being almost entirely a scholarly product, the work of academic rather than literary translators, a fact too frequently forgotten. So total has the triumph of academic theory been, so thoroughly has it suppressed rival genres or driven them to the wall, that its principles have finally come to seem self-evident; and for this reason it has proven exceptionally tenacious. The scholar has been able to maintain his position as translator to the age by using the massive weight of his own expert authority to police his theory and discredit his rivals. (What does it mean, one might ask in passing, that the two authors of this introduction are writers who earn their bread in an academic community? It probably further demonstrates the universities' hungry assimilation of all cultural activities, from defense of traditional values to passionate revisionism.)

In a period deferential to expert authority and impressed by a show of 'scientific' accuracy, rival genres were easily discredited. And none was more easily discredited than the 'literary' mode—that great genre created and developed by generations of writers and poet-scholars from Hellenistic times on, and which dominated European literature until the last century.[1] The differences between these two genres are, of course, immense, but the essential difference lies in their attitude to present and past, familiar and alien. Unlike his literary rival, the academic translator characteristically attempts to think and feel his way into the forms and experience of his original, not with an eye to re-creating them in his own terms, but rather bending and even distorting his own language into the shape of the original. That is, the spirit of his work is essentially *antiquarian,* motivated by a feeling of deep historical piety and empathy, but directed always more at the understanding of the past than the delight and illumination of the present. If, at its worst, academic translation is conceived in an archaizing and literal-minded spirit that destroys both liveliness and urgency, at its best (as in Jebbs' *Sophocles* and Donald Frame's *Montaigne*) it is a valuable form of scholarship and textual understanding. But in either case the final product is quite unlike the literary version, where the crucial goal is the *re-creation* of the past; by rendering an ancient or an alien experience contemporary or familiar, the translator renews it, and this

[1] In the Appendix we have gathered a group of representative statements of the 'literary' translator's position, ranging in time from Cicero to Pope, and in attitude from the extreme permissiveness of Cowley to the more modest freedom allowed by Samuel Johnson. The collection could be greatly expanded (and it is our hope that it may stimulate a second volume of collected texts on translation). But our purpose here was merely to show in a brief collection of classical statements how much the literary tradition of translation diverges from academic tradition, and how very recent is the domination of academic translation. In some sense, of course, academic translation has always been with us, and for obvious reasons. But by and large it has flourished in the past only when strict accuracy was mandatory (as it usually is in both religion and philosophy), or when fidelity was easily possible and compatible with elegance (as in Hoby's translation of Castiglione's *Courtier*).

renewal is the heart of his labor. This is why literary translators are, to the acute distress of scholars, so often careless of the literal words of their originals, and so attentive to the spirit (by which is often meant the meaning of the original to the translator's time rather than its meaning to its own). Both genres possess the deficiencies appropriate to their basic purposes and chosen loyalties, and the exponents of either genre are naturally quicker to notice the cost of their rivals' practice than their own. Scholars will presumably go on echoing Bentley's complaint against Pope's *Iliad* ('Charming . . . but you must not call it Homer'), and literary men will almost certainly reply by pointing out that most academic translation is inherently stillborn. And both will almost certainly be right.

But because the popular notion of translation-as-literal-copy tends to support the academic theory, it is literary translation whose principles are not understood today and which therefore stands in need of friendly defense. Here, for instance, is Nietzsche in a classic statement of the traditional literary view:

> One can judge the degree of historical sense possessed by an age in the way it makes translations and tries to assimilate past periods and literatures. The French of Corneille's time, even the French of the Revolution, appropriated Roman antiquity as we no longer have the nerve to do—thanks to our 'higher' historical sense. As for the Romans, how violently and yet naively they appropriated everything of value and sublimity in the Greek world of the past! How they translated that literature into the Roman present! With what conscious unconcern they brushed away the wing-dust of the butterfly-moment! This was the way Horace now and then translated Alcaeus or Archilochus; in which Propertius translated Callimachus and Philetas (in *my* opinion, the equals of Theocritus). What did it matter to them that the original poet had experienced a certain feeling and expressed that feeling in a poem?

> As poets, they had no use for that prying antiquarianism which is a condition of the 'historical sense'; as poets, they simply removed personal traits, names, details of a particular city, coast, or century in its dress and masks, and proceeded to put the present and the Roman in their place. They seem to us to be asking: 'Shouldn't we make the old new for ourselves, relate *ourselves* to it? Shouldn't we be allowed to breathe our own spirit into this dead body? Because it *is* dead now: how loathesome is everything dead!' They, of course, were ignorant of the joys of the 'historical sense'; what was past and alien was a nuisance to them, and as Romans, it was an incitement to Roman conquest. In fact, they conquered what they translated—and not only by omitting the historical. No, they even added allusions to the present; above all, they struck out the name of the original poet and inserted their own in its place, not with a feeling of theft but with the good conscience of the *imperium Romanum*.[2]

And Nietzsche's intuition here is surely correct. *This,* one recognizes immediately, is just the proud, violent, appropriating spirit in which the great classics of literary translation must have been done; *this* is how it was, not only with Horace and Philetas and the Alexandrian scholar-poets, but with Golding, Chapman, Urquhart, Adlington, and North; and also in our own day with Pound's *Homage to Sextus Propertius* and Robert Lowell's 'imitations.' It is this spirit, and not merely a difference of talent, that separates literary translation so sharply from the academic translation of the modern period.

But Nietzsche is also right in emphasizing the competitive element, the writer's belief that the greatest works of the past are not merely models to be imitated but achievements to be surpassed. It was in precisely this

[2] *Fröhliche Wissenschaft,* 83.

spirit of emulation and rivalry that Plautus and Terence 'translated' Menander and Greek New Comedy, that Vergil 'translated' Homer, and Dante in turn 'did' Vergil. These poets are, as it were, competitors of the classic, cultural translators who typically take a past greatness at its peak and attempt to struggle that greatness across time and space into their own culture, there to domesticate it and, if possible, surpass it. For obvious reasons such attempts have always required the radical boldness and pride of genius, and 'translation' may seem like stretching things or too tame a word for the effort involved (though it is our own modern usage that had made of translation a tame affair). But if we readily see the originality of these attempts, it is time again to see that they are only extreme, and extremely great, examples of the old literary tradition of translation—a tradition which, as a rule, refused to draw invidious distinctions between 'original' work and 'translation' and which regarded fidelity as a scribe's virtue. Translation, that is, was a crucial cultural device—and one which often enjoyed a corresponding dignity—for the simple reason that it enhanced the present by giving life to the past. Hence the agent of that enhancement was placed on equal terms with the original poet because both were thought of as doing the same thing: turning experience—whether individual or national did not matter—to life-giving advantage. Since formal beauty as well as content was highly regarded, there was no necessary distinction of talent to be made between poet and translator: both were required to triumph over their material, and in success were therefore equal.

Needless to say, translation of this kind will inevitably offend the scholar's piety to the past[3] and impress him as

[3] Because scholars tend to exaggerate the claims and rights of the past as opposed to the present, they often create the very problems they later come to regard, correctly, as 'insoluble.' In no case is this clearer than in the area of literary 'influence' and 'borrowing.' Thus in dealing with Plautus and Terence the standard scholarly problem is the assessment of the indebtedness ('con-

a typical literary *hybris*. And the writer might justifiably reply that no higher respect to the past can be shown than that which treats it with the seriousness and urgency of life. In our own time the literary genre of translation has been revived, but so profound has been the scholar's hold on the imagination of the age that the revival has usually seemed a heresy and its principles paradoxical. Indeed, among many scholars it is still suspected that 'free' translation is something first invented, with characteristic perversity, by Ezra Pound, who is, in fact, nothing more than the latest exponent of a millennial tradition (though the hostility his name arouses is an indication of how lamentably that tradition has been eclipsed).

Nietzsche, of course, seems to imply that the great literary translations of the past depended largely upon their positive lack of the 'historical sense.' But when he speaks of the historical sense possessed by an age, he means, not modern culture as a whole, but precisely that spirit of antiquarian piety that characterizes modern scholarship and academic translation. For if the scholar dominates the age, it cannot be inferred that the scholar's historical sense is typical of the period, except perhaps in a taste for fake archaism or historical novels. Certainly academic translation *assumes* the popular existence of a 'historical sense,' but anybody who has ever had the experience of teaching, say, the *Iliad* in the translation of Lang, Leaf and Myers (an archaizing translation if ever there was one) or any standard anthology version of *Aucassin et Nicolette*, knows

---

taminatio') to Greek New Comedy on the part of the Latin writers. But the problem only arises because scholars uncritically retroject into antiquity their own (basically Romantic) notions of literary 'originality' and 'property.' They fail to see, that is, that Plautus and Terence are precisely 'translators' in the Nietzschean sense, and that the problems of 'originality' and 'indebtedness' are radically altered by this fact. Indeed, if scholars could only widen their sense of both 'translation' and 'originality,' many of the problems presently gathered under the rubric of *Quellenforschungen* would disappear or assume different—and more meaningful—guise.

to his cost how little historical sense, or even interest, most students possess. Indeed, how could it possibly be otherwise? Most academic translations tend, in fact, to threaten the development of the student's historical sense by systematically shutting him off from a *literary* encounter with his text. An archaizing translation of Homer, for instance, is useful only to a teacher who proposes to treat Homer not as a literary object but as a historical and archaeological one (indeed, it was with this kind of instruction in mind—a kind now happily waning—that the academic translations were first devised). In any case, the literary translator cannot allow himself to be frightened off by fear of the historical sense, but must everywhere take the risk of his talents and convictions, re-creating as vividly as he can the life he sees in alien and classical places. And he can perhaps take comfort from signs—the increasing popuage is less prone than it once was to worship the authority of the scholar or to respect an expertise so limited by its knowledge that it cannot speak to living men.

If so much be granted, we should see to it that our habits do not paralyze our resolves. Consider for a moment the respectable practice of publishing a translation with the original *en face*. Obviously students and scholars going about certain essentially linguistic tasks must be able to refer back and forth rapidly between texts in an activity that sometimes resembles watching a tennis game. We have there one useful category of translation, but why do we have an *en face* text for the poet-translator as well? Do we really need it? How did it get there? Such a format, now standard publishing practice for poetry established by the well-meant insistence of the powerful scholarly community during the past few decades, sets up the original to glare implacably across at its offspring and all too often to suffocate the poet in the translator. It obliges him to think more often of a finished poem in a foreign language than of a nascent one in his own. And even if the poet emerges victorious from this duel, the reader may still be hypnotized by the format into the old tennis game of split reading that prevents him from entering fully into the flow of either version. The conclusion is categorical and emphatic. In translations of poetry by poets intended to be read as poetry, let's throw out the original altogether, welcome all the risks that such liberation entails, unclutter the format, and cut costs to boot. If for some reason the original is not available to those who really want it, it could be kept under wraps in an appendix. We may not bring about either better or more translations of foreign poetry this way. But we will at least clear the air and know whether we hold in our hands a volume of poetry in English or an accurate trot for specialists. The distinction is crucial for the craft of translation.

Our point here is not to take sides with the literary translator against his academic rival, but to show why and how the traditional literary approach was displaced, and what the effect of that displacement has been. Certainly the disastrous fall in the prestige of the translator's craft can be directly linked to the present domination of academic theory. Traditionally, as we have seen, there was was translation unfavorably contrasted with original work. little tendency to draw an invidious distinction between 'original' work and translation; when Pope translated the *Iliad*, he had no thought that his translation was in any way less valuable or less creative than his own poetry, and in this he seems to have had the agreement of his contemporaries. Indeed, not until the early nineteenth century larity of good literary translations, for instance—that the The reasons for this change were, of course, the Romantic cult of the 'original' genius and the emergence of professional scholarship and its own theory of translation. But by the close of the century the contrast had become axiomatic for the simple reason that academic translation was, in fact and by principle, profoundly uncreative. Thus the old belief in translation as a form of creativity gave way to the present view of it as a useful, yet modest and basically unoriginal activity. Historically speaking, there is no reason why literary translators should accept a view of translation derived from academic practice and assumptions. Yet essentially this is what they are now doing. Until translation once again becomes creative, until the writer once more assumes his old historical task of renewing the past, the translator's craft as a whole will remain the prisoner of academic principles.

We should like here to record our gratitude to the Humanities Research Center of the University of Texas, which generously supported both the original symposium and its hardcover publication, and particularly to Chancellor H. H. Ransom whose enthusiastic support made this project possible.

William Arrowsmith
Roger Shattuck

Austin, Texas
March, 1964

Contents

Part One

THE CRAFT OF TRANSLATION

D. S. CARNE-ROSS

Translation and Transposition

D. S. CARNE-ROSS, *a former Talks producer for the BBC Third Programme, now teaches Italian at the University of Texas. His translations include the* Hippolytus *of Euripides and* Dialoghi con Leuco *by Cesare Pavese. He is the co-editor of* Arion, *a classical quarterly published by the University of Texas.*

I suppose that the broadest distinction one draws between ways of transferring literary matter from one language to another is the distinction between translation and crib. And the broadest account of that distinction is that where a crib proposes to take care of the letter of the original, a translation must attend to its spirit. But that is broad indeed, an Asian landmass of a distinction, and for the purposes of this paper I intend to insert a middle term between translation and crib. The term I propose is 'transposition'. Transposition, in the sense I choose to give it, occurs when the language of the matter to be translated stands close enough to the language of the translator—in age, idiom, cultural habits and so on—for him to be able to follow the letter with a fair hope of keeping faith with the spirit. Turning a modern French novel into English is thus mainly a matter of transposition. Poetry is more difficult, because its verbal organization is usually more concentrated and more personal; nonetheless a good deal of modern verse can usefully be transposed. Take the English version of the poems of Cavafy by Professor Mavrogordato. It is, in a perfectly honorable sense, essentially a first rendering; yet as an account of the matter (and metre) of

Cavafy it is very serviceable and will stand until such time as someone is moved—and of course permitted by the laws of copyright—to attempt a poetic re-creation; or, in other words, a translation. A somewhat more ambitious example of transposition is the version of Rilke's *Duino Elegies* by Leishman and Spender. It reads like poetry, of a sort, it seems to reproduce something of the spirit of Rilke's poem, and yet it is close enough to the letter of the original to help the reader with next to no German to decipher Rilke's German words.

The further one moves back in time, the more transposition must approximate to translation. There is nonetheless a definite element of what I am calling transposition even in the finest modern rendering of a poem relatively as distant as the *Divine Comedy*. In the sense that Laurence Binyon worked out a modern English equivalent for Dante's medieval Italian, this is true translation. But since Dante's language and the procedures of his poetry are still just within hailing distance, Binyon was also able to transpose. He could for example take over Dante's *terza rima* metre; English allowed him to reproduce, though to a lesser extent, the elision which helps to give Dante's line its peculiar concentration; he was often able to follow the contour of the syntax and even the patterning of the stresses. Let me quote a single tercet:

Io venni in luogo d'ogni luce muto,
che mugghia come fa mar per tempesta,
se da contrari venti è combattuto.
Inferno, V, 28–30

I came into a place of all light dumb
That bellows like a storm in the sea-deep
When the thwart winds that strike it roar and hum.

The first two lines hug the curve of the original very closely; if the third line is a little freer, it is perhaps better in English than in Italian—certainly 'thwart' is stronger than 'contrari'—and, in spite of Dr. Johnson's view to the contrary, there is no rule that the translator may not try to surpass his original. My point however is not simply the closeness of the rendering, but rather that the English and the Italian fall on my ear as the same *kind* of poetry. Binyon did not have to reproduce, to re-create, his original in some radically different medium.

I think that one should transpose when one can; and only translate when one must. I mean that the liberties which translation usually demands are not justifiable unless they are unavoidable. I suggested just now that the further one moves back in time the more one is driven to translate, but of course it is not merely a matter of time. Modern literature often requires the kind of total re-creation for which I am reserving the word translation. But ancient literature—by which I mean classical Greek and Latin literature—must always be re-created. Here there is no middle way between translation and crib. Faced with a different organization of language, a great many idioms which approach familiar experience with an unfamiliar strategy, a set of key words—particularly in Greek—for which there are no precise, or constant, equivalents, the translator's work begins many stages further back than with a modern language. It begins, in fact, at the pre-verbal level; the sentence, often the word, has to be dissolved, atomized, and its elements then reconstituted in a new form.

It is here, then, that I believe the translator is tested most revealingly; here, since this is the extreme case, that the theorist of translation is most likely to find something worth saying.

At its highest, a translation comes into existence in the same way as a work of original literature: a man experiences something—in this case, a foreign text—which he has got to find words for if he is to have any peace. More often, of course, a translation arises from an act of will. A better occasion is perhaps a summons. With the more ambitious sort of translation, it is encouraging to feel that someone wants your work, that it is going to serve some public purpose. I am sure that it would help the translator of Greek tragedy, for example, if he could feel that he was providing the text for a stage production. Some possibility of *regular* production, indeed, not just the occasional amateur performance, would be a great thing. For the problems involved in translating a Greek play are not literary problems alone. The unreality of so much translated Greek drama–on the page or on the stage–is due partly to the difficulty of finding equivalents for a set of conventions which are theatrical as well as literary. Take the case of the messenger's speech which turns up in almost every Greek tragedy, the big formal narration, lasting anything up to a hundred lines, describing the disaster which has just overtaken the hero. The translator's problem is that there is so little precedent in his own literary tradition to draw on–there is the messenger's speech in Milton's *Samson Agonistes*, of course, and Pirithous' description of Arcite's fatal accident in *The Two Noble Kinsmen*, but not much else. The problem of the producer, and of the actor, is that they too lack any precedent, any theatrical precedent, to draw on. They cannot even relate the convention to any familiar human reality, for this long recitation hard on the heels of disaster is in no sense a formalization of any known Anglo-Saxon pattern of behavior. Faced with disaster, the Mediterranean is liable to talk. During the war I heard an Italian woman give a long, circumstantial and very dramatic account of an air-raid which had taken place a few days before, and it struck me at the time that this was the raw material out of which the ancient dramatists fashioned the convention of the messenger's speech. The Anglo-Saxon, in similar circumstances, doesn't make a speech; he simply swears and tries to put the fire out.

As things stand at present, this brilliant artistic convention, one of the high moments of almost every Greek tragedy, defeats the translator and leaves the actor, should the thing ever be performed, with a long and embarrassing piece of versification on his hands. The problem is one that could only be solved by a corporate effort. The translator, having done his best to devise an effective rhetoric, should submit his text to actor and producer and modify it according to their technical criticism; actor and producer would have to devise a style of performance to fit the words the translator was giving them and to express the spirit he detected behind those words. With the additional help of musician and, ideally, of choreographer, the big choral odes would have to be tackled in the same way. And so on with the rest of the elements of the play.

I put it in this way, not because I can quite envisage so complex a corporate effort being mounted, even in this rich country, but because I think the difficulties are on this scale and of this sort. They are emphatically *not* difficulties which can be solved by a single man sitting down with a typewriter and a copy of Sophocles.

Another incentive to improved translation in this field would be to aim, as the University of Chicago has aimed, at the creation of a canon, a body of work covering the whole range of Greek drama. Like a modern bomber fleet, it ought to be under constant revision, with models being scrapped as soon as they become obsolete and replaced by new ones. In one sense, this is now a mere necessity, since so many people have to approach Greek drama through translation or not at all. However I am not thinking of translation as a substitute for the original, something 'to send one's students to,' a relatively painless way of acquiring cultural background. True translation is much more a commentary on the original than a substitute for it. Like criticism, to which it is closely allied, its role is interpretative. Every age has to work out its own relations to the creative achievements of the past, and the task of the translator, like that of the critic, is to define those works of other times and places which are most living and reveal those aspects of them which we most need today.

Only when translation is seen in this way, as essentially an instrument of criticism, is it going to be allowed the liberty it needs. Where it is seen as a substitute for the original, the stress is likely to fall on literal accuracy. If we are looking for a faithful account of the letter of the original, we should use a crib, not a translation. (There is of course no reason why a crib should not be decently literate. John D. Sinclair's prose version of the *Divine Comedy* is a crib, but a crib that is well enough written to teach one something about Dante's poetry.) The accuracy of translation is of a very different kind. A great deal of local distortion, of amplification and even excision, may be necessary if the translator is to follow the curve of his original faithfully.

I stress this point because I want to go on to argue that the translator must be given all the liberty he needs, and at the same time to criticise what I think is a current tendency in classical translation towards a rather conservative literalism. It is present in the Chicago series of Complete Greek Tragedies for example. In a sense I suppose this is inevitable, for translation reflects the spirit of the time and this is no longer a revolutionary period in literature. The pity is that the revolutionary decades of this century, the second and the third, didn't produce more good translation. For when taste changes, existing translations begin to seem either opaque–they have solidified into literature in their own right, the transparence of true translation lost–or unreadable. The new vantage point seems to offer a chance of tackling the masterpieces of the past with a new hope of success.

One detects this note in a venture like the Poets' Translation Series published by the Egoist Press just after the first world war. In his celebrated little essay on Gilbert Murray, T. S. Eliot commented on H.D.'s translations from Euripides and remarked: '. . . allowing for errors and even occasional omissions of difficult passages, [they are] much nearer to both Greek and English than Mr. Murray's. But H.D. and the other poets of the Poets' Translation Series, have *so far* [the italics are mine] done no more than pick up some of the more romantic crumbs of Greek literature.' None of them, Eliot goes on to say, has 'yet' shown himself competent to attack the *Agamemnon*. The suggestion, however, is distinctly that this is going to be done soon. Ezra Pound, with his belief that modern poetic techniques were in some way akin to those of Greek poetry since the Greeks employed a kind of *vers libre* in their choric odes[1], was probably the presiding figure in this as in so many ventures, not only through his actual translations, but also through the Greekish lyrics in *Ripostes* and *Lustra*. 'A brilliant improvisator translating at sight from an unknown masterpiece,' Yeats called him.

In the field of Greek translation, however, the most interesting work was done not by Pound but by H.D., most successfully in her fragmentary sketches from the *Iphigeneia in Aulis*, published by the Egoist Press in 1919. Here, to my mind, she suggested certain elements in the Greek lyric better than they have ever been suggested before or since. She leaves out an enormous amount. She is not interested in the syntax, in the elaborate weave of the Greek lyric; and she shows little dramatic feeling. She is hardly concerned with the 'sense,' it is the picture—the 'image'—that she is after, and that is what she presents, a sequence of images as fresh and unexpected as though they had just been disinterred from the sands of Egypt. The Imagist technique was particularly well equipped to present certain aspects of the Greek lyric. The legato English line is too soft for the fiercely edged musical phrases out of which the Greek lyric is built. The Imagistic, Poundian insistence on clarity of outline—avoiding the English, or anyway the

[1] See the essay 'The Tradition', section II, published in *Literary Essays of Ezra Pound* (New Directions, New York, 1954), pp. 92–3.

late Victorian muzziness which Eliot rightly objected to in Murray—and the whole mystique of perfect phrasing, composing 'in the sequence of the musical phrase, not in sequence of a metronome'—all this provided the happiest promise of turning Greek lyric into English:

I crossed sand-hills.
I stand among the sea-drift before Aulis.
I crossed Euripos' strait—
Foam hissed after my boat.

I left Chalkis,
My city and the rock-ledges.
Arethusa twists among the boulders,
Increases—cuts into the surf.

In her complete version of the *Ion* of Euripides, published a good many years later, in 1937, H.D. tried to stretch the fragmentary Imagistic discipline to cover a complete play. I suppose it's a failure—the lack of rhythmical and syntactical continuity makes it very hard to read on—but if so, it's a failure that's worth a good many successes. One sees her, in the translation itself and in the rather mannered prose notes between the sections—really grappling with the problems a Greek play presents: what to do about the big bland speech from the god at the beginning, how to handle the rapid criss-cross exchange of stichomythia, trying to decide how much this or that passage really means, working her way to the reality of gesture and emotion behind the stiff, splendid words.

If one compares H.D.'s *Ion* with Louis MacNeice's *Agamemnon*, published a year earlier, in 1936, one finds something like the contrast I was trying to draw earlier on between translation and transposition. H.D. took her play to pieces, broke it down to a pre-verbal level and then set about reconstituting it in her own terms. MacNeice's version is the work of a poet and a scholar, but it starts very much farther along the line. He takes the words as they come and turns them into the best English words he can find. There is little trace of the effort which I believe every Greek play demands, to 'make it new,' to devise a new set of formal equivalents. Where H.D.'s *Ion* is modern, MacNeice is content to be modernistic. The diction is in fact quite often old-fashioned academese, slightly tightened up ('The altars are destroyed, the seats of the gods, / and the seed of all the land is perished from it') and fitted out with some contemporary trimmings. The watchman, for example, is made to speak of the stars as 'shining Masters *riveted* in the sky.' Industrial imagery was of course popular in the poetry of the Thirties, but the adjective 'riveted' is none the less badly lacking in propriety. It destroys the overtones of religious awe which the original carries, and it is wrong visually, since stars are essentially moving, flickering points of light whereas 'riveted' suggests something immobile.

However, if MacNeice's *Agamemnon* must be reckoned a failure to continue the search for a genuinely modern translation of Greek tragedy, compared with later British work in this field it stands out as a solitary peak. It was I think Mr. Rex Warner, whose versions from the Greek began to appear in the late Thirties, who showed that classical translation was not the problematic business it had once appeared. In his handling of the odes, Mr. Warner was not, like H.D., influenced by a particular school of modern writing, but rather by what Eliot once called 'the rumour that verse has been liberated.' Observing that the right-hand margin of contemporary poetry was not infrequently jagged, Mr. Warner took his place confidently within the modern tradition. Let me quote a strophe from his version of the *Hippolytus*:

No more can I look with a mind undisturbed
upon things unexpected,
Now the brightest of stars
Of Hellas, of Athens,—we saw it—
Is sent by the rage of his father
To foreign countries abroad.

O sands of the shores of my city,
O glades in the mountains where he
Slew wild beasts with his swift-footed hounds,
And holy Dictynna was with him!

Mr. Warner moves with such dexterity from one metrical effect to another that I think a contemporary band of Troezenian huntsmen would have difficulty in scanning his verses correctly. The first line breaks new ground metrically, though a glance at the Greek confirms the dactylic intention which one's ear discerns. The line 'O sands of the shores of my city,' suggesting an early enthusiasm for Swinburne, is less revolutionary, and this Swinburnian movement is continued in the next line, beginning

O glades in the mountains—

But then, with a metrical inventiveness beyond Swinburne and indeed beyond Euripides, Mr. Warner halts the rhythm he has set in motion with the two strong monosyllables—'where he'—leaving us with the puzzling line:

O glades in the mountains where he—

The last line, 'And holy Dictynna was with him,' draws in an interesting and once again quite unexpected manner on the healthy vernacular tradition of the limerick.

The freedom of Mr. Warner's choric odes is countered by his strictly disciplined iambics. His line is based upon the observation that the Greek tragic line contains twelve syllables, or thereabouts. Let it then, one may say, have twelve syllables in English too. The difficulty is that the unrhymed dodecasyllabic line is not a native English metre and that unless you are very clever with your caesuras, it tends to turn into no metre at all. Let us take a few lines from Theseus' speech in the same play to see what Mr. Warner makes of it:

O mind of man! To what lengths will it not proceed?
Where will a bound be set to reckless arrogance?

For if in every generation this swells up,
If the younger comes to an excess of shame beyond
The former generation, then the gods will have
To add another world to this one, which will hold
The evil men who are by nature all depraved.

Since the war, the Penguin Classics have published translations from the greater part of Greek tragedy. Sophocles has fallen to Mr. E. F. Watling, while first Euripides and then Aeschylus have gone to Mr. Philip Vellacott. Now, following Penguin's lead, the BBC Third Programme has broadcast a number of these translations. Mr. Watling's odes do not readily submit to exact metrical analysis; in the scenes he has relaxed the rigor of Mr. Warner's dodecasyllabics and inclined more to an off-the-shoulder blank verse. At moments of heightened emotion, he sometimes has recourse to prose:

'In what manner Oedipus passed from this earth, no one can tell. . . . We know he was not destroyed by a thunderbolt from heaven, nor tide-wave rising from the sea, for no such thing occurred. . . .'

Mr. Vellacott usually prefers to translate the scenes entirely into prose, reserving his verse for the odes:

You have heard of the rocky fountain
Where water gushes streaming from the heart of earth,
Where they dip pails in the pool:
A friend of mine was there,
Rinsing rich-coloured clothes in the rill-water. . .[2]

I have gone into this melancholy episode in British literary history at some length, because I think it throws some light on one of the problems of classical translation: the problem, quite simply, of general disinterest. Nobody minds if it's bad. The ordinary classical scholar can't tell; the texts he is used to dealing with are all supposed to be good, so he has never had occasion to develop a method of

[2] *Hippolytus,* 121 ff.

distinguishing good from bad. And the general literary public isn't very interested one way or the other. But is it really so small a thing that in this vital encounter—the encounter between the two greatest bodies of poetry known to us, Greek and English—English should be represented by so shoddy an instrument and that translators should ignore the creative achievements of this century and take the art of classical translation back to the point at which Gilbert Murray picked it up?

Wyndham Lewis' Tarr described sex as a German study. Classical translation is now an American study and I pass with relief from the British to the American scene. The work I most admire has been done jointly by Dudley Fitts and Robert Fitzgerald, notably their *Oedipus Rex* which is I think the finest existing translation of any Greek play. Their handling of the choric odes is in places extremely free and occasionally they almost seem to be writing a poem of their own inspired by the original. But where Sophocles is splendid, they are splendid too, and with a splendor I would dare to call Sophoclean:

What is God singing in his profound
Delphi of gold and shadow?
What oracle for Thebes, the sunwhipped city?

Fear unjoints me, the roots of my heart tremble.

Now I remember, O Healer, your power, and wonder:
Will you send doom like a sudden cloud, or weave it
Like nightfall of the past?

Speak, speak to us, issue of holy sound:
Dearest to our expectancy: be tender!

That is very free, of course, but the liberties it takes are the kind of liberties one must take in dealing with passionate, high-wrought poetry in which a great poet is straining language to make it carry an enormous burden of suggestion. This isn't the occasion to examine the strophe in detail, but let me quote for comparison the opening lines of a much more literal rendering of the same passage by Mr. David Grene, published in the University of Chicago series of Greek tragedies:

What is the sweet-spoken word of God from the shrine of
Pytho rich in gold
That has come to glorious Thebes?

Greek poetry is very rich in adjectives, compound and simple; Greek poets love to cosset their nouns with these beautiful but sometimes rather empty words,—'swelling epithets,' as Milton called them in a saddening passage, 'thick laid / As varnish on a harlot's cheek.' Mr. Grene, trying to *transpose*—in my sense—a passage that can only be *translated*—has brought them all over literally—the 'sweet-spoken word of God,' the shrine of Pytho 'rich in gold' 'glorious' Thebes. The result is nearly meaningless. Compare what Fitts and Fitzgerald have done. The 'sweet-spoken word of God' has become 'What is God singing'—the action handed over to the verb which performs it much better. They have done something to re-create the note of awe which the passage conveys, the awe with which the message from the Delphic oracle is expected, by building up the image of Delphi. (*Delphi*, not *Pytho*, as Mr. Grene has it. There is no point in bogging one's text with this sort of surface obscurity.) The shrine becomes God's 'profound / Delphi of gold and shadow.' There is no 'shadow' in the Greek, certainly; what there *is* in the Greek, which Mr. Grene's fidelity misses, is the *response* to Delphi which Sophocles could count on from his Athenian audience. The modern reader has not worshipped at earth's central shrine; he has not stood in the blinding sunshine and seen the golden images in the temple's shadow. And yet if he is to understand the burden of this passionate song, he must in imagination have stood there. The translator's job is, if necessary, to build into his versions the overtones which the Greek words carry. I recognize the dangers of this doctrine of the compensatory gloss but sometimes there is no other course.

In the introduction, dated 1938, to his versions from the Greek Anthology, Mr. Fitts made a brief statement of his principles. 'I have not really undertaken translation at all,' he wrote, 'translation, that is to say, as it is understood in the schools. I have simply tried to restate in my own idiom what the Greek verses have meant to me.' In a note, dated 1956, to a new edition of the book, he claims that he has radically altered his theories of translation. Whatever exactly he means by this, he has not denied himself the proper liberties of his earlier work. Elsewhere in modern American translation of the classics, there is a greater emphasis on the letter and a reluctance to experiment. Rather than comment on some of the work in the Chicago Series which seems to be definitely bad—and bad partly for this reason—I prefer to take a somewhat earlier translation which in its own way succeeds. I refer to the version of the *Oedipus at Colonus* by Mr. Robert Fitzgerald, first published in 1941. This is unmistakably a poet's translation; it has insight and delicacy, but often I find myself wishing that Mr. Fitzgerald did not have to be so traditional. Let me quote a few lines from the great ode in praise of Athens:

The river's fountains are awake,
And his nomadic streams that run
Unthinned for ever, and never stay:
But like perpetual lovers move
On the maternal land—

These are chaste and beautiful lines, but I should never have supposed that they came from the Greek. Their beauty is a gently lyrical English beauty, whereas the passage from the *Oedipus Rex* which I quoted just now seem to me both Greek and Sophoclean. I would not want to lay it down as a principle that traditional English forms are always unsuitable for Greek lyric—it's hard enough to translate as it is, without having one hand tied behind one's back. Nonetheless, I am sure that the verbal and metrical possibilities offered by modern poetry provide the translator with an instrument which has not yet been fully exploited. I fancy that a good deal more might be done with quantity in English, particularly the dactylic and trochaic rhythms which are the basis of Pound's lyrical writing.

Mr. Richmond Lattimore is, I suppose, the most widely respected classical translator. He has not been afraid to tackle the greatest names in Greek poetry—Homer, Aeschylus, Pindar. His *Oresteia,* with its admirable introduction, is certainly the most impressive account of Aeschylus' trilogy that we possess. I complained of Mr. Fitzgerald just now that he approximated too closely to the traditional form of the English lyric; with Mr. Lattimore, I am sometimes worried by the way he sticks to the metrical form of the Greek lyric. He is too much of an artist to attempt complete metrical correspondence—always a quite hopeless undertaking—but in his versions of the *Choephoroe* and the *Eumenides,* he has kept so close that the reader without Greek would, I think, here and there have difficulty in scanning his verses correctly. This desire for the closest fidelity is reflected in the translation as a whole. One guesses that for Mr. Lattimore the attempt to 'restate in his own idiom what the Greek verses have meant to him' would not rank as translation at all, but as paraphrase. If so, I can only say that I wish he would let his remarkable gifts have their head rather more and allow himself to be more paraphrastic.

A developed taste for Greek tragedy is a relatively modern acquisition, made possible by the textual labors of nineteenth century scholars and also by the experiments in Greek dramatic form of a series of nineteenth century poets. To modern poets, it has offered the charged compression of its language, the presentation of a single action on different planes of reality; to playwrights interested in poetic drama it has offered a way of escape from the long dominance of Shakespeare. Homer, by contrast, if he has been with us longer, has no particular relevance to contemporary literary interests. If he has survived undiminished, that is simply because he is, presumably, the best poet in the world. But to translate Homer today is to find a living form for a dead genre. For epic is doubly dead; it died once when poets lost the art or the will to write it; and it died a second, a critical, death, with the romantic, or post-romantic insistence on the brevity of the poetic emotion. The phrase, 'a long poem,' Edgar Allan Poe said, is a logical impossibility, a flat contradiction in terms. What place was there for this old leviathan of letters when poetry was contracted to the isolated point of poetic emotion?

I had this critical prejudice very much in mind when a few years ago I produced a 'radio Iliad' for the BBC Third Programme. The original intention was to invite someone to translate the whole poem, but our house poets had other fish to fry and the project was handed over to me to do what I liked with. I could think of no living poet capable of evolving a style, a diction, a metre which could be prolonged for fifteen thousand lines and retain the strong poetic excitement which hardly ever fails in Homer. I had also in mind that radio is an impatient medium; the binding matter which the *Iliad* contains like all other long narrative poems, the links and passages and bridges, are perfectly acceptable in one's experience of the poem on the page; I was not convinced that they would always hold the attention on the air.

So I set about constructing a minimum *Iliad*, a sequence of about 5,000 lines—roughly a third of the total poem—intended to give the main narrative action and to present the principal characters. I then invited about a dozen people to try their hand at single passages. Within the limits of a few hundred lines, I hoped that the members of the team would be able to devise a style, a form of speech, that would be faithful to this ancient poetic masterpiece *and* to their own poetic practice. For I saw the venture less as an exercise in translation than as a challenge to contemporary writers. No conditions were laid down, but I hoped that the use of a language standing in some relation to the language of modern poetry would produce something like a common style. And to play down the inevitable stylistic differences, I had the whole series read by a single actor, Mr. Denis McCarthy.

A good deal of variety, in diction and metre and tone, did of course remain. One or two versions were so old-fashioned that they would have disconcerted Matthew Arnold. One translator tried to find a local equivalent for Homer in *Beowulf* and fitted out his version with ring-prowed ships and so forth. The majority of translators used some variant of what has become the standard metrical equivalent for the hexameter, the free six-beat line which Lattimore employed in his *Iliad* and Day Lewis in his *Aeneid*. Blank verse was also employed, but only in the hands of Robert Fitzgerald did it yield distinguished poetry. The one attempt at an unmistakably modern style was made by the young English poet, Christopher Logue.

Translators were chosen for the excellence of their English rather than the excellence of their Greek, and several, some of the most successful, in fact, knew no Greek at all. Some people, I know, regard this as little short of immoral: all I can say is that it works. If a man is a poet, and the right kind of poet for the job in hand, he can *guess* what the original is like from a crib—as unliterary a crib as possible, and preferably written out in verse lengths. It helps if he has someone who knows the language at hand to warn him when he is going wrong, but the essential communion—the vision of the thing to be rendered—can take place. If it still sounds immoral, I can only say that many poets lack the necessary languages and that only a poet—a poet, possibly, in some way *manqué*, but still a poet—can translate poetry. *The Oxford Book of Greek Verse in Translation* is there as horrid evidence of what happens when people whose only claim is that they can read Greek, try to write English.

I propose to conclude this paper with some extracts from my radio *Iliad*. The first exhibit is taken from Book I and forms part of the great slanging match between Achilles and Agamemnon. Achilles, you will remember, has backed the prophet Calchas who has declared that the only way to placate the anger of Apollo, who is savaging the Greek army, is to hand back to her father the girl Chryseis whom Agamemnon has taken. The translator is Peter Green, a classical scholar and the author of two novels with a classical setting.

. . . So saying, Calchas sat down, and after him the noble
Son of Atreus rose, wide-ruling Agamemnon,
Choked black with rage, his eyes glinting like points of fire.
First he turned to Calchas, face eloquent with hatred:
'You long-faced quack, have you ever prophesied good?
Doom's your delight, disaster your stock-in-trade—
Never a cheerful omen declared, much less fulfilled!
And now you stand up here with your miserable cantrips
And swear this plague from Apollo is all my *doing—*
Because I turned down rich ransom, and kept the girl Chryseis!
Why shouldn't I? I want her. I'd rather have her than my wife,
Yes, rather than Clytemnestra. She's better all round—
Prettier, nicer figure, more sense, and a damned sight handier
About the house. Still, even so I'm willing
To hand her back, if the public good demands it.
I have a responsibility for my men, I can't stand by
And see Achaeans slaughtered. But if I release the girl,
You'll have to find me another prize to replace her. How

Would it look if I was the only Argive chief among you
Without a share in the booty? Think of it this way,
All of you: it means that I kiss my prize goodby.'
Then Achilles, the godlike, the swift of foot, replied:
'Most noble Agamemnon, high prince of covetousness,
How shall we, the Achaean warriors, find you a prize?
We are no tradesmen with a hoard of public funds;
Whatever we took when we sacked those towns has already
Been shared out. We cannot decently beg it
Back from its owners now. But if you are willing
To surrender this girl to the God, then we Achaeans
Will pay you back triple, no, fourfold, if Zeus grant us
To storm the giant walls and citadel of Troy.'
Then the lord Agamemnon answered him in these words:
'Fine soldier you may be, Achilles, and like a god,
But don't try your tricks on me. It's a waste of time.
You'll neither outwit nor persuade me. What are you after?
It's all right for you to say, "Give up the girl"
While your own prize is in no danger. Am I to agree to that?
No, I say. Either you get me a prize of equal value
To the one I'm losing, something well to my taste,
Or else, if you refuse, I shall help myself
To one of yours—your own, perhaps, Achilles, or yours,
Odysseus, or, Ajax, yours. We shall see how well you react
In the same position. But this can wait till later.
Our first concern is to fit out a ship, and take
Chryseis home. That means collecting a crew, to begin with,
And freighting cattle aboard for sacrifice, and choosing
A captain. One of our senior princes, naturally—
Ajax, Idomeneus, perhaps our good friend Odysseus,
Or even yourself, Achilles, with your unrivalled
Military reputation—to offer up sacrifices
And appease the Sky-Archer.'—

The Homer who emerges from that passage is a Homer

with a good sense of humor, an eye for character and an ear for the cadences of speech, a feeling for the everyday reality of the life he is describing. A Homer, in short, who has undergone the influence of the novel. I think this is inevitable and quite proper. If translation is to be more than an academic exercise, it has to be related to living literary interests. Pope could turn the *Iliad* into an Augustan epic because the civilization he belonged to still believed that epic was, in Dryden's words, 'the greatest work which the soul of man is capable to perform.' But for better or worse, the only great living form today is the novel, and it is inevitable that we should bring to our reading, and so to our translation, of the great narrative poetry of the past demands and preoccupations which we have learnt from our reading of the novel.

My next exhibit is quite different. It is from the very unhomeric episode in Book XIV describing how Hera deceived her husband Zeus in order to conceal from him the help which his brother Poseidon is giving the Greek army. The translator, Iain Fletcher, is a poet not greatly interested, perhaps, in the larger human realities of the novel, but filled with what Mario Praz, speaking of D'Annunzio, called 'il gusto sensuale della parola.' Here is a part of the scene: Hera at her dressing table.

So off she went to the private room her son Hephaistos
had built her
With a properly fitting door and a secret bolt,
And once inside, with the door shut safely behind her,
First with suave ambrosia washed off the slightest stain
From her brilliant skin; then richly sweetened herself
With a swift and vividly scented oil of Olympos.
If that oil were shaken in the bronze dominion of Zeus
An erotic odour would be rained over Heaven and Earth.
She fondled this into her flesh and then softly combed
And plaited the intense fall of hair with her hands.
Then gently drew on a glinting dress that Athene

Had carefully designed for her, hatched with a hundred patterns,
And pinned it across her breasts with a golden clasp,
Rounding her waist with a belt flaring out in a hundred tassels.
She hung ear-rings with three clustering drops
Like mulberry berries in the pierced
Lobes of her ears, and O, how liquidly they glistened!
Then lastly the goddess secreted herself in a slender
Fresh veil that smiled as sweetly as sunlight
And bound finical sandals round her dazzling feet,
And all this finished, her finery fluent about her,
Left the boudoir, and beckoned her step-daughter, Aphrodite,
Apart from the other gods, and Hera said this to her . . .

No other passage in the Iliad could be treated in this way: the beautiful conventional epithets caressed into new, surprising life, the verbs nudging the action into subtly unexpected directions, the march of the Homeric hexameters relaxed into sliding, sensuously playful cadences. Fletcher has taken great liberties with his text, but this Alexandrian, almost Restoration treatment seems to me to suggest, as a more conventional handling couldn't, how far the smiling grace of this Milesian interlude is from the heroic seriousness of Homer's characteristic manner. I wonder if a poet more conventionally grounded in Greek would have ventured to take such liberties?

My third passage could only have been written by a poet with very good Greek. The scene at the beginning of Book XVIII in which Achilles, desperate for the loss of his friend Patroclus, goes down to the sea shore and calls out to his mother Thetis, is one of the most affecting in the whole poem. From the depths of the sea, Thetis hears Achilles' cry and accompanied by the Nereids, she laments the fate that is soon to befall him too. But before the lament starts, Homer inserts a long list of the Nereids. The passage has not been to all tastes and some ancient commentators condemned it as a Hesiodic interpolation. I gather that modern scholars consider the passage genuine and the names probably Homer's own invention. Certainly it is no mere catalogue; it has, as Wilamowitz noticed, a structural importance. 'The enumeration,' he said, 'sounding like the ripples of a quiet sea, soothes our agitation, turns us away from the agitating scene, and makes us ready for the calm of the words between mother and son.' It is, however, a passage which presents the translator with a severe problem. If he simply gives the names as they appear in Greek, one is left with an unreadable piece of enumeration:

For Glauke was there, Kymodoke and Thaleia,
Nesaie and Speio and Thoe, and ox-eyed Halia;
Kymothoe was there, Aktaia and Limnoreia—

so Mr. Lattimore. But this is not even transposition, it's mere transliteration. Pope also catalogues the names, but he enlivens his catalogue with a few strokes which help to suggest something of the charm of the original:

Thalia, Glauce, ev'ry wat'ry name,
Nesaea mild, and silver Spio came:
Cymothoe and Cymodoce were nigh,
And the blue languish of soft Alia's eye.

That is better, but it still doesn't go far enough. The difficulty is that in Greek they are not really proper names at all; as one reads the passage in Homer, the firm outlines of these mythological young persons dissolve into a glimmering sequence of images, all the delicate play of wind and water and light and rock and shore. William Arrowsmith, in his version, chose the difficult, the only solution and re-created in English the fluid succession of sea pictures which rise up before the mind's eye as one read the lines in the original Greek:

Then, out of his grief and anguish, Achilles cried aloud,
a terrible, awful cry, and his goddess mother heard him
where she sat in the depths of the sea at the side of her agèd father,
and she too gave a cry, and the goddesses gathered around her,
all those who were daughters of Nereus in the depths of the sea
Seagreen and Shimmer, the goddesses Blooming and Billow
and those who are names of the islands, those who are called for the caves,
and She-who-skims-on-the-water, and Spray with the gentle eyes
like the gentle eyes of cattle, naiads of spume and the shore,
the nymphs of marshes and inlets and all the rocks out-jutting,
and Dulcet too was there and Wind-that-rocks-on-the-water
and Grazer-over-the-sea and she whose name is Glory,
and the naiads Noble and Giver, and lovely Bringer, and Nimble,
and Welcomer too, and Grace, and Princess, and Provider,
and she who is named for the milk, the froth of the curling breakers,
glorious Galateia, and the famous nymphs of the surf,
and Infallible and Truth, true daughters of their father,
and goddesses over the sand, and she who runs from the mountains
and whose hair is a splendor, and all the other goddesses
who are daughters of Nereus along the deep floor of the sea.

Now for my fourth and last exhibit, the battle of Achilles and the river Scamander, from Book XXI, translated by Christopher Logue. One of the paradoxes of Homer's poetry is that using a traditional, conventional style—Homer thinks in clichés, someone said—he manages to convey a sense of the pressure of everyday, surrounding reality more strongly and continuously than any other poet. The translator's problem is to release this pressure of reality—realities of gesture and movement and light and sound—from its stiff formulaic encasement. Pope wrote of the 'unequal fire and rapture which is so forcible in Homer that no man of a true poetical spirit is master of himself while he reads him. Everything moves, everything lives, and is put in action . . .' This aspect of Homer's poetry seems to me to have been brilliantly caught by Chistopher Logue. This is the scene by the bank of the river as Achilles is slaughtering the unfortunate Trojans.

—Then Achilles,
Leaving the tall enemy with eels at his white fat
And his tender kidneys infested with nibblers,
Pulled his spear out of the mud and waded off,
After the deadman's troop that beat upstream
For their dear lives; then, glimpsing Achilles' scarlet plume
Amongst the clubbed bullrushes, they ran and as they ran
The Greek got seven of them, swerved, eying his eighth, and
Ducked at him as Scamander bunched his sinews up,
And up, and further up, and further further still, until
A glistening stack of water, solid, white with sunlight,
Swayed like a giant bone over the circling humans,
Shuddered, and changed for speaking's sake into humanity.
And the stack of water was his chest; and the foaming
Head of it, his bearded face; and the roar of it—
Like weir-water—Scamander's voice:—

That is of course extraordinarily free. The transformation of the river god into human form is done in two words in the Greek; Logue spends eight lines on it. But the thing has happened; we have seen the swollen water rise up before our eyes and confront the astonished superman. If you say that this isn't translation at all, but paraphrase, a new poem suggested by Homer, I can only repeat the sentence from Dudley Fitts which I quoted just now—'I have simply tried to restate in my own idiom what the Greek verses have meant to me'—and ask what the translation of poetry can be if it is not the re-creation in a new language, by whatever means are open to the translator, of an equivalent beauty, an equivalent power, an equivalent truth.

Let me, to end, quote one more passage from the same translation. It is not quite so free as the last one, but it is still full of detail that is not in the Greek text. Logue has tried to *see* the scene which Homer presents; and if his account does not tally with Homer's point for point, that is because no two observers will describe something in exactly the same words. But I think he has seen what Homer saw: the greatest of heroes in headlong flight as the river swarms terribly after him:

Hearing this,
The Greek jumped clear into the water, and Scamander
Went for him in hatred: curved back his undertow, and
Hunched like a snarling yellow bull drove the dead up,
And out, tossed by the water's snout onto the fields,
Yet those who lived he hid behind a gentle wave.
Around the Greek Scamander deepened. Wave clambered
Over wave to get at him, beating aside his studded shield so,
Both footholds gone, half toppled over by the bloodstained crud,
Achilles snatched for balance at an elm, Ah!, its roots gave,
Wrenched out, splitting the bank, and tree and all
Crashed square across the river, leaves, splintering branches,
And dead birds blocking the fall. And Achilles wanted out.
Scrambled through the root's lopsided crown, out of the ditch,
Off home.
But the river Scamander had not done with him.

Forcing its bank, an avid lip of water slid
After him, to smother his Greek breath for Trojan victory.
Aoi!—but that Greek could run!—and put and kept
A spearthrow's lead between him and the quick,
Suck, quick, curve of the oncoming water,
Arms outstretched as if to haul himself along the air,
His shield—like the early moon—thudding against
His nape-neck and his arse, fast, fast
As the black winged hawk's full stoop he went—
And what is faster?—yet, Scamander was near on him,
Its hood of seething water poised over his shoulderblades.
Achilles was a quick man, yes, but the Gods are quicker than men.
And easily Scamander's webbed claw stroked his ankles.

KENNETH REXROTH

The Poet as Translator

KENNETH REXROTH, *the well-known American poet, has published poetry in translation from six languages.*

When discussing the poet as translator, from time immemorial it has been the custom to start out by quoting Dryden. I shan't, but in the course of these remarks I will try to illustrate Dryden's main thesis—that the translation of poetry into poetry is an act of sympathy—the identification of another person with oneself, the transference of his utterance to one's own utterance. The ideal translator, as we all know well, is not engaged in matching the words of a text with the words of his own language. He is hardly even a proxy, but rather an all out advocate. His job is one of the most extreme examples of special pleading. So the prime criterion of successful poetic translation is assimilability. Does it get across to the jury?

If we approach the great historic translations this way it is easy to understand why they are great. It is obvious on the most general survey of English literature that the classic translations of the classics accompany the classics of English, occur in the periods of highest productivity and greatest social—what shall we say? cohesion? euphoria? Tudor, Jacobean, Caroline, Augustan, Victorian, many of the translations are themselves amongst the major English works of their time. Malory's *Morte d'Arthur*, North's Plutarch, Pope's Homer—and of course the King James Bible. All the great translations survive into our time because they were so completely of their own time. This means simply that the translator's act of identification was so great that he speaks with the veridical force of his own utterance, conscious of communicating directly to his own audience.

Of course many such translations are ethnocentric to a degree. Sometimes to the degree that they have turned the original into something totally different. This is not true of many of the greatest translations but it is true of some. Is Fitzgerald a translation of Omar? Here the two cultures are so radically different, all that can be said is that he is probably all of medieval Persia that Victorian England was prepared to assimilate. The only real problem is Urquhart. It is hard to imagine anything less like the benign humanism of Rabelais than this crabbed and cracked provincial euphuism. The point of Rabelais is that he is the opposite of eccentric—he is profoundly, utterly normal. Urquhart produced a Scotch classic and for Englishmen Rabelais will always be an oddity. This is unfortunate, but then, is Rabelais' normality normal in the British Isles? I think not. Perhaps his Gallic magnanimity could only cross the Channel tricked out in a tartan-striped harlequinade.

It is the custom to deride Pope's Homer. Nothing could be less like Homer. But the Eighteenth Century certainly didn't think so—on either side of the Channel—this was the Homer they were prepared to accept. Of course, Pope was a neurasthenic, a dandy in Baudelaire's sense, or Wallace Stevens', a thoroughly urbanized exquisite who had professionalized his nervous system. Whatever his formal commitments—he was a Roman Catholic—his real system of values was only a specialized hierarchy of nervous response. Certainly, nothing less like Homer could be imagined. But each age demands its own image. The other Eighteenth Century Homers are not Homer either, they are just mediocre or bad. Is Butler Homer? I suppose he is for those of us who are rationalist, utilitarian, humanitarian. He is a fine Reform Club Homer. I still prefer Butler to Butcher and Lang or William Morris, let alone T. E.

Lawrence. However, it is simply not true that Butcher and Lang is any more false to the text than Butler. Butcher and Lang is Homer for the readers of *The Idylls of the King*.

I am not proposing to dissolve all questions of authenticity in some sort of vulgar pragmatism. The text is always there as a control. The recent hair-raising performance of Robert Graves, for instance, both violates the text and fails to transmit anything resembling Homer. This is not Homer for the readers of *Punch*, it is the invasion of the text of Homer by the text of *Punch*. Here we have passed the limits of eccentricity. Pope's whole age was eccentric, as was Urquhart's. Theirs is a viable eccentricity, Graves' is not; it is an unpleasant eccentric eccentricity.

The first question must be, Is this as much of Homer, or whoever, who can be conveyed on these terms to this audience? Second, of course, Is it good in itself? Lord Derby or T. E. Lawrence are simply not good enough English. Graves is simply in bad taste and the Heroic Age, by definition, was before bad taste was invented. It is possible of course that a given audience cannot assimilate enough of the original to justify the efforts or to ever achieve a significant resemblance. How much of *Les Liasons Dangereuses* could be translated into the world of William Law? How much does Proust mean to a Chinese collective farmer and vice versa? Imagine Dante translated by Dorothy Parker or Shakespeare by Tristan Tzara. You don't have to imagine. Dante has recently been translated by someone not unlike Dorothy Parker. Read it.

As time goes on all translations become dated. Before the language changes the society changes. Butcher and Lang are repugnant to us because society has changed, but has not changed so much that it has become strange to us. Pope on the other hand, speaks a language that, purely linguistically considered, seems closer to our own, but his world has receded so far that we read him for his special and extraordinary insights and distortions. At length language changes so much that it becomes liturgical. This is a natural thing and can never be imitated. The Nineteenth Century made the mistake of thinking it could. Nothing sounds less like liturgical English than William Morris trying to imitate it. This led to terrible waste—I doubt if Morris' wonderful Saga Library was ever readable by anybody—and there the great sagas are, locked up in that ridiculous language. On the other hand, we never think of the Prophets as speaking like a committee of Jacobean Bishops, we think of the Jacobean Bishops as speaking like the Prophets. At last the language becomes really foreign. Chaucer's wonderful rendering of the *Consolation* of Boethius sounds splendid to us, and certainly seems by far the best ever made in any language. It didn't sound that way to generations closer to Chaucer, not even as far away as Dryden and Pope. They read Chaucer as still in their own language. We do not, but in another that we have no difficulty translating as we go along. Of course, there is here the special factor: Chaucer was an incomparably finer poet than his original.

What I have been thinking about behind these introductory remarks, and trying to convey indirectly, is what the poet does in the living relationship of translation, the actual act. Or at least what I think he does and what I presume I do myself. Before going on let me read you a poem of H.D.'s. It may seem dated to those who are not old enough to have mellowed to H.D.'s enthusiasms, to those who are not young enough to have never heard of her. Its language is very much the argot of Bloomsbury aestheticism with a strong lacing of the Chautauqua Circuit. Still, I think it does convey, all allowances being made, the excitement of translation of great poetry. It certainly does recall very vividly to me my own experience—my first translation from the Greek, a whole evening till after midnight spent in the continuously exalted discussion of one small Sapphic fragment with a friend who was then an undergraduate student of Paul Shorey's.

Here is the H.D.[1]:

HELIODORA

He and I sought together,
over the spattered table,
rhymes and flowers,
gifts for a name.

He said, among others,
I will bring
(and the phrase was just and good,
but not as good as mine,)
'the narcissus that loves the rain.'

We strove for a name,
while the lights of the lamps burnt thin
and the outer dawn came in,
a ghost, the last at the feast
or the first,
to sit within
with the two that remained
to quibble in flowers and verse
over a girl's name.

He said, 'the rain loving,'
I said, 'the narcissus, drunk,
drunk with the rain.'

Yet I had lost
for he said,
'the rose, the lover's gift,
is loved of love,'
he said it,
'loved of love;'
I waited, even as he spoke

1 HELIODORA, p. 222, *Collected Poems of H.D.*, Liveright 1925.

to see the room filled with light,
as when in winter
the embers catch in a wind
when a room is dank;
so it would be filled, I thought,
our room with a light
when he said
(and he said it first,)
'the rose, the lover's delight,
is loved of love,'
but the light was the same.

Then he caught,
seeing the fire in my eyes,
my fire, my fever, perhaps,
for he leaned
with the purple wine
stained on his sleeve,
and said this:
'did you ever think
a girl's mouth
caught in a kiss
is a lily that laughs?'
I had not.
I saw it now
as men must see it forever afterwards;
no poet could write again,
'the red lily,
a girl's laugh caught in a kiss;'
it was his to pour in the vat
from which all poets dip and quaff,
for poets are brothers in this.

So I saw the fire in his eyes,
it was almost my fire,
(he was younger,)
I saw the face so white,
my heart beat,

it was almost my phrase:
I said, 'surprise the muses,
take them by surprise;
it is late,
rather it is dawn rise,
those ladies sleep, the nine,
our own king's mistresses.'

A name to rhyme,
flowers to bring to a name,
what was one girl faint and shy,
with eyes like the myrtle,
(I said: 'her underlids
are rather like myrtle,')
to vie with the nine?

Let him take the name,
he had the rhymes,
'the rose, loved of love,
the lily, a mouth that laughs,'
he had the gift,
'the scented crocus,
the purple hyacinth,'
what was one girl to the nine?

He said:
'I will make her a wreath;'
he said:
'I will write it thus:

I will bring you the lily that laughs,
I will twine
with soft narcissus, the myrtle,
sweet crocus, white violet,
the purple hyacinth, and last,
the rose, loved of love,
that these may drip on your hair
the less soft flowers,
may mingle sweet with the sweet

of Heliodora's locks,
myrrh curled.'

(He wrote myrrh curled
I think, the first.)

I said:
'they sleep, the nine,'
when he shouted swift and passionate:
'that *for the nine!*
above the hills
the sun is about to awake,
and today white violets
shine beside white lilies
adrift on the mountainside;
today the narcissus opens
that loves the rain.'

I watched him to the door,
catching his robe
as the wine bowl crashed to the floor,
spilling a few wet lees,
(ah, his purple hyacinth)
I saw him out of the door,
I thought:
there will never be a poet
in all the centuries after this,
who will dare to write,
after my friend's verse,
'A girl's mouth
is a lily kissed.'

What H.D. has been doing in this rather precious and rather dated little drama is objectifying the story of her own possession by the ghost of Meleager. Whatever else she has done, she has conveyed the poignancy of that feeling of possession and the glamour of the beautiful Greek words as they come alive in one's very own English. Most of the epithets can be found in the lovely 147th epigram of the 5th Book, and who will ever forget the first time he ever saw them, bright with their old Greek life on the page? That 147th epigram has been translated by most of these who have taken the Anthology to English, but only H.D. brings over the glamour and excitement of the language.

Now I will read you a selection of the great number of translations of Sappho's *Orchard*, the poem I translated so long ago under identical emotional circumstances, and finally my own.

. . . And by the cool waterside the breeze rustles amid
the apple-branches, and the quivering leaves shed leathargy;

J. M. Edmonds

And round about the cool water gurgles through apple-boughs,
and slumber streams from quivering leaves.

Wharton

And by the cool stream the breeze murmurs through apple
branches and slumber pours down from quivering leaves.

Cox

Cool waters tumble, singing as they go
Through appled boughs. Softly the leaves are dancing.
Down streams aslumber on the drowsy flow,
My soul entrancing.

T. F. Higham

Through orchard-plots with fragrance crowned
The clear cold fountain murmuring flows;
And forest leaves with rustling sound
Invite to soft repose.

John H. Merivale

All around through branches of apple-orchards
Cool streams call, while down from the leaves
a-tremble
Slumber distilleth.

J. Addington Symonds

By the cool water the breeze murmurs, rustling
Through apple branches, while from quivering leaves
Streams down deep slumber.

Edwin M. Cox

. . . about the cool water
the wind sounds through sprays
of apple, and from the quivering leaves
slumber pours down. . . .

K. Rexroth

I hold no brief for my own translation, but at the time I did it, it was an entirely original experience with me, or with us—there were two of us worked on it; as in H.D.'s poem, we were neither of us familiar with any other English version. That evening was one of the memorable experiences of my life, just because of the completeness of projection into the experience of that great dead Greek woman. On inspection of these various versions it is obvious that what matters most is sympathy—the ability to project into Sappho's experience and then to transmit it back into one's own idiom with maximum viability.

There is a special factor here, something that comes up in most all translations of Sappho from Catullus to our own day. It seems as though there was a special, vertiginous exaltation about her language, not just about the phrases of a poem like the one to Anactoria, which is about such a state, but a special quality to two or three words surviving as a fragment, sometimes even only one. Both H.D. and those two very exalted ladies who called themselves Michael Field not only felt this, but they all wrote poems which are expansions of tiny fragments of Sappho, and which in each case attribute to the inspiring fragment precisely this supernatural lustre. Is there any basis for this in fact? It is easy to see what an Englishwoman of Sappho's sexual temperament could do with *optais amme*, 'you burn me . . .' but is there anything actually inflammatory about Fragment 106: *Met' emoi meli mete melissais*, 'Neither honey nor bees for me.' Does it bear H.D.'s almost hysterical expansion? I think not. Actually it means, 'If I can't have roses without thorns I won't have them at all,' and is a proverb quoted by Sappho. I will read you a poem by Michael Field which is an expansion of Fragments 109 and 110: *Kotharos gar o chrysos io* and *Dios gar pais est' o chrysos/ kenon ou sees oude kis/ dardaptois. o de damnatai/ kai phrenon brotean kratiston.*

Yea, gold is son of Zeus; no rust
Its timeless light can stain.
The worm that brings men's flesh to dust
Assaults its strength in vain.
More gold than gold the love I sing,
A hard, inviolable thing.

Men say the passions should grow old
With waning years; my heart
Is incorruptible as gold,
'Tis my immortal part.
Nor is there any god can lay
On love the finger of decay.

This is a rather lovely little poem, perhaps the best of their volume of reconstructions of Sappho, *Long Ago*. But it is not Sappho–it is very specifically the *fin de siècle* Lesbian sensibility that flourished alongside the poetry of Wilde and his friends. It is part of the same myth as *Les Chansons de Bilitis* and the poems of Renée Vivien. The amusing thing about it is that the Greek 'originals' are not originals at all, but paraphrases in Sappho's metre from indirect references in Pausanias and a scholiast on

Pindar. The Sapphic legend was so powerful that anything was enough to set off her late born sisters. Here sympathy achieves a kind of translation when the source does not even exist. In a few of the translations of the *Apple Orchard* lack of sympathy leads to ludicrous effects—to words, for instance 'gurgles' that would never have occurred to anyone who bothered to project himself imaginatively into Sappho's experience.

Still there is the question of the awesome lustre of Sappho's simplest words. Is it there or do we read it into her fragments? Partly it is a function of attention. If you isolate two sentences of a skillful description of passion or of Nature and say—'pay attention, these are by the greatest lyric poet who ever lived,' the mind will find values in them which may have been there, but which would normally have been passed over. Prisoners with nothing else to do, their eyes focused on the stained ceilings of their cells for hours, can find more than Sistine Chapels to look at. True, her apple orchard or her waning moon have all the intensity of Japanese *haiku*, but so do Frances Densmore's schematic translations of Chippewa and Teton Sioux—and we should never forget, so do hundreds of mediocre English translations of Japanese *haiku* themselves which transmit none of the special virtues of the originals. I am afraid that I must admit that the supernatural gleam that seems to emanate from *oio polu leukoteron* (fragment 62) 'far whiter than an egg' is a delusion, on a par with the mystical vision which comes with staring too long at an unshaded electric bulb or from taking one of Aldous Huxley's pharmaceutical nirvanas. But, still, in Sappho as in Homer, the simplest sentences do have a wonder, never to be equalled again in the West and never to be translated to any other language.

I am going to give you a little anthology of translations, all of them I think successful. They are not all of them successful for all the same reasons, and one of them is definitely eccentric, but I think they all exemplify a very high degree of imaginative identification with their originals:

LUGETE, O VENERES CUPIDINESQUE

Weep, weep, ye Loves and Cupids all
And ilka Man o' decent feelin':
My lassie's lost her wee, wee bird,
And that's a loss ye'll ken, past healin'.

The lassie lo'ed him like her een:
The darling wee thing lo'ed the ither,
And knew and nestled to her breast,
As ony bairnie to her mither.

Her bosom was his dear, dear haunt—
So dear, he cared no lang to leave it;
He'd nae but gang his ain sma' jaunt,
And flutter piping back bereavit.

The wee thing's gane the shadowy road
That's never travelled back by ony:
Out on ye, Shades! ye're greedy aye
To grab at ought that's brave and bonny.

Puir, foolish, fondling, bonnie bird,
Ye little ken what wark ye're leavin':
Ye've gar'd my lassie's een grow red,
Those bonnie een grow red wi' grievin'.

Catullus
G. S. Davies

ME NIVE CANDENTI PETIT MODO JULIA

White as her hand fair Julia threw
A ball of silver snow;
The frozen globe fired as it flew,
My bosom felt it glow.

Strange power of love! whose great command
Can thus a snow-ball arm;
When sent, fair Julia, from thine hand
Ev'n ice itself can warm.

How should we then secure our hearts?
Love's power we all must feel,
Who thus can by strange magic arts
In ice his flames conceal.

'Tis thou alone, fair Julia, know,
Canst quench my fierce desire;
But not with water, ice or snow,
But with an equal fire.

Petroniana
Soame Jenyns

THE RIVER MERCHANT'S WIFE: A LETTER

While my hair was still cut straight across my forehead
I played about the front gate, pulling flowers.
You came by on bamboo stilts, playing horse,
You walked about my seat, playing with blue plums.
And we went on living in the village of Chokan:
Two small people, without dislike or suspicion.

At fourteen I married My Lord you.
I never laughed, being bashful.
Lowering my head, I looked at the wall.
Called to, a thousand times, I never looked back.

At fifteen I stopped scowling,
I desired my dust to be mingled with yours
Forever and forever and forever.
Why should I climb the look out?

At sixteen you departed,
You went into far Ku-to-yen, by the river of swirling eddies,

And you have been gone five months.
The monkeys make sorrowful noise overhead.

You dragged your feet when you went out.
By the gate now, the moss is grown, the different mosses,
Too deep to clear them away!
The leaves fall early this autumn, in wind.
The paired butterflies are already yellow with August
Over the grass in the West garden;
They hurt me. I grow older.
If you are coming down through the narrows of the river
Kiang,
Please let me know beforehand,
And I will come out to meet you
As far as Cho-fu-Sa.

Li Po
Ezra Pound

AN ELEGY

I

O youngest, best-loved daughter of Hsieh,
Who unluckily married this penniless scholar,
You patched my clothes from your own wicker basket,
And I coaxed off your hairpins of gold, to buy wine with;
For dinner we had to pick wild herbs—
And to use dry locust-leaves for our kindling.
. . . Today they are paying me a hundred thousand—
And all that I can bring to you is a temple sacrifice.

II

We joked, long ago, about one of us dying,
But suddenly, before my eyes, you are gone.
Almost all your clothes have been given away;
Your needlework is sealed, I dare not look at it. . . .
I continue your bounty to our men and our maids—
Sometimes, in a dream, I bring you gifts.
. . . This is a sorrow that all mankind must know—
But not as those know it who have been poor together.

III

I sit here alone, mourning for us both.
How many years do I lack now of my threescore and ten?
There have been better men than I to whom heaven denied a son,
There was a poet better than I whose dead wife could not hear him.
What have I to hope for in the darkness of our tomb?
You and I had little faith in a meeting after death—
Yet my open eyes can see all night
That lifelong trouble of your brow.

Kiang Kang-Hu
Witter Bynner

L'OMBRE DES FEUILLES D'ORANGER

La jeune fille, qui travaille tout le jour, dans sa chambre solitiare, est doucement émue si elle entend, tout à coup, le son d'une flûte de jade;

Et elle s'imagine qu'elle entend la voix d'un jeune garçon.

A travers le papier des fenêtres, l'ombre des feuilles d'oranger vient s'asseoir sur ses genoux;

Et elle s'imagine que quelqu'un a déchiré sa robe de soie.

Le Livre de Jade
par Judith Gautier

THE SHADOW OF THE ORANGE-LEAVES

The young girl who works
all day in her solitary chamber
is moved to tenderness if she
hears of a sudden the sound of
a jade flute.

And she imagines that she
hears the voice of a young boy.

Through the paper of the
windows the shadow of the
orange-leaves enters and sits
on her knees;

And she imagines that some-
body has torn her silken dress.

'Tin-Tung-Ling'
Stuart Merrill's English of
Judith Gautier's French

Davies' Catullus has been put down, by a Sasenach, as a charming trick. Perhaps it is, but it is a moving poem in its own right and makes a comparison made many times before—the Celtic Catullus and the curiously Roman Burns. Also, Englishmen never really believe that Scots speak their own language. I prefer to think that Davies was so deeply moved and identified himself so closely with Catullus that he naturally turned to his most natural idiom—the Doric.

Soame Jenyns, not the curator at the B.M., but the Eighteenth Century churchman, seems to me to have achieved something very rare—a perfect translation of the most untranslatable type of Latin verse—those light lyrics and erotic elegies and little satires which are grouped in the Petroniana and which have otherwise only been captured by Ben Jonson and Herrick, and in their cases have been actually paraphrases. Not only is the English as close as possible to the metric of 'Petronius', but the Latin and the English can both be sung to the same melody, 'Phillis why shoulde we delaie?' by Waller with music by Henry Lawes. This can be found in Potter, *Reliquary of English Song* and you can try it yourself if you like. Jenyns catches not only the tone, but he handles language in exactly the same way. The only thing that is missing is the deep hidden undercurrent of iron disillusion and memory of blood that haunts all these little poems and that led to them being attributed to Petronius in the first place.

The greatest translators of Chinese, Judith Gautier, Klabund, Pound, knew less than nothing of Chinese when they did their best translations. In fact, Judith Gautier's lover and informant was a Thai, and himself had only the foggiest notions of the meanings of the Chinese text. Stuart Merrill was America's greatest poet between the New Englanders and the Post-War I moderns. He is practically unknown in the USA because he lived and wrote almost exclusively in French. His English is definitely Edwardian or McKinleyan, and suffers from all the vices of *The Yellow Book*. Yet who could quarrel with this 'translation'? It is a perfect transmission of one of the dominant themes of Chinese poetry and conveys exactly the neurotic lassitude and weakness of the sex starved girls and deserted concubines who fill Chinese literature.

Pound worked from the mss. of Fenollosa, who was himself badly informed by two Japanese whose knowledge of Chinese was already out of date, hopelessly Japonified for even the Japan of their day. Nevertheless this is one of the dozen or so major poems to be written in American in the twentieth century, and still the best single translation from the Chinese.

I have given you Witter Bynner's translation of Yuan Chen's *Elegy For His Dead Wife* because I think it is again, one of the best American poems of this century, incomparably Bynner's best poem, and, of all these poems, it conveys an overwhelming sense of identification with the situation of the original author. Mistakes, or at least dubious interpretations of a few words have been pointed out since it was made, and Bynner has discarded all the obliquity and literary reference of the original. Still, I think that from every point of view it is the second ranking single translation from the Chinese out of all we have so far done.

Not only have the best 'translators' not known Chinese, there is only one great translator who has, and only one in the second class—Arthur Waley, of course, and Bernhard Karlgren. Waley is a special case. He is a fine poet who has deliberately limited himself, as a kind of rigorous aesthetic discipline—a little like the self-imposed rigors of Paul Valéry—to translation from the Chinese and Japanese. Karlgren must be a special case, too, because he is the only Sinologist in any language who is any good at all. Possibly this is because he translates not into his own Swedish but into another foreign language—English.

I think this is due to the primitive state of Sinology. Most Sinologists are philologists. They are all too close to the language as such and too fascinated by its special very un-English and yet curiously very English-like problems to ever see the text as literature. The grammarian takes over in the decadence of the study of a language; but he also takes over—in fact he is essential—in its infancy. Karlgren does as a matter of fact seem to sit very easy to Chinese, you can hear him ordering a meal in Cantonese or bawling out a bureaucrat in the National Language.

A bit of the GI approach to language: Où sont les cigarettes, les girls, le restaurant, le W.C.? would be a great help to contemporary Sinologists and would go a long way to overcome their barbarism. After all, you can do nothing whatever with poetry until you comprehend that it too is about 'the necessities of life.'

One of the most engaging Hellenists of our time, Robert Byron, believed that all ancient Greek should be given the modern pronunciation. There is something to be said for this. Homer certainly did not sound like the waiter in the corner beanery, but it is possible that he sounded even less like the German and American professors, and it is certainly great fun to sit and eat pie à la mode after midnight and swap quotations with a lonely counterman. Somehow Pericles seems more available. This again is the virtue of the Italian and Roman Catholic pronunciation of Latin.

The *Tantum Ergo* of Aquinas known to children in the slums of Youngstown or Belfast, shades imperceptibly into the chirr of Horace's bracelets and back to the old Saturnian stomp. Communion is as important to the poet translator as communication. I was taught the correct pronunciation of Latin, but I have never been able to take it seriously. On the other hand, who has ever forgotten the first time, on the streets of modern Rome, that he looked down at his feet and saw SPQR on a manhole cover?

Sympathy can carry you very far if you have talent to go with it. Hart Crane never learned to speak French and the time he wrote his triptych poem *Voyages* he could not read it at all. His only informant was Allen Tate, a doubtful guide at best in this field, and his image of Rimbaud was an absurd inflation of the absurd Rimbaud myth. Yet *Voyages* is by far the best transmission of Rimbaud into English that exists—the purest distillation of the boyish hallucinations of *Bateau Ivre*.

Sympathy, or at least projection, can carry you too far. All sensible men to whom English is native are distressed at the French enthusiasm for M. Poe, the author of *Jamais Plus*. Nobody in France seems to be able to learn, ever, that his verse is dreadful doggerel and his ratiocinative fiction absurd and his aesthetics the standard lucubrations that go over in Young Ladies' Study Circles and on the Chautauqua Circuit. The reason is, of course, that the French translate their whole culture into Poe before they even start to read him. They think his formalism is their formalism and his scientific speculation the speculation of d'Alembert. They think the giddy early nineteenth century misses in Baltimore who swooned over the architectonics of *Eureka* are the same over-civilized courtesans who once bestowed their favors on the brocaded inventors of ingenious mathematical machines and, for that, on the homespun Le Bon Franklin. In this they are exactly like the brave French Jesuits whose adroit questions taught the Iroquois to expatiate on the mysteries of the Great

Spirit, a deity who had migrated unnoticed through the empyrean across the Atlantic from the court of Louis XV.

Finally, what does all this mean to the poet himself? What has it all meant to me? As Eliot, paraphrasing Dryden, has said, inspiration isn't always at its peak. Today we demand practically unrelieved intensity of poetry. The versified agricultural handbooks of the past are not for us —not even the verse novels of the Victorians. No poet ever could meet such a demand every day in the week. Translation however, provides us with plenty of poetic exercise on the highest level. It is the best way of keeping your tools sharp until the great job, the great moment, comes along. More important, it is an exercise of sympathy on the highest level. The writer who can project himself into the exaltation of another learns more than the craft of words. He learns the stuff of poetry. It is not just his prosody he keeps alert, it is his heart. The imagination must evoke, not just a vanished detail of experience, but the fullness of another human being.

Last and not least, translation saves you from your contemporaries. You can never really model yourself on Tu Fu or Leopardi or Paulus the Silentiary, but if you try you can learn a great deal about yourself. It is all too easy to model yourself on T. S. Eliot or William Carlos Williams or W. H. Auden or Alan Ginsberg—fatally easy—thousands do it every day. But you will never learn anything about yourself. Translation is flattering too. I don't at all like feeling like T. S. Eliot or Alan Ginsberg. All over the world's literature there are people I enjoy knowing intimately, whether Abailard or Rafael Alberti, Pierre Reverdy or Tu Fu, Petronius or Aesculapius. You meet such a nice class of people.

SMITH PALMER BOVIE

Translation as a Form of Criticism

SMITH PALMER BOVIE, *formerly of Indiana University and now chairman of the classics department at Douglass College in Rutgers University, has translated the* Georgics *of Vergil, the* Satires *and* Epistles *of Horace, and is presently working on a translation of Lucretius.*

Translation, like psychology, covers a multitude of sins. Like psychology, too, it flourishes in contemporary gardens, and therefore deserves to be asked what sort of flower it is, and what sort of gardeners cultivate it. How shall we identify the new plant, name it, arrange it neatly alongside other more deeply rooted varieties of natural exuberance? How shall we describe its habits?

Original species of poetry raise few such questions. They just grow, and we can admire or cultivate them as we will. In his *Definition of Poetry*, Boris Pasternak lists 'The stifled sweet pea on the vine' in a series of poetic items that begins:

It's a whistle's precipitous rise,
It is icicles broken and ringing,
It is night when the frost on leaves lies,
It's a duel of nightingales singing.

Auden, in *Music Is International*, rummaging among ramblers, comes out with the perfect blossom of a word to describe the coin-operated record player: 'hideola.' Keats may look up from the scene of his labors to catch the cadence of poetry in 'A pigeon tumbling in clear summer air'; or look down again, to treasure 'the wealth of globed peonies.' Such mature results are easy and innocent and only need to be looked at to be known.

But entering into the subject of translation is more bewildering. One book is a seed catalogue and a fiercely technical discussion of methods of comparative gardening. *On Translation* (ed. R. Brower, Harvard 1959) makes sixteen different inroads upon the scene, and lists some 277 bibliographical items beginning with Cicero and Horace and ending with Pasternak and the papers read at the Moscow conference on machine translation, May 15–21, 1959 (and, I trust, tape-recorded on a collectiveola). What has happened? Criticism has set in. Translated words are being further translated, into the laboratories to be further analyzed. We now have a botany of artificial flowers.

I think that translation itself is a form of criticism and therefore I wince at the new book which offers to bear us on past this idea into the land of the criticism of criticism, where it is hard to keep one's intellectual bearings. And I think that if the subject has become somewhat cluttered and complicated, rudimentary spadework is called for. I propose to dig up the earth around poetry and its hybrid, translation, for a while; then, to leave the things to their own original devices.

First, I would prune back art and criticism to some semblance of their original shapes; 'modern' art must go, and along with it 'new' criticism. 'New criticism'! The name alone is poisonous, the leafage and offshoots many, and correspondingly weak, the clinging vines parasitic. What was the old criticism? And the middle? What will follow the new? And what is 'modern' art? Something preceded by ancient art, or medieval art, something to be succeeded by future art? These epithets clamor for attention, but they tell us nothing. They want to be sign-posts, but in reality they are flags fluttering at the masthead of time, or guidons heading up a parade of devoted followers.

There is no such thing as modern art, or as new criticism. There is art, the joining together in palpable form of the fragments of life we endure as momentary passion, wonder, action, and dismay. There is criticism, the commonplace and widely distributed faculty of reasonable discernment, man's way of assuming responsibility for the experience he accumulates. Art and criticism are always with us, and therefore need lay no special temporal claim to our allegiance. They are today what they have always been. In fifth-century Athens *ho krites* witnessed and judged the poetic contest, and the relation of art and criticism is still like that. Art performs, acts on life, proposes marriage to the desirable soul of the audience. Criticism sits and watches, reads all the clauses in the marriage contract and disputes details of the dowry. Art flies and falls; criticism plots and plans. Art vibrates. Criticism shudders. Every last eye of Argos the watchful was sealed shut by Hermes, teller of tales.

Literary art includes poetry and fiction, two words long separated, but perhaps in need of being joined together again. And I would suggest that poetry means doing something with the forms of *language*, fiction doing something with the forms of *experience*. Admittedly, literary art in these two aspects has survived with miraculous hardiness for some two millennia, and literary criticism has trudged hopefully along at its heels, *non passibus aequis*. There is little more to say about the facts of artistic growth than this.

To simplify further and clarify my own interest, let me dismiss the idea of fiction and confine myself to poetry and its translation. Here again, I think that we can touch bottom readily enough. Translation is the carrying over of an original work in parts or as a whole into another language. The reliable judge of the result is a person in command of both languages.

Those who most need translations are those unfamiliar with the original language, whereas those who make the most use of *translation* belong to the ranks of original poets and their competent judges, or 'informed' critics. The existence of translations being granted, *translation* itself serves readers somewhat the way criticism does, by putting art to use. Through either medium something besides immediate cognition is gained. The original is reread, examined under a different light, subjected to interpretation. By being translated it undergoes experiences similar to those it meets by being criticized. It will be remembered, for instance, that Horace in *The Art of Poetry* included counsels appropriate to the art of translation and to the art of criticism.

Horace expected the three things to be linked together; certainly, from Horace's example alone we would infer the original poet's right to translate, transfer, criticize, and adapt the work of others, for he re-uses situations, themes, and phrases from elsewhere; he imitates and transforms; he criticizes poetic results, both his own and others'. At its farthest reach, such wholesale translation may be likened to American aircraft carriers being sold for scrap metal and towed to Japan, whence they will return to us in the form of toy pistols for small Americans to brandish on the streets of small towns. The extremes of usage seem to be of this sort: total re-use produces toy pistols; total neglect produces disarmament. The optimum between these extremes, then, would somehow preserve what is being put to use. A handy example of the workings of the subtle spirit of translation presents itself in Horace's adaptation of Terencė in the *amator exclusus* passage of the Third Satire of Book II[1]:

[1] For the book's original voyage, on its primary mission to triumph, compare Horace, *The Art of Poetry*, lines 345–6:

hic et mare transit
et longum noto scriptori prorogat aevum.
This book will . . .
travel across the sea, and extend
It's author's fame a long distance into the future.

For the *amator exclusus* passage I quote see my translation, *The*

LOVER:

To go now, or not to go now, when she herself calls me?
Or, thinking more deeply upon't, why not end my troubles?
She herself shut me out, she herself calls me back: shall I go?
No! Even if she begs me.
[Enter his slave, much smarter.]

SLAVE:

Oh master, a matter that doesn't submit
To methodical handling or rational wit

Satires and Epistles of Horace, Chicago, 1959, *Sermones* II.3. 259–271.

Compare also Terence, *Eunuchus*, lines 46 ff.:
Phaedria, the lover, speaks:—

Quid igitur faciam? non eam ne nunc quidem
quam accersor ultro? an potius ita me comparem,
non perpeti meretricum contumelias?
exclusit; revocat: redeam? non, si me obsecret.

Parmeno, the slave, replies (vss. 57 ff.):—

ere, quae res in se neque consilium neque modum
habet ullum, eam consilio regere non potes.
in amore haec omnia insunt vitia: iniuriae,
suspiciones, inimicitiae, indutiae,
bellum, pax rursum; incerta haec si tu postules
ratione certa facere, nihilo plus agas
quam si des operam ut cum ratione insanias.

And Horace, loc. cit.:

amator
exclusus qui distat, agit ubi secum, eat an non,
quo rediturus erat non arcessitus, et haeret
invisis foribus? 'nec nunc, cum me vocet ultro,
accedam? an potius mediter finire dolores?
exclusit; revocat: redeam? non, si obsecret.' ecce
servus non paulo sapientior: 'o ere, quae res
nec modum habet neque consilium, ratione modoque
tractari non volt. in amore haec sunt mala, bellum,
pax rursum: haec si quis tempestatis prope ritu
mobilia et caeca fluitantia sorte laboret
reddere certa sibi, nihilo plus explicet ac si
insanire paret certa ratione modoque.'

Will not be conquered by reason or rules.
In love the feelings are wicked tools.
First it's war, then it's peace, then both together:
La donna è perpetuum mobile, just like the weather.
The situation is fluid, subject to chance:
The scenes shift, and *their inhabitants,*
And it's done in the dark. To eliminate sadness
By a rational scheme to promote your gladness
Would be only as right as devising a method for madness.

Horace was perhaps not so much translating as quoting, but he was of course putting Terence to use in a different context and in a different meter, and he did add that passage about the weather to the original. I felt free, therefore, in translating Horace's translation of Terence, to work back toward the comic style by means of rhyme and to quote Shakespeare, Verdi and Irwin Edman as faithfully as Horace quoted Terence. A good gardener, like Horace, I think, knew just when to transplant from Terence, and I can only hope that the passage, uprooted and reset in English soil, stands up to the northern weather.

Another routine instance from Horace is his editorial version of a report of the first line of the Odyssey:

(*rursus quid virtus et quid sapientia possit*
utile proposuit nobis exemplar Ulixen)
qui domitor Troiae multorum providus urbis
et mores hominum inspexit, latumque per aequor
dum sibi, dum sociis reditum parat, aspera multa
pertulit, adversis rerum IMMERSABILIS *undis.*

(*On the other hand, Homer gives us a useful example*
Of virtue and wisdom at work in the noble Ulysses:)
The tamer of Troy, whose piercing glance traveled into the hearts
Of men, as he entered into their cities. Borne to the ends
Of the world to discover the homeward path overseas for his friends,

He tossed on his troubles, UNSINKABLE, a true man of parts.[2]

Here I went to rhymed hexameters to indicate the preservation of Homer's account in Horace's report of it, and felt that the superb Horatian editorial epithet IMMERSABILIS (a word heard here once, and heard no more, in Latin poetry) demanded being acclaimed as a capital achievement. Vergil and Horace alike handled this kind of translation nimbly, making use of others and thereby becoming the source of words that could be made use of by still others. It may be a weakness, like a loss of strength that is best repaired by a blood transfusion from the right type of donor. For instance, at the hair-raising crisis in the underworld, his re-encounter with Dido, Aeneas probably felt faint, and therefore 'quoted' Catullus, to bolster up his premises. In Catullus, the Lock of Berenice had defended its abrupt departure from the head of the queen by saying: *invita, o regina, tuo de vertice cessi.* Quick-witted, but nervous, Aeneas, protests to Dido: *invitus, regina, tuo de litore cessi.*[3]

But I suspect that translation like this, quotation with a vengeance, is more like Dubonnet *avec un zeste* than blood transfusion. Tossing off lines from his predecessors, the

[2] Horace, *Epistles* I.2. 17–22.

[3] Catullus LXVI. 39 (the whole poem derived from Callimachus' original). Vergil, *Aeneid* VI. 460. Vergil's wit often carried him to zestful quotation: he transplants and parodies a timely piece of Epicurean advice from Lucretius, in *Georgics* I. 158–9:

heu magnum alterius frustra spectabis acervum
concussaque famem in silvis solabere quercu.

And so turns Lucretius' saying inside out:

suave, mari magno turbantibus aequora ventis,
e terra magnum alterius spectare laborem.
(*DRN* II. 1–2)

Servius says that Vergil transformed Ennius' 'solid black line of elephants' into a 'solid black line of ants,' when appropriating to his own use his predecessor's *it nigrum campis agmen*, at *Aeneid* IV. 404. This is perhaps a form of translation by truncation.

poet feels the glow of originality mounting to his head. He raises a toast to the past and plunges on into the present adventures of his own work. Whatever subtle spirit generates these effects, quotation and immediate use are rudimentary forms of translation as the preserving of another original. And, even at this stage, they amount to evidence of the critical faculty which selects, excludes, and applies. Consider, for instance, the fate of Horace in the hands of Pope, his eighteenth-century protector. We are safe in saying that a good deal of Pope's originality consists in his unique imitation of Horace, of Horace's mien (and mean), of Horace's views, of Horace's self-confidence and fastidious perfectionism. Pope tells us as much simply by writing the *Essay on Criticism* to disarm his critics before they can join battle, and to indicate that his art, like Horace's, requires the exercise of intelligence and the shepherding of one's best talents. Art must be witty, Pope demonstrates in this essay on witticism; that is, clear *and* brilliant. And so an affinity for Horace is well painted:

Horace still charms with graceful negligence,
And without method talks us into sense,
Will, like a friend, familiarly convey
The truest notions in the easiest way.
He, who supreme in judgment as in wit,
Might boldly censure, as he boldly writ,
Yet judged with coolness, though he sung with fire;
His precepts teach but what his works inspire.
Our Critics take a contrary extreme,
They judge with fury, but they write with fle'me:
Nor suffers Horace more in wrong Translations
By Wits, than Critics in as wrong Quotations.[4]

Pope is slightly ambiguous here (as might be expected when a writer is dealing simultaneously with two subjects, his own and his predecessor's critics), as is reflected in the final couplet, usually taken to mean that 'Horace suffers

[4] *Essay on Criticism*, 653–664.

no more from poet's mistaken translations of his poetry than from critics' mistaken interpretation of his criticism.' In other words, he suffers both ways, Pope may imply. Certainly, some such fate dogged a singularly fine line in Horace's *Epistle to Florus* through the 17th century and caught up with it at last in *The Dunciad*. Horace wrote:

> *vehemens et liquidus puroque simillimus amni*[5]

This gave Denham occasion to write in *Cooper's Hill* (1642):

> *Oh could I flow like thee and make thy stream*
> *My great example, as it is my theme!*
> *Though deep, yet clear, though gentle still not dull,*
> *Strong without rage, without o'erflowing, full.*

And paved the way for Pope's parody in *The Dunciad* (1728):

> *Flow, Welsted, flow! like thine inspirer, Beer;*
> *Though stale, not ripe; though thin, yet never clear;*
> *So sweetly mawkish, and so smoothly dull;*
> *Heady, not strong; o'erflowing, though not full.*[6]

Deliberate cultivation of a Horation flower has turned it into a weed.

Of course, more important than the particular consequences I have been reviewing is the whole decision to choose and embrace another author. Adaptation of the original to new purposes which ensue is like that criticism which listens to the concert for the music it offers, not that for which it fidgets, waiting for the performer to blow a bad note. And under this dispensation we can sense the importance to Horace of his originals, Pindar, Alcaeus, Sappho, and the comic poets; to Vergil of Theocritus, Hesiod, Homer, Euripides; to Milton of Homer and Vergil, plus the Bible; to Pope of Homer and Horace.

[5] *Epistles* II.2. 120.
[6] *The Dunciad* III. 169–172.

Shakespeare, who surely deserved to be knighted for his successes, as much as Sir Francis Drake and Sir John Hawkins, boarded *friendly* vessels, cheerfully relieving them of their burdens. Having captured the captivating Ovid, for instance, and lifted effects wholesale from the good ship *Metamorphoses,* Shakespeare himself was sometimes astonished at the result. 'Bless thee, Bottom! bless thee!' exclaims Peter Quince, 'thou art translated.'[7] Transcendental as the verb has become, all of *Midsummer Night's Dream* has the touch of Midas without the curse. A major portion of Ovid's *discors concordia* steals into its magical wit, not the least glittering of which are the very mistranslations of the misinformed and twice translated Bottom, the displaced poet:

I will move storms; I will condole in some measure
. . . my chief humour is for a tyrant: I could play Ercles
rarely, or a part to tear a cat in, to make all split.
The raging rocks
With shivering shocks,
Shall break the locks
Of prison gates:
And Phibbus' car
Shall shine from far,
And make and mar
The foolish Fates.

This was lofty![8]

Add to this a rather too particular reworking of Pyramus and Thisbe, grievously met at 'Ninny's tomb,' and no wonder Theseus' consternation is complete when he is presented with the playbill so altered from its Ovidian beginnings:

A *tedious brief scene of young Pyramus,*
And his love Thisbe; very tragical mirth.[9]

[7] M S N D III.1. 19.
[8] M S N D I.2. 27 ff.
[9] M S N D V.1. 56–7. And thus, to Theseus' consternation, Ovid is brought not to new birth but to a new misconception. Something of the same playful pirating of Ovid's freight,

Shakespeare's larger interest in Ovid was not with the forms of language, but with the forms of experience, which he willfully transplanted to his own garden, as in Sonnet LX or in *Venus and Adonis*. There he combined several narrative elements from the *Metamorphoses*, to outstrip Ovid's story, and prefaced the new work with an epigraph from the *Amores*. By the fifth stanza he is ready to make use of Narcissus' *inopem me copia fecit:*[10]

---

the spiriting away of the spirit of Ovid, steals into AYLI also, I would conjecture, where Jaques is a personification of *discors concordia*, whose dissonant antitheses (which owe something to Ovid) grate against the romances being performed and transformed in this pastoral retreat:

TOUCHSTONE:
I am here with thee and thy goats, as the most
capricious poet, honest Ovid, was among the Goths.

JAQUES (aside):
O knowledge ill-inhabited! worse than Jove
in a thatch'd house.

TOUCHSTONE:
When a man's verses cannot be understood, nor a man's
good wit seconded with the forward child
understanding, it strikes a man more dead than a
great reckoning in a little room.–Truly, I would
the gods had made thee more poetical.

AUDREY:
I do not know what poetical is: is it honest in
deed and word? is it a true thing?

TOUCHSTONE:
No, truly: for the truest poetry is the most
feigning: and lovers are given to poetry: and what
they swear in poetry may be said, as lovers, they do
feign. III.3. 7–27

In spite of Touchstone's rapid-fire fooling here, isn't Shakespeare's schooling having its say as well? Ovid was spirited off to an all too pastoral retreat among the 'Goths,' knowledge of his work was variously lodged, not always adequately; what he feigned in verse he didn't necessarily act out in life. What happened to Ovid was in a way as disastrous as what happened to Marlowe, a pointed quotation from whose translation of Musaeus' Hero and Leander also figures in the text of AYLI.

10 *Metamorphoses* III.466.

Here come and sit, where never serpent hisses,
And being set, I'll smother thee with kisses.
And yet not cloy thy lips with loath'd satiety
But rather famish them amid their plenty,
Making them red and pale with fresh variety,
Ten kisses short as one, one long as twenty.[11]

Sparks like these struck from the anvil of Ovid may undergo the ultimate transformation of being asked to form a halo around the head of an even more interesting 'Roman' original, Cleopatra:

Age cannot wither her, nor custom stale
Her infinite variety: other women cloy
The appetites they feed: but she makes hungry
Where most she satisfies.[12]

Bless thee, Ovid! bless thee! thou art at last translated! Throughout *Venus and Adonis*, Shakespeare simply outdoes Ovid, the main interest centering in Venus' incapacity to evoke love for herself. She waxes eloquent, and soliloquizes like any heroine in Ovid you may care to name. Adonis wishes she would stop talking. Her ardor increases, like that 'flame' consuming any heroine in Ovid you may care to name. Adonis' boredom mounts. Ovid had remarked that in this whole plight Venus acted like Diana tucking her tunic above her knees and sprinting about the landscape with her favorite huntsman. Shakespeare makes her even more of a self-contradiction:

But all in vain. Good queen, it will not be!
She hath assay'd as much as may be proved.
Her pleading hath deserved a greater fee:
She's Love, she loves, and yet she is not loved.[13]

This is not translation: it's how to give a wrong synopsis

[11] *Venus and Adonis* 17–22.
[12] *Antony and Cleopatra* II.2. 240–243.
[13] *Venus and Adonis,* 607–610.

of the verb *amo* when you intend to leave it in the passive voice. And could anyone ask for a more wilful handling of original Latin?

Shakespeare certainly could translate. For instance:

> LUCENTIO (reads):
> *Hac ibat Simois; hic est Sigeia tellus;*
> *Hic steterat Priami regia celsa senis.*[14]
>
> BIANCA:
> *Construe them.*
>
> LUCENTIO:
> *Hac ibat, as I told you before,–Simois, I*
> *am Lucentio–hic est, son unto Vicentio of*
> *Pisa,–Sigeia tellus, disguised thus to get*
> *your love;–hic steterat, and that Lucentio*
> *that come a-wooing,–Priami, is my man Tranio,*
> *–regia, bearing my port,–celsa senis, that*
> *we might beguile the old pantaloon.*[15]

This manifests Shakespeare's great power of negative capability when applied to the art of translation, and proves that although he could translate, he didn't need to.

So, poets are translators; and more than that, weavers, joiners, stainers, incarnadining the multitudinous seas of other poets' work, making the old one new. Major exam-

[14] From Ovid, *Heroides* I. 33–4.

[15] *The Taming of the Shrew*, III.1. 26 ff. And, among other odd instances of Shakespeare the translator there is the old grey doe of *Love's Labour's Lost* IV.2, who isn't quite what she seems to be:

SIR NATHANIEL:
I assure ye it was a buck of the first head.
HOLOFERNES:
Sir Nathaniel, haud credo.
DULL:
'Twas not a haud credo: *'twas a pricket.*

Not to mention Holofernes' wholly infernal Latin throughout. Or again we have the schoolbook small Latin translation that was to live on and on, *Et tu Brute*, for the lesse Greek of Suetonius.

ples, multifarious instances of translations and translation, are too many, too important and too familiar to submit to excerpting. And so I have settled for syndromes rather than recite case histories. The relatedness I seek to stress is traceable to the simple fact that many poets have been adept at translation.

They have also, more often than not, been blessed and cursed with keen critical insight. Pope is a strong contender in the ranks of classical critics—as Coleridge, Arnold, Eliot were to become in due time. And Pope's best criticism is usually to be found in his sprightliest verse. After all, he worked out an epic of poetry and criticism, whose heroes are all bad poets and myopic critics. Seeing farther into art than they, he scored off their partial views:

The critic Eye, that microscope of Wit,
Sees hairs and pores, examines bit by bit.[16]

And, heavily conscious of the weight of learned lumber critics carry in their heads, Pope addressed the Muse of Dullness in tones of genuine anxiety:

For thee we dim the eye and stuff the head
With all such reading as was never read:
For thee explain a thing till all men doubt it,
And write about it, Goddess, and about it.[17]

Or, he pierced his own pensive criticism with classical allusions and shafts from *L'Allegro:*

As erst Medea (cruel, so to save!)
A new Edition of old Aeson gave;
Let standard Authors thus, like trophies born,
Appear more glorious, as more hacked and torn.
And you, my Critics! in the chequered shade
Admire new light through holes yourselves have made.[18]

[16] *The Dunciad* IV. 233–4.
[17] Ibid. IV. 249–252.
[18] Ibid. IV. 121–126.

The more intemperate plebeian, Swift, went so far as to measure the critical impulse in poets by the rule of envy, and to transfigure the result in a new version of Hobbes' classic statement of the war of every man against every man:

Hobbes clearly proves that every creature
Lives in a state of war by nature . . .
If on Parnassus' top you sit
You rarely bite, are always bit:
Each poet of inferior size
On you shall rail and criticize
And strive to tear you limb from limb;
While others do as much for him.
The vermin only teaze and pinch
Their foes superior by an inch.
So, naturalists observe, a flea
Has smaller fleas that on him prey;
And these have smaller still to bite 'em,
And so proceed ad infinitum.
Thus every poet, in his kind,
Is bit by him that comes behind[19]

It is probably true, moreover, that the power of negative thinking in poets can become a preoccupation with one's own destiny, and a critical effort to preserve one's identity, perhaps by attacking others. Paul Valéry's *Variations sur les Bucoliques,* the introduction to his verse translation of Vergil's *Bucolics* aptly focuses this critic vision: 'At moments, as I fiddled with my translation, I caught myself wanting to change something in the venerable text. It was a naive and unconscious identification with the imagined state of mind of a writer of the Augustan age . . . I could not help looking at the text of the *Eclogues,* as I translated them, with the same critical eye as at French verse, my own or another's.'

And a more comprehensive and precise account of the

[19] Swift, *Poetry: A Rhapsody.*

whole relationship of poet, translator and critic can be derived from Valéry's account along the length and breadth of this introductory essay than can be learned from Swift or Pope. In essence, it tells us that the poet is himself a kind of translator 'poised between his fine ideal and his nothingness . . . a singular form of translator, translating conventional discourse, modified by an emotion, into the language of the gods.'[20]

II

So much for poets as translators and critics. Next, I wish to regard translators as poets and critics. And while this is not the same thing as saying that they are numerous,[21] we may begin with the fact that they are and ask why.

Like nature, translators abhor a vacuum, and therefore become instrumental today, as they have always been, in resolving the modern reader's dreadful suspension between *his* beau idéal and *his* rien. Like criticism, translation has set in, with a vengeance, and has taken root. And among the reasons for its proliferation today are the same old reasons as well as several new ones. In the United States, languages are less well known than they were, and less well handled. Out of this dangerous nettle, ignorance, we pluck this flower of a safety device, translation, and raise the supply by increasing the demand. But the aristocracy too, who dominate the republic of letters, have been perceptibly shaken by the shift of sensibility which accompanied the tremors of Eliot's early poetry, and disarmed the immediate past of its conventional pseudo-

[20] Paul Valéry, *Traduction en Vers des Bucoliques de Virgile*, Paris, 1956, pp. 25–8 passim. The first part quoted here is translated by Jackson Mathews in *On Translation*, p. 76.

[21] Sir Ronald Storrs, in *Ad Pyrrham* (London, Oxford U. Press, 1959) has assembled a 'Polyglot Collection of Translations of Horace's Ode to Pyrrha' from 1590 to the present. Some 451 'discovered' translations of the poem, into 26 different languages (including back into Latin), are listed.

dignities. New sensibility scolded, and old sensibility shook in his boots. Certainly these are two reasons that can be offered. A third is generated by the educational style we have adopted, of soaring over whole documents in the humanistic tradition. The wings are translations, preferably mass produced in cheap editions for Sibylline consumption in classrooms. A fourth reason may derive from some general need that is growing in us for an international attitude toward time—the history that all men have in common. Time, like Hell, is full of other people, but particularly of people speaking other languages. Our translations embrace these eternal fellow citizens, and perhaps here lies the humanistic counterpart of the more grisly, because more precise, international scientific yearning for space.

The old reasons, I think, make as much sense and have even more chance of longer life than the topical obsessions. Like the Elizabethans, like 18th Century Augustans, like the Romans, our translators strive to be poets and manage to exercise good judgment. They are persistent gardeners, however exposed to competitive gardening they may be. The hardy Random House *Complete Greek Drama* (1938–$5.00 for the two volumes) is now exposed to the Chicago *Complete Greek Tragedies* attractively done up at the pre-Christmas price of $16.95 for the four volumes. And I suppose that the New York publishers are muttering the long-rehearsed Roman political sentiment, *delenda est Chicago*. Abroad, Penguins glide unruffled on their air patrol, sure to intercept and shoot up any enemy craft, at least, if not shoot it down. But fortunately, our concern is not with the cold war of every translation against every translation: it is with that standard type of gardener, the translator, busy today wearing out his hands with spadework.[22] Translators today are poets and so earn their right to labor as they will. Day Lewis is insouciant, direct, deft;

[22] As Vergil says of the beekeeper: *ipse labore manum duro terat.* (*Georgics* IV. 114).

Rolfe Humphries, fleet-punning, fertile in metrics, a man of many moods. And their translations are correspondingly original. It is now *Lattimore's* Iliad, as it was Pope's, or Chapman's. Valéry's Canticle of the Columns has become Louise Bogan and May Sarton's splendor of Ionian white and gold. Mary Barnard's versions of Sappho are shapely counterparts of their originals. Richard Wilbur's translations from the French have perfected a principle of 'ordre et beauté,/ Luxe, calme et volupté,' by themselves manifesting 'grace and measure, richness, quietness, and pleasure.'

All along the rows of our decades Mr. Eliot has cleverly shored up from other originals fragments of language, constructing a ruin for himself that never fell in, and has now gone on to transform Euripidean dramatic contexts, making highly original puzzles out of the same old pieces of psychology and poetry. If we place Pound alongside Eliot we see how close the relationship of poet and translator can be. Eliot of course is no mere translator, but he is fertile in translation, like Shakespeare, and has always put the literary originals of the past to good uses in his poems, which are transfigured versions, as well as true poems. He is the translator who became a poet, just as Pound is the poet who became a translator. Eliot has become the poet in residence at the University of the West, Pound the Translator in Exile.[23]

I suspect that a bittersweet longing for the old dispensation impels our translators and sharpens their critical faculties. In a curious way Yeats hit on the thing when he said 'I have put myself to school where all things are

[23] And in view of Ovid's continuing fascination for English writers from Shakespeare to Joyce, compare Pound's remarks in the *ABC of Reading* (p. 113) about Golding's translation: 'I do not honestly think that anyone can know anything about the art of lucid narrative in English, or let us say about the history of the development of English narrative-writing (verse or prose) without seeing the whole of the volume . . . the most beautiful book in the language.'

seen: A Tenedo tacitae per amica silentia lunae.' Even if we fail to decipher the precise Celtic code that Yeats' allegiance to Vergil is written in, we can be grateful for this impulse leading to the essay, for it contains the appealing aphorism:

> *We make of the quarrel with others, rhetoric,*
> *but of the quarrel with ourselves, poetry.*[24]

Where had he been? To a line from the second book of the *Aeneid*. And what had he seen? The Greek fleet stealing back to render Troy? The essence of Vergil, shimmering in the moonlight, and stealing from Homer to fashion the first epic poem to have a worrier, not a warrior, as its chief character? Had Yeats seen that empires are built on anxiety, and had he known immediately that poems are too? At least it can be argued that translators, like poets, are anxious to do something with poetry, and *if* they cannot write *Paradise Lost*, can transplant some of its native products. If they are gardeners of adamant, furthermore, like Rilke or Pasternak, they cultivate the common earth with remarkable results, strengthening and fertilizing it; they end by making it more proof against soul-erosion than it originally was.

When Rilke became convinced that Valéry was the greatest living poet, he dropped everything else and proceeded to translate.[25] Pasternak, whose mighty powers of refusal[26] loom large today, could not be ordered to

[24] *Per Amica Silentia Lunae*, 1917–1918. pp. 492, 507–8, *Essays* Macmillan 1924.

[25] Norbert Fuerst, in *Phases of Rilke*, Indiana U. Press, 1958, describes the further result as follows: 'His satisfaction with the translations was almost as great as his admiration for the original . . . a steppingstone toward his own French poems . . . Valéry himself . . . used his prestige to introduce this new *French* poet Rilke.'

[26] Replacing *Safe Conduct* with *I Remember*, Pasternak becomes the first self-critic to write two autobiographies. *I Remember* is interesting for its mode, as a kind of abstraction of *Safe*

write, but could order his art to sustain itself on translation. And now, like Schiller's Ode to Joy in the Ninth Symphony, *Dr. Zhivago* bursts on our ears in translation, and we hear in the United States a new Ode to Freedom. I sense in the keen sensibility and the rugged grandeur of Pasternak a new Prometheus, critical of Zeus in whatever shape that tyrant may momentarily assume, bent on bringing to humanity the fire of life and hope, and at the same time caustically scornful of any mercurial messengers truckling to the powers that be and hustling into his presence to enlist the hero's 'cooperation' on behalf of a western union.

The power of translation as a form of criticism is as forceful as the Titanic conduct and aesthetic range of a Pasternak is complicated, and I cannot pretend to explain it fully. The best approach to this part of the subject may be to back away from it, to let remembrance of things past do the work, and recall what we already know. Chiefly, I would argue that the critical judgment evident in the energy of translating is like a musical score, immediately

---

Conduct, and for its tone of Promethean humility: 'Above I have described my ambivalent attitude toward my own poetic past and to that of others. I would never lift a finger to bring back from oblivion three fourths of what I have written. Why then, it may be objected, do I let someone else publish it? There are two reasons for it. First, there are often grains of truth, aptness, and acute observation in the mass of what is deplorable and annoying about those things of mine. Secondly, quite recently, I completed my chief and most important work, the only one I am not ashamed of and for which I can answer with the utmost confidence, a novel in prose with a supplement in verse.'

I would also like to draw attention to the following words from a facsimile of a letter written in October 1958 (to David Magarshak, translator and editor of *I Remember* [?]) which appears on p. 127 of the Pantheon Books edition: 'I take the opportunity to repeat you, that except the "Dr. Zh." which you should read, all the rest of my verses and writings are devoid of any sense and importance. The most part of my mature years I gave off to Goethe, Shakespeare and other great and voluminous translations. Thankfully yours, B.P.'

sensed by being diffused rather than analyzed. If one heads for the subject, translation as a form of criticism, it recedes, like the shores of Italy, so long as Aeneas was heading for them, *semper cedentia retro.* Or like Augustine's definition of time, it becomes a matter which we can fully comprehend, but which will not stand still long enough to be apprehended.

Criticism reveals itself (1) in the translator's kinship with his author, (2) in the irreversible decision he makes to take possession of his original, and (3) in the techniques used to implement that decision. There is in the first place a deep affinity, and a workable *ménage à trois* embraces the poet, his faithful translator and best critic. Or rather, the bonds of art effect the marriage of true minds in lifelong friendship. The kinship will always assume individual form and the relationships differ as the persons forging them differ. Pope loved Horace, but in his own way. Shakespeare felt perfectly free to take liberties with Ovid. Milton admired Vergil to the point of transforming his worrier into a husband, which comes rather close to doing away with heroics entirely. Every new writer in every new generation likes Homer, as the chronology of translations testifies. And most translators will defend their judgment when asked why they do this work by saying 'I like the way he writes.' Dante serves best as the symbol of fellowship between original writers and their followers, for he was even more the friend than the translator—although wonderfully phrased and artfully rephrased lines from the *Aeneid* blaze out in the *Comedy*. The critical and austere medieval follower, the son of the 'dolcissimo padre' did not translate Vergil: rather, he was transported by Vergil toward the sublimities of poetic truth, and left there to administer poetic justice.

Dante's example is worth remembering because of the topical situation today. Why is he himself being so ardently translated, and what kinship do his imitators reveal? What are they after? The restatement of his fiery critique of human understanding? The English equivalent for a Latinate Italian form of expression? Royalties? Why is Dante so prominent a great book? The majority of his translators are critics, several are poets. All seem interested in executing the kind of poetic justice on Dante that Dante exemplified in his relationship to Vergil. All peer into the meaning of an original where more is meant than meets the eye, and so enable us to see it better. Many have a way of writing poetry that is akin to Dante's.

Granting that the translator as critic finds merit in his friend's work, what causes him to take possession of the original? His judgment that the worth of the past can be measured by its contiguity in time and space with the present. By translating, then, he makes the past contemporary and renews the old. This involves a selection and exclusion, choice and discernment, and the methods a new necessity for translating must invent. The translator, in effect, pronounces a major judgment on another work when he says: this is in fact ours, and we will not lose it through ignorance, oversight, or neglect. He thereupon presents the reader with the past, carrying the cargo across the gulf of time on the bridge of style.

A third form of criticism is seen in the style of adaptation, once the papers for adoption have been filed. It is widely and variously seen in the technique of the imitative craftsman. It partakes of self-criticism. Out of the quarrels the translator has with others in this case, he makes poetry. *On Translation* is one long soliloquy on the technical judgment of the translator, and its debated lines need not be rehearsed here: it is enough to remember that hundreds of points are made and details of decisions reviewed by the contributors to the volume, who number many of the most recent and most gifted translators, all of whom turn out to be critics. The book itself is like an army critique: after the decisive moves have been made and the battle won, the officers confer and discuss how the campaign might have been waged. Or, it is like an orchestra tuning up again, after the concert.

Between the decision to befriend and take possession of the original and the methodological afterthoughts, meanwhile, has intervened the performance, the translation itself not as form of criticism but as a diffusion of truth.

And there I leave the whole matter to its original devices. Like a garden, it will grow, and it might prove interesting to continue taking stock, rewarding to bring in tangible fruit. One consideration apropos of stock-taking would require the quintessential effort to do justice to the critic himself, whom I have, I hope, regularly belabored. His attitude is always Stoical enough to invite such treatment. But to the four propositions, the poet as translator, the poet as critic, the translator as poet, the translator as critic, a fifth could be added. Critics are translators. Much criticism is a species of translation. Our carpenter critics raise the roof—of the original work in question—over their own heads and take shelter under it. Often enough, criticism is telling us what the poet really said, but saying this in the other language, the language of criticism. If the poet, in Valéry's conception, translates ordinary discourse into the language of the gods, our critics translate the language of the gods back into ordinary discourse. Perhaps criticism is most instrumental in leading us back to particular aspects of the original, and serves as this kind of fragmentary and *ad hoc* job of work. Translation carries on the work, leading us back to the whole original.

Only one more move is necessary, and this one is left up to the reader. The criticism and the translation which free us from confinement in ignorance and release us from the present, bring us to the point where we can finally enter the realm of the original and, with some work, make of its language what we will. Furthermore, the amiable cooperation of poetry, criticism and translation has perhaps been *not* so much a carrying over of the precious past into the greedy present, but rather a carrying of us to it. The little known has become better known, thanks to the mediators: but their mediation has acquired a magical power to restore our sight. It has made us realize and gradually perceive that there is as much light at the other end of the tunnel.

Surely this is the light that can best illuminate the whole subject I have been going through. Streaming from so particular a source as Vergil's Third Eclogue, for instance, it shows us two poets, rivals, and a third a critic and judge. Palaemon, the critic, has arrived on the scene opportunely just as Damoetas and Menalcas reach the crisis in their pastoral affairs by introducing the question, 'Which of us is the true poet?' With Palaemon to preside, the two shepherds put their powers to the practical test, and as the challenging and responsive couplets smoothly run their course, we hear in our ears what Palaemon will eventually have to decide. Neither is best because both keep improving by virtue of mutual inspiration. Neither drowns out the other because both excel at their common task, which, in this imaginary setting somewhere in Arcadia, is simply to work at the composition of poetry. Is not this an idyllic version of poetry being handed on and being adjudged well worth the breath to utter it?

We remember how it ends, with Palaemon's judgment:

Non nostrum inter vos tantas componere lites;
et vitula tu dignus et hic, et quisquis amores
aut metuet dulcis aut experietur amaros.
claudite iam rivos, pueri: sat prata biberunt.

So great a quarrel is not mine to end;
Ye both deserve the heifer; so do all
Who fear love's honey or who taste its gall.
Shut off the waters, for the fields are moist.[27]

An alert and unfoolable critic, Prof. H. J. Rose, puts the scene in scholarly perspective by explaining in his com-

[27] Vergil, *Eclogues* III. 108–111.

mentary the extent of Vergil's indebtedness to Theocritus in this poem. And he reminds us sharply that the highly original touch Vergil applied to the critic Palaemon transformed his role from the conventional one of stodgy yes-man to that of absent-minded fellow artist:

> '. . . we may suppose Palaemon to have spent much thought and sung over his love, whoever she may be, and it needs but a few notes of music to set his mind on that familiar theme once more . . . Therefore, when the singers pause, as they do unbidden, it dawns on the poor umpire that he had not really been listening, and is in no position to decide which has done better. So he hastily declares a draw, and assures them that they have sung enough:
>
> *claudite iam rivos, pueri, sat prata biberunt.*'[28]

True. These are the critic's final words: this is the judge's sentence. But perhaps not true enough, as a critique of Palaemon. Like the one poet Menalcas, and the other poet, Damoetas, Palaemon speaks for Vergil. And Vergil speaks for all poets and their rivals, as well as for all critics, and for all who 'fear love's honey or who taste its gall.' For all who would balance one word, like *amores*, against another, *amaros*. Palaemon has the best word, then, the last word, when he decides that it's time to stop, for this day the garden has been well tended, and the idyllic contest of art well attended.

[28] H. J. Rose, *The Eclogues of Vergil*, Berkeley, 1942, p. 42.

JEAN PARIS

Translation and Creation

JEAN PARIS *has served as 'visiting professor' in French and comparative literature at Brandeis, University of Nebraska, University of Buffalo, and Smith College. Among his translations into French are: Lorca's* Poeta in Nueva-York, *Behan's* The Hostage, *and Shakespeare's* The Tempest.

In one of his remarkable fictions, Jorge Luis Borges tells of a certain Pierre Ménard whom we could regard as the ideal translator. Not only is he mad enough to devote his whole life to a single book–namely *Don Quijote*–but this work he painfully tries to rewrite in Spanish, with the very same words, sentences and order as in Cervantes. No one will ever go further. And we may well wonder if Borges has not the right to call him the *autor del Quijote*. In the same way, with his odd kind of wit, the Argentinian writer relates the drama of a geographer obsessed by an ever increasing need for precision, who draws larger and larger maps until finally they become as great as the country itself and cover it entirely.

These stories are meant to point out the traditional limit of translation, that is, the original. How close we can get to it is a problem which torments, or should torment, all translators. But it is a naïve question, for we may choose various ways of reproducing the work, according to its elements. The most common, and also the most unaesthetic, is the mere transcription of the 'meaning.' The rationalist translator is satisfied when he has expressed what he believes to be 'the ideas of the author,' with a minimum of misinterpretations. Furthermore, he may be tempted to repeat the sounds or rhythm of the text, regardless of its precise signification. Although this approach is not usual, a Hungarian scholar in Paris, who is now writing a thesis on this topic, maintains that we are perfectly entitled, as far as poetry is concerned, to render, for example, the English substantive 'soul' by the French adjective 'soûl', which means 'drunk'. This may seem an extreme statement, leading to a drastic revolution in literature, but such an assertion brings the translator back to the problem of his own justification.

The problem is this: does not the transforming of a written work from one language to another utterly alter its character? And, in performing this metamorphosis, does not the translator commit, if not a sacrilege, at least an offense against art and spirit? These questions, themselves serious enough for an essay, become crucial as soon as poetry is at stake. The higher we go in literary hierarchy, the more difficult it is to separate a work from its own original expression. If we may hope, at least theoretically, that a translation from Descartes or Heidegger convey the essentials of their thought, it is obvious that Donne or Dylan Thomas lose everything when they lose their own language. There is no such thing in poetry as an abstract 'meaning', independent of its form, reducible to a formula, translatable in all idioms. Here the word constitutes its own universe, obeys its own laws, shapes its own significance, and the poetic principle remains of such a private, intimate nature that to violate it is also to destroy the secret core of the work—which is precisely what a translation ought to preserve.

Naturally, the drama is less intense when the two languages bear a close kinship. Shakespeare found his second best home in Germany, and Pushkin is likely to be less betrayed by Polish than by Chinese. When the roots are the same, when the rules are sisters, when both tongues have in common a certain syntax, climate and resonance, the translator is able to convey not only the meaning but the tone, the atmosphere; to reproduce not only the skeleton, but the flesh. Dutch and Flemish, Danish and Norwegian, Czech and Serbo-Croat would be good illustrations of this paradise. However, my concern is not with facilities, but rather the reverse, in comparing the two most incomparable, two most incompatible tongues of the Western world: English and French.

It is rather sad, yet quite understandable, that each culture should accuse the other of lacking poets and poetry. For centuries, each could read the other's authors only in translation, and I wonder how a Briton could admire Racine in English, or a Frenchman appreciate Keats in an approximate Gallic. Here the translator discovers his own hell: on the one hand, a Saxon idiom complicated with Latin and Scandinavian—on the other, a Latin dialect altered by Celtic, Frankish, etc. But the differences I am referring to are less a question of grammar and vocabulary than a question of spirit, spirits which ten centuries of literature have finally led to extreme opposites.

The secrets of English will always defeat us. The phonetic complexity of this language, its power to reproduce thousands of natural sounds—the roaring of the waves, the howling of the wind, the dripping of the rain—make it a perfect instrument for suggestion. Compare, for instance, 'profond' and 'profound': while the French adjective is purely nominative, the English one seems to possess in itself the quality it indicates: profundity is the very substance of the word; we can almost hear a voice sinking into its depths. It is this splendid music of diphthongs of which we, the French, are dreadfully deprived. No wonder Shakespeare was British; he derived his aesthetics from his language; the words themselves provided him with a cosmic background where he could hear the 'oak-cleaving thunderbolts' and find 'tongues in trees, books in the running brooks, sermons in stones and good in everything'.

Thus, in English discourse, the words seem to be counterpoints, they extend in great complexes of echoes and correspondences, which suggest behind the logical sense an obscure world where dreams can travel indefinitely. 'The isle is full of noises, sounds and sweet airs, that give delight.'

We must also admit that English has shown more vitality than French in assimilating foreign imports. The fact that the British flag covered an enormous range of human races and territories is not sufficient in itself to explain this amazing capacity. For, after all, the French also had some business with India and Canada and, for a little while, with the whole of Europe, but their only profit from fifteen years of Napoleonic wars was the word 'bistro.' English, on the contrary, has welcomed so many foreign elements–from Celtic Irish to Negro poetry, from Asiatic mysticism to American slang–that it is impossible now to trace its frontiers. English has become the languages of the universe itself, and it is this protoplasmic quality which enables it to swallow almost everything. Compared to this oceanic language, what could French be but a language of stone?

And, indeed, it is that petrifying function which has affected French since the classical age. Once upon a time, we probably had a language as great as Shakespeare's own, and an approach very similar to his. But the rejection of the boundless vocabulary of Rabelais and Montaigne for the pedantic euphuism of a Malherbe, the adoption of a minimum number of basic words which recur in Racine's style as well as in Mallarmé's, became the rules of our literature. *Je suis belle, ô mortels, comme un rêve de pierre.* Drastic rules, indeed, against which poetry had to reconquer its own kingdom, and from Hugo to Claudel, from Rimbaud to St.-John Perse, starts a desperate battle. But the tragedy remains in the French language; a sharp conflict between this deliberate poverty, this *obstinée rigueur* as Valéry said, and the lasting nostalgia for a land where the soul could recover *sa douce langue natale*. It is certainly in France that Western thought reached the extreme of its divorce from the universe, a state of separation in which man could only verify his utter loneliness. Thus, while English appears constantly as an *open* language, French is *closed,* closed into itself, into its own, unbearable purity—and the *Hérodiade* of Mallarmé is certainly a dramatic picture of this self-entombment. But thanks to their barren language, the French writers were obliged to invent the great style, to develop habits of precision, of balance; writing became for them the setting of words into sentences like diamonds into a crown. Eventually, the deficiencies gave birth to astounding mastery and virtuosity. 'They have a rather poor instrument', as Joyce used to say, 'but they play wonderfully well.'

Thus we could see in English and French the two complementary principles of culture, roughly corresponding to the two instincts that Nietzsche saw in the origin of the theater. One, an opening of each word on a vast horizon of evocations and symbols; the other, enclosing all sentences in themselves and reducing them to the clearest, the most precise meaning. The sea and the stone. A convincing example of this contrast is given by Shelley's *Ode to the West Wind* and Baudelaire's *Rêve parisien*, or, better, by the works of Claude Lorrain, a painter equally admired on both sides of the Channel. In his views of Greek harbors, a mysterious sea beyond the proud, marmorean, rigid architecture of palaces, invites long voyages, and reflects a golden, ambiguous light which could come as well from a promising sunrise as a threatening sunset.

If we abide by the traditional concept of translation, it is obvious that these two worlds will never coincide. I could list hundreds of examples of this pathetic impossibility, from the *sauvage vent d'ouest* which fails to evoke the superb music of the 'wild west wind', to *dans la chambre les femmes vont et viennent, parlant de Michel* Ange which has so little to do with Eliot's couplet:

In the room the women come and go
Talking of Michelangelo.

But we may wonder if this antithesis could not be taken in a dialectical way, in other words, if a new concept of translation could not replace the old ones.

Until now, translation has fluctuated between two limits, which are also its negations: extreme freedom and extreme slavery. The former is to literature what parody is to theater—and the best, or rather the worst example of it, is certainly Ducis' versions of Shakespeare's plays. Not only did this 'honnête homme' take the liberty to add or cut some lines or to alter whole scenes, to change the names of the characters and rebaptize them according to the allegoric tradition, but he also forced the most subtle rhythms of blank verse into the stiff corset of the alexandrine. Naturally, the result was anything but Shakespearean, and it is surprising that such piracy could have flourished on French stages until the first world war. But should we call it a piracy? Translation had not yet discovered the notion of 'alterity', and the copy remains so far from the original that we may rather think Ducis made use of Shakespeare as Shakespeare himself made use of Bandello or Belleforest.

Perhaps an interesting parallel could be drawn here between literature and painting. It does not seem that painters were ever obsessed by our problems with translation, although copying the old masters was for a long time an essential part of their apprenticeship. But the fact that a painter has to be a copyist before becoming an artist encourages him to see only in the original an opportunity of discovering his own genius. So we may be struck by the liberties he allows himself. We may be struck for instance, by Degas' copy of Mantegna's *Crucifixion,* where the expression is definitely sacrificed to composition; or by Van Gogh's version of Delacroix's *Le Bon Samaritain,* which is certainly more concerned with problems of color and movement than with the psychological tone of the scene. And yet these scandalous betrayals are more significant than a flat imitation; they reveal explicitly an element that was merely implicit in the original; in other words, they produce a new aspect, a new epiphany of the work, and a translator would probably benefit from meditating upon this. But it is also true that some other painters, and great painters, sometimes approached the problem of imitation in an almost scholarly spirit. Rubens is certainly the best example of this fidelity; his copies of Van Scondrel's *Portrait of Paracelsus* and Titian's *Rape of Europa* show how much he tried to forget his personal genius and to render the original as accurately as possible—a fact which we may well regret.

Now, when the translator imitates Rubens and keeps too closely to the text, we reach the other pole of translation, mere mechanical reproduction, a genre which is to real translation what a photograph is to a portrait. It belongs to the positivist tradition, which still prevails in many universities, and provides us with those incredible bilingual books, where beside the verse of Milton or Coleridge we find the stalest, flattest, and most unprofitable *ersatz*. To be sure, these translations are accurate to a degree, but this accuracy concerns only the meaning and practically never the spirit of the work. The reader feels only too grateful when he is allowed, here and there, to catch a glimpse of the author's genius. Thus, thanks to the pens of distinguished specialists, we see 'get thee to a nunnery' reduced to *va dans un couvent!*; not to mention Rimbault's appalling versions of Faulkner, the word 'bra' ('soutien-gorge') rendered by 'brassière' ('infant's bodice'). It is difficult enough in this perspective for a novel to keep its aesthetic value, but for poetry, such interpretation results in complete non-sense, as it tends to reduce a poem to a logical arrangement of words, and a clear meaning, which is precisely what the poet wants to keep obscure.

What, then, should be done? If we turn our back on the original, we may produce monstrous fantasies à la Ducis, but if we are overwhelmed with respect, we can also betray the beauty, the nuance. And yet, the history of literature does not always show disasters, and translation does not appear, *a priori*, as a 'genre maudit'. Goethe even preferred his *Faust* in Gérard de Nerval's version, and beside too many failures it is easy to point out some masterpieces, from Urquhart's translation of Rabelais to Proust's translation of Ruskin, from Rossetti's transcriptions of François Villon to Pierre Leyris' version of Gerard Manley Hopkins. The time has come to wonder what made such victories possible and to deduce from them, if not a definite method, at least a new concept.

The most current error which has impaired the spirit of translation is the belief that one must necessarily imitate the written text. I am not trying to encourage infidelity, but to determine at which level and for what element fidelity must be intransigent. Since French and English are so obviously antagonistic, I propose that it is futile to hope to obtain literal accuracy without betraying the music, or to reproduce the music without altering the meaning. It will always be impossible, for instance, to produce in a French reader of *The Waste Land* the exact impressions that an English or an American reader may expect. But, after all, does every American or Englishman get the same feelings from this poem? Clearly not, and the contrary would mean complete failure. Therefore, behind the various interpretations, we can imagine the poem itself as a version of some absolute poem which would be less the sum of its meanings, symbols, images, than their source, structure and secret essence. This absolute poem, of which Mallarmé dreamt his life long, would then be to the written one what Plato's Forms or Aristotle's Archetypes were to visible things: their supreme reality.

And I do think that a poet is first a translator; the translator of an unknown world to which he gives tangible form, sensitive expression. Art is less invention than discovery, for it is insofar as the artist becomes rooted in what Shakespeare called 'nature's infinite book of secrecy', that he can become a creator of our universe. The greater he is, the further he goes, the more closely he will approach this book written somewhere in the stars. 'It is no mere appreciation of the beauty before us, but a wild effort to reach the beauty above,' said Edgar Allan Poe, and he praised 'the multiform combinations among the things and thoughts of time, to attain a portion of that loveliness whose very elements, perhaps, appertain to eternity alone.' But it is clear that, if we cease to mistake the poem for the secret order it translates more, or less, successfully, the translator finds himself in a similar position and becomes the co-creator of the work of art, as the artist is the creator of reality.

To be sure, this position is not comfortable. It requires primarily a deep insight into the nature of the work, which means the translator has to be a critic, an analyst as well as a linguist and a poet, too. He has to submit the poem to a series of experiments in every possible field: linguistics, psychology, sociology, metaphysics, etc.[1] Many

[1] Modern criticism now provides us with very good techniques in this respect. I would call your attention to the works of the French school, especially Gaston Bachelard. Bachelard has a method for interpreting poetry, midway between psychoanalysis or phenomenology and poetry itself. It is an effort to trace the dream process which has given birth to a poem or even a single image. Bachelard discovered that all these images were more or less connected with an element: earth, air, fire, water. He started to classify them according to their basic content, and in his six books (*La Psychanalyse du feu, L'Eau et le rêves, L'Air et les songes, La Terre et les rêveries du repos, La Terre et les rêveries de la volonté,* and recently, *La Poétique de l'espace*) he studied the long chains of images, the unconscious process we may find at work in almost every literary work. This method was followed by Georges Poulet (*Essais sur le temps humain*) who studied

years may pass before he is able to grasp this platonic form of the poem, and then he must reconstruct its whole structure, its whole universe of images, its whole network of symbols, intuitions and correspondences; in other words, the absolute of which the written text is but an approximation. When this process comes to an end, the most difficult part of the job begins, namely, to give an expression to this spiritual architecture without betraying it. The translator has to work in his own language exactly as the poet did in his, putting forth the same effort to organize the same images and to shape similar rhythms. The result may sometimes prove disappointing, but in this regard translation ceases to be a minor genre and becomes an equivalent of a genuine creation.

I would go even further. Thus understood, translation may sometimes be more difficult than poetry itself. The translator must retrace the initial intuition, the root of the work; he must devote his whole intelligence and sensitivity to the research of what may have been, for the poet, a mere illumination, a gift from the gods. Then, having worked out the core of the poem, having rebuilt the spiritual process according to its numerous elements, he has, finally, to go to more trouble than the artist himself; he must pass from this construction to the concrete, written expression, and with no freedom whatsoever, try desperately to adjust every word, every line, every single cadence to the transcendental model. When this effort is carried out satisfactorily, the translation may be considered as an equivalent of the original, and becomes in its turn another facet of the form, another facet which may even be able

---

the various concepts of Time which one meets in novels and poems. It is also the same techniques which led Jean-Pierre Richard (*Littérature et sensation, Poèsie et profondeur*) to a phenomenological approach in literature, an approach which has proved extremely interesting: a study of the physical sensations which can be regarded as the basis of a poem. *Example: Goethe.* Thus all these critical tools may enable us to penetrate much deeper than before into the world of poetry.

to modify, sharpen and deepen the first one. For, as long as translation demands elements of genuine criticism, it is very like a comment; as long as we have to choose among several possible solutions, to select the all-embracing one, it may well happen that the translated poem is better than the original, more revealing, closer to the Ideal. If I dared to phrase it in family terms, I would say a successful translation should rather be the brother than the son of the original, for both should proceed from the same transcendental Idea which is the real but invisible father of the work. And finally, a book is but the endless series of its own metamorphoses, and through its various epiphanies tends to become universal, to coincide with its archetype, as a mathematical series approaches the infinite without ever reaching it, or as a hero, like Don Juan or Faust, progresses from one author to another, toward his ideal image. Today, *Ulysses* is no longer limited to James Joyce's text, but includes also the admirable French version (by Auguste Morel, Stuart Gilbert and Valery Larbaud), and others, from German to Japanese, to say nothing of the innumerable books of comments, analyses and criticism which it constantly occasions.

Though extreme, this conception is not utopian. I would like to end with a concrete example: *The Raven* translated by Baudelaire and Mallarmé, two versions which, owing to the prestige of their authors, have become, in the poetic sky, two satellites of this magnificent black sun. As everyone knows, Edgar Poe has himself given the most penetrating comment on its genesis. Far from being a spontaneous, gratuitous creation, the poem is a reflection of Poe's poetics, which are but a reflection of his whole world picture. It did not grow at random or by inspiration, but from precise combinations, as a geometric theorem, and the explanations given in *Philosophy of Composition*, may well serve to illustrate the process I ascribe to the translator.

The writer started by defining the length (100 lines), the field (Beauty) and the tone (sadness) of the work to come. Then, to express this sadness, he discovered that the essential element should consist in variations of a leit-motiv, a key-word which would include, for musical reasons, the dreariest sounds, 'o' and 'r', which are combined in 'more' and by extension 'evermore', 'nevermore'. Then, considering the difficulty in reconciling this monotonous refrain with the discourse of a rational creature, Poe imagined the word could be said by a parrot or, better, a raven. Then, searching for a theme that could fit this image of a bird repeating at the end of every stanza the sole word he knows: 'nevermore', the poet found that the most striking would be Death, which, combined with Beauty, leads to the picture of a fair maiden mourned by her lover. Then, looking for a way to vary the initial leit-motiv, he conceived that the raven could answer the lover's questions and then acquire a prophetic symbolism. The questions would have to proceed from the most banal to the most dramatic, as though the lover felt at the same time bitter grief and a secret pleasure, an ambiguous feeling culminating in utmost despair. Starting from this point, that is from the end, Poe composed the climax stanza and moved toward the beginning, *à rebours*, in a series of descending gradations, according to the pattern he had chosen: an alternance of acatalectic octameters, catalectic heptameters and catalectic tetrameters. We can therefore regard the creation of this poem as a result of successive and triumphant deductions—like the discovery of the treasure in *The Gold Bug*—and see it as a perfect example of what a translator should do before taking up his pen.

Fortunately neither Baudelaire nor Mallarmé had to undertake this painful reconstruction, since Poe had been good enough to pave their way unto the threshold of language. Instead of trying to attain an almost impossible literality, both decided to sacrifice the form to the content, the verse to the mystical atmosphere of the scene. *Dans le moulage de la prose appliquée à la poésie, il y a nécessairement une affreuse imperfection; mais le mal serait encore plus grand dans une singerie rimée*—as Baudelaire said. And he recognized the impossibility of giving *une idée exacte de la sonorité profonde et lugubre, de la puissante monotonie de ces vers, dont les rimes larges et triplées sonnent comme un glas de mélancolie.* Mallarmé, also despising all attempt to render the rhythms and the rhymes, preferred to give his own version of the 'supernatural loveliness' at which Poe had been aiming. This is now a sample of the two first stanzas:

Baudelaire:

Une fois, sur le minuit lugubre, pendant que je méditais, faible et fatigué, sur maint précieux et curieux volume d'une doctrine oubliée, pendant que je donnais de la tête, presque assoupi, soudain il se fit un tapotement, comme de quelqu'un frappant doucement, frappant à la porte de ma chambre. 'C'est quelque visiteur—murmurai-je—qui frappe à la porte de ma chambre; ce n'est que cela, et rien de plus.'

Ah! distinctement je me souviens que c'était dans le glacial décembre, et chaque tison brodait à son tour le plancher du reflet de son agonie. Ardemment je désirais le matin; en vain m'étais-je efforcé de tirer de mes livres un sursis à ma tristesse, ma tristesse pour ma Lénore perdue, pour la précieuse et rayonnante fille que les anges nomment Lénore—et qu'ici on ne nommera jamais plus.

Mallarmé:

Une fois, par un minuit lugubre, tandis que je m'appesantissais, faible ou fatigué, sur maint curieux et bizarre volume de savoir oublié—tandis que je dodelinais la tête, somnolant presque: soudain se fit un heurt, comme de quelqu'un frappant doucement, frappant à la porte de ma chambre—cela seul et rien de plus.

Ah! distinctement je me souviens que c'était en le glacial décembre: et chaque tison, mourant isolé, ouvrageait son spectre sur le sol. Ardemment je souhaitais le jour—vainement j'avais cherché d'emprunter à mes livres un sursis au chagrin—au chagrin de la Lénore perdue—de la rare et rayonnante jeune fille que les anges nomment Lénore:—et de nom pour elle ici, non, jamais plus!

I do not like to discount these interpretations, especially Mallarmé's, which is better and was admired by such connoisseurs as Swinburne and Payne. But Mallarmé himself was aware of many imperfections, which were charitably listed by his friend Vielé-Griffin. And we have to admit that these versions convey only the plot of the poem, fail to give the slightest impression of its music, and pay no attention to Poe's commentaries. In spite of their quality, they, too, are victims of the old prejudice for rational accuracy, for they only respect what the author considered to be but the ninth stage of his work, namely, the phrasing. Now, we have seen that the basic clue, the very first source of the poem, previous to any expression or theme, was the discovery of a word, 'more,' whose sound was able to have an almost infinite dreary echo. It seems surprising that a poet like Baudelaire did not realize that such a dream-like word could hardly be suggested by the French adverb 'plus', which closes the voice on a rather grotesque note, while the last syllable of 'jamais' opens it in an almost English way. It is also surprising that Mallarmé did not render 'nevermore' in this manner, did not lay the stress on music, even at the expense of meaning, and did not try to find a French equivalent for Poe's subtle rhythms and correspondences of sounds. In other words, the insufficiency of these versions can be explained by the fact that both proceeded from the written text, instead of starting from the Form which had given it successively its length, nature, tone, leit-motiv, characters, themes, symbols, movement and meters. By following this order, which Poe himself has defined, it should be possible to establish the hierarchy of the elements which absolutely must be represented, and of the ones which could possibly be sacrificed, and the result, still far from perfection, would be these new stanzas with which I would like to conclude:

Jadis par un morne minuit, comme je songeais, lourd d'ennui,
Sur maint rare et curieux volume d'un savoir désuet—
Et dodelinais, somnolent, un coup fut frappé brusquement
Tel quelqu'un heurtant doucement, heurtant ma porte de chambre
—C'est un visiteur, marmonnai-je, frappant à ma porte de chambre
Et rien qu'un visiteur, mais . . .

Distinctement je me remembre, ah! c'était au glacial décembre
Chaque tison mourant seul ciselait son spectre au parquet
Et j'aspirais tant au matin—ayant dans mes livres en vain
Cherché sursis à mon chagrin—à mon regret de Lénore
De la rare et radieuse vierge qu'anges nomment Lénore—
Mais ici sans nom désormais.

WERNER WINTER

Impossibilities of Translation

WERNER WINTER, *Associate Professor of Linguistics at the University of Texas, has a wide background in European and Slavic languages and has translated poetry by T. S. Eliot into German.*

It seems to me that we may compare the work of a translator with that of an artist who is asked to create an exact replica of a marble statue, but who cannot secure any marble. He may find some other stone or some wood, or he may have to model in clay or work in bronze, or he may have to use a brush or a pencil and a sheet of paper. Whatever his material, if he is a good craftsman, his work may be good or even great; it may indeed surpass the original, but it will never be what he set out to produce, an exact replica of the original.

In a nutshell, we seem to have here all the challenge and all the frustration that goes with our endeavors to do the ultimately impossible. We know from the outset that we are doomed to fail; but we have the chance, the great opportunity to fail in a manner that has its own splendor and its own promise.

What I propose to do is to present a linguist's views and reflections on the reasons why the translator must necessarily despair of achieving a completely faithful rendering of his original. Of necessity, I have to concern myself not with the delicate artistic aspects of translation, which, as I take it, reflect above all an individual's selections from the raw material of the languages at his disposal, but rather with the most general problems of transfer from one language to another. It is the background to the translator's endeavors in which I am primarily interested; but it seems to me that such an interest is essential for any attempt to objectify one's reactions to the results of a translator's work—whether this translator happens to be a stranger or oneself.

To translate is to replace the formulation of one interpretation of a segment of the universe around us and within us by another formulation as equivalent as possible. We speak of translation even within the framework of one single language in the case of stylistic shifts, for instance, when we find ourselves asked to make plain and intelligible a highly esoteric statement we have just made. This use of the term is, however, rather marginal, even though the basic characteristics of the process are all present. As a rule, we may inject into our definition the further qualification that translation involves the replacement of an interpretation in one language by another in a second language.

I do not want to devote much time to statements about languages and Language in general, but it is important for the course on our deliberations that we keep a few essential points in mind. *Languages are systems of arbitrarily selected, but conventionalized signs which serve to convey arbitrarily selected, but conventionalized meanings.* We want to note several things at this moment. One, sign and meaning cannot be dissociated from one another; an utterance, a sound or a sequence of sounds, is part of a language only if it is employed in signaling a reference to something different in substance from the mere physical utterance; a meaning does not exist in itself, but only insofar as it becomes manifest in a linguistic feature. Second, signs and what they stand for owe their existence to arbitrary selection and their preservation to conventionalization of this selection; the arbitrary origin makes for almost unlimited diversity in languages, a diversity which is reduced only when languages are related to one another in a broad historical sense, covering both genetic and contact relationships. Third, no sign and no meaning exists by itself, but only as part of a system.

The next point we have to make seems utterly trivial. While languages may be similar to each other, they are never identical. If we insert what we just said about languages in general, we can expand this trivial statement into something more meaningful: The system of form and meaning in language A may be similar to that in language B, but is never identical with it.

This statement has a very simple, yet very important corollary: *There is no completely exact translation.* If an interpretation of reality as formulated in language A does not exist in any isolation, but only as part of the system total of this language, then its correlative in language B cannot be isolated from the overall system of B, which must be different from that of A.

There is no completely exact translation. There are only approximations, and the degree of similarity possible between original and translation depends on the degree of similarity between the systems of form and meaning in the two languages involved. The more serious the deviations from one language to the other, the less of the original can be salvaged in the process of transfer.

To be sure, there are partial exceptions to this. One-to-one correspondences are possible as long as one confines oneself to utterances of limited size outside a larger context (the rendering of an English cry *Fire!* by German *Feuer!* would be a fairly good example), but this observation does not invalidate the overall statement.

However, it may be asked: Is it not possible to convey in a second language completely, without omission or addition, the CONTENT of a statement in the original language—even if one has to grant that the formal properties of the two utterances have to be different? Isn't it the same thing whether we express a certain semantic unit by *father* or *Vater* or *père?*

The answer must be No. Meaning and form, as I have already pointed out, cannot be dissociated from one another. So if forms differ, *a priori,* semantic equivalence cannot be expected. Let me illustrate.

Take first the result of the multiplication process 3 × 30 in a number of closely related languages. In English, the numeral used would be *ninety,* with formal indication that the semantic unit 90 is to be analyzed as 'nine decadic units'. When we turn to Russian *devianosto,* the form suggests a very similar, but not identical interpretation, *viz.,* 'nine decadic units, one unit away from one hundred' (*deviat'* being 'nine', *sto*—'one hundred'). French *quatre-vingt-dix* requires a quite different analysis, namely, 'four score and ten', and Danish *halfems,* finally, has to be paraphrased as 'half of the fifth score', with the type of elliptic formulation as found in German *anderthalb* 'half of the second' = 'one and one-half'.

We clearly observe two systems of semantic organization of the field of numerals and two variants of each of the systems. Taken in isolation, *ninety* may appear to be the perfect match of *quatre-vingt-dix,* but in the context of their respective systems, the two forms signal two different semantic configurations. That the equivalents of the linguistic items in the world of reality seem to be identical here is not of crucial importance; what matters for our understanding of language is the interpretation of reality, not reality itself. *Three-score years and ten* and *seventy years* cover identical time spans; but linguistically, the two formulations are different, and it is no wonder that they can readily be used for quite different communicative purposes: the one, *seventy years,* as a flat, colorless, matter-of-fact statement, the other, with its unmistakable biblical ring (cf. Ps. 90.10), for solemn oratory.

Still, we may want to grant linguistic diversity and yet continue to insist that the agreement in the use of the linguistic units is so great as to make the difference negligible. For the examples cited, one can hardly deny that the gain or loss in the transfer is minute. However, if we proceed to other cases, we will find that the differences may take on quite forbidding proportions.

I mentioned before the example of apparent semantic equivalence of *father* : *Vater* : *père* 'genitor.' The natural logic of such a term and such a notion strikes us as inevitable. A living being has to have a father, the relationship father : mother : child is provided for in nature. Nonetheless, if one goes out to western Arizona and asks speakers of Mohave for their equivalent of English *father*, one will get not one term, but two—not stylistic variants of the type of *father* and *dad*, but mutually exclusive, contrasting terms. One of them can be paraphrased 'father of male referent,' the other, 'father of female referent.' Clearly, there is no difference between the biological facts of the father-child relationship in Parker, Arizona, and in Austin, Texas; yet the linquistic interpretation of this relationship is totally different, and a translation without loss or addition is not possible.

Thus not even 'basic notions', central points in a human sphere of experience, stand outside the area of arbitrary segmentation and arrangement and subsequent conventionalization; and the extent to which semantic boundaries as determined by linguistic form and linguistic usage coincide with absolute boundaries in the world around us is negligible. It is interesting to note in passing that all attempts to compile lists of semantic entities supposedly universally valid have had the same fate: they had to be reduced constantly in the light of new data which showed that even the most elementary assessments of natural phenomena were not conditioned by the phenomena, but by the language which served to make these assessments.

It would be easy enough to document this claim that virtually no 'natural' semantic units are confirmed by the sum total of linguistic data. For our purposes, a few more examples will suffice.

For instance, the spectrum of colors is not divided up in any 'natural', consistent way by speakers of different languages. *We* would never hesitate to affirm the importance of the difference between 'green' and 'blue'—whereas the Yuman languages (of which Mohave is one), although otherwise employing a set of basic color terms very similar in application to our own, do not have separate forms to indicate these two colors, and consequently do not have separate meanings 'blue' and 'green' (though speakers of these languages will note the physical difference between a dark blue and a light green without hesitation).

For us, 'grey' is a unified meaning field, whether the word is applied to the color of a wall or a person's hair; Russian has two different terms and therefore two meanings correspond to our one. For us, 'high' and 'low' are 'natural' categories; *mons altus* and *mare altum* indicate that we cannot say the same for the Romans. 'Round' we apply to a ball or a hoop without further differentiation; in Yuman languages, the two terms used in this connection have nothing in common with each other except possibly a feature of reduplication.

And these examples could be multiplied, but the point is clear already. Even the simplest, most basic requirement we make of translation cannot be met without difficulty: one cannot always match the content of a message in language A by an expression with exactly the same content in language B, because what can be expressed and what must be expressed is a property of a specific language in much the same way as *how* it can be expressed. It is only so that the area of agreement in the analysis of the world around us is usually very much greater than the area of agreement in the formal expression of this analysis. As a result, we get the impression only too easily that the content of the original message can always be transmitted in the second language.

What we have touched upon so far is only one aspect of meaning, and in many ways the least complex aspect. We have been concerned only with the immediate, denotative meaning of the original utterance and the problem of its transfer into the other language. It is, however, rather the exception than the rule that a specific form evokes only one precise meaning in isolation. We know very little about the organization of meaning structures and their storage in the human mind. There are, however, strong indications that we can get a fairly reasonable picture of this unknown reality by assuming that in the human memory bits of meaning are associated with other related bits, and not stored in a random fashion. We find, for instance, that when one particular linguistic item is called for, another one will simultaneously be 'pulled out'—if this simile is permissible—causing frequent formal distortions; and that this item or these items 'pulled' by mistake are related semantically to the item wanted. Such an interpretation of what seems to happen accounts very simply for developments such as Vulgar Latin *grevis* 'heavy' in lieu of the usual Latin *gravis*—*grevis* owing its—*e*—to interference from *levis* 'light'.

This peculiarity of semantic storage, in which the term 'related item' would cover a wide variety of classes, likewise seems to be in its specific form, a property of every individual language and not of Language in general. The range of items evoked by meaning association will therefore vary from language to language. A German item *älter* is associated with both *jünger* and *neuer*; so is English *older* with *younger* and *newer;* but English *elder,* another correlative of German *älter,* does not pair with *newer,* nor does Latin *senior* seem to be associated with *novior.*

There are indications that such alignment of a semantic unit with others in the semantic structure is rarely unique. The criterion of phonological interference which we have met with *gravis* becoming *grevis* beside *levis,* allows us to conclude that such a word as 'second' in Sanskrit is associated equally with the word for 'two' and the word for 'third'. For other semantic units, the affiliation with certain subgroups of meaning may be much more complex.

The meaning of a form conditions, and is conditioned by, its occurrence. Memory storage apparently includes not only information about related semantic bits, but also information about the occurrence, the distribution of a form in previous utterances of the same language. In a very primitive sense, such stored information allows us to use linguistic forms in a grammatically correct, or 'established' way. In a more sophisticated sense, this type of stored information permits us to grasp the total semantic field of the item chosen.

Special types of such distributional information are familiar to all of us. When we say that a particular word has certain undesirable connotations, this means that we remember, perhaps in a very loose sense, a context in which this word was used, say, in a rude or overly slangy fashion. Or when we note that a given word evokes certain literary reminiscences, this indicates that apart from the mere meaning information we remember distributional facts of a very special sort.

Both classes of semantic association seem to be basic properties of languages. But again, the exact arrangements and groupings within these classes appear to be strictly structural characteristics of each individual language. A transfer from one language to another of the sum total of what is usually—though none too aptly—called 'connotative meaning' is an even more hopeless task than the transfer of plain, straightforward denotative meaning. As a result, the degree of difficulty in approximating the content of the original increases with the relative importance that connotative meaning properties possess in the text to be translated. When we deal with a scientific treatise, (which is—or should be—as free as possible from all recourse to allusion, subtle reference, *double-entendre*, etc.), a fairly satisfactory matching of the *semantic* content can usually be achieved. On the other hand, a lyrical poem or a critical essay full of hidden pointers to data known to the educated native reader, may present insurmountable problems. It is certainly no chance development that plans for mechanical translation tend to be limited entirely to the field of scientific prose. I doubt that the considerations of practical usefulness are, in a final analysis, crucial; rather it seems to me that what appears to be wise restraint is due to the insight that the task of teaching a machine to absorb the immense range of ramifications of connotative meanings in one language and then to convert that into an equally immense variety of such meanings in the other, is a task which cannot even be considered at this moment. After all, it is in this area of understanding connotative meaning that even the most capable of translation 'machines'—the mind of the human near-bilingual—fails most miserably.

Up to this point, we have been concerned only with problems of meaning and organization of meaning. We will now turn to a brief discussion of matters of form.

We know that the area of formal agreement between two languages is sometimes, in the case of closely related languages, fairly large, but much more often it is discouragingly small. Innumerable problems arise for the translator who wants to preserve essential formal patterns of the original and to avoid inappropriate patterns of the replica language. There must be a vast array of stories about such labors. I have always particularly liked the story told me by Kenneth Pike.

A missionary, brought up in the tradition of down-to-earth, up-to-date, close-to-the-people sermon topics had his words translated to an attentive audience by a very competent native interpreter. He noticed that his helper, who had started out with great vigor and persuasiveness, began to halt and hesitate until he finally turned to the missionary and declared: 'I am most sorry, but I cannot translate what you say.' The missionary's topic had been announced as: 'God's Navy', and there were three parts to the sermon, one discussing Fellowship, one Stewardship, and the third another ship whose name slips my mind.

Or there is the other story about the formidable difficulties to be overcome in the teaching of the doctrine of the Trinity to speakers of Arabic, since the words in Arabic for Father and Son are properly masculine, but the word for Holy Ghost is feminine.

But the problems of replacing formal properties of the original by something at least roughly equivalent are constantly present in the translator's work. Decisions must be made as to what to sacrifice, what to preserve. The matter of the role of sound as a musical and secondarily symbolic factor comes to mind; the matter of word length, of choice from various syntactic alternatives. To select a single example, the morphological clarity of Greek and Latin allows for great flexibility in word order. This in turn permits the use of complicated metrical patterns with relative ease and the introduction of stylistic devices such as the chiasm. One important characteristic of Latin poetry is split constructions which create an effect similar to that of retardation and resolution in music, and which one might call suspension. A good example:

Aequam memento rebus in arduis servare mentem.

This string cannot be cut off at any point before the close of the line, and a very strong impression of controlled compactness is achieved for the entire sentence. A language without the formal properties of Latin or, for that matter, Greek or Russian, cannot match this suspension effect. When a writer like Hölderlin tries to do it in German we get a stanza like this:

Nun! sei in deinem Adel, mein Vaterland
mit neuem Namen, reifeste Frucht der Zeit!
Du letzte und du erste aller
Musen, Urania! sei gegrüsst mir!

By so doing, he seems to me to overtax the potential of the German language and to achieve only a rather poor quasi-classical effect without real poetic weight. Of course, in other poems where the same archaic mannerism is practiced, the poet's artistic achieving of the right word and the right balance far outweighs the shortcomings; for instance, in the opening of *Hälfte des Lebens*, the classical suspension has been matched in perfect beauty:

Mit gelben Birnen hänget
und voll mit wilden Rosen
das Land in den See,
ihr holden Schwäne . . .

What can succeed only in the exceptional case in German, cannot be done at all in English. For the function of a form in a sentence is generally indicated in English not by the form itself, but by the position of the form. The freedom of arrangement, which makes possible the classical effect of suspension, does not exist; the content-equivalent of our Latin line will, therefore, have to lack an important stylistic property or else new English ways have to be found to express the property of the original.

A simpler example, but without the complications which the translation of poetry involve, is visible in the particular compactness which is achieved in a paragraph of German by placing an object first in certain sentences. *Müller erzielte zuerst in einem wichtigen Versuch dieses Resultat; den gleichen Versuch wiederholten dann Schmidt und Schulze einige Jahre später*. 'Müller achieved first, in an important experiment, this result', would be rough but still syntactical translation for the first clause; the following clause, however, cannot be rendered by a parallel translation. We have to choose either to break down the order—which appears to be stylistically relevant—or to shift the entire sentence from the active to the passive, a choice which seems fully justified but which takes us a significant distance from the syntactic pattern of the original.

However, in the translation of scientific prose or newspaper texts such distortion would not matter much, since a form is there treated as though it were merely an accidental concomitant of a meaning-complex to be conveyed, and so long as the meaning-content is left fairly intact, the formal manifestation does not seem to make much difference.

Such a casual attitude is, of course, completely out of place in literature and literary translation. If scientific prose is easily translated because it concentrates on direct, denotative meaning and form is only of secondary importance, other genres and forms present more formidable problems. To be sure, an exact ranking by order of difficulty is hard to achieve, since genres are apparently never quite pure, except for those which are formally most controlled. Thus while a prosy novel would rank low in the hierarchy of difficulty, certain passages in it may well show high concentration of controlled form or of association stimuli; and these passages would of course be harder to translate. In general, the role of allusions, etc., probably cannot be confined to one genre or one set of genres; the degree of formal control, however, is more easily stated. Thus, newspaper texts, excluding *feuilleton*, would probably rank immediately after scientific prose, very low on the scale of difficulty; next one may place letters, prose plays, and non-poetic novels; after that, poetry in free form and poetry in flexible form, such as blank verse, and last, and most difficult of all, poetry in rigid form. As one moves up the scale, the number of instances in which one has to give up all hope of duplicating the original increases; at the same time, of course, the number of opportunities for the translator-poet increases.

To sum up. Transfer of denotative meaning, though difficult and at times impossible, can, as a rule, be exacted in a more or less satisfactory manner; the closer the cultural bonds between the speakers of the two languages, the more acceptable the results become. Associative meaning is very much harder to convey; adequate success can be hoped for only in exceptional cases. Form differs from language to language; still, for all literature which depends on form to become an artistic whole, means for transferring as much of the original form as possible must be found or else replaced by other formal features which fulfill a function equivalent to that of the original forms.

Can one, in translation, justly and profitably set up a hierarchy of properties of the original to be preserved or, if need be, sacrificed? It is this question which most concerns me, and though my conclusions are, of course, quite tentative, these are the rules as I would formulate them at this time.

In order to achieve maximum equivalence, we should match the following properties of the original in the order indicated by the arrows:

I. Semantic:	(a) direct;→	(b) associative.
	↓ ↘	
II. Formal:	(1) overt;	(2) distributional;
	↓(a) metre;	↓(a) peak position;
	(b) rhyme;	(b) position in specific line, etc.;
	(c) sound.	(c) arrangement in specific order.

If a sacrifice has to be made, maintain (a) over (b), (b) over (c), etc. Usually, in an arrangement of rigid form, lower ranking positions will have to be neglected. These suggestions refer definitely to the translation of texts in the European tradition.

As a test of the usefulness of these notions of hierarchy, I would like to discuss in some detail a number of actual translations, calling attention, whenever necessary, to the linguistic conditioning of some of the difficulties encountered.

My first set of examples consists of two German translations of a movement from T. S. Eliot's *Four Quartets*, one by Nora Wydenbruck, published in Austria in 1948, the other my own, unpublished as far as I know.[1]

The fourth movement of the first Quartet, *Burnt Norton*, reads:

Time and the bell have buried the day,
The black cloud carries the sun away.
Will the sunflower turn to us, will the clematis
Stray down, bend to us; tendril and spray
Clutch and cling?
Chill
Fingers of yew be curled
Down on us? After the kingfisher's wing
Has answered light to light, and is silent, the light is still
At the still point of the turning world.

The most striking features of the overall structure of the original are a rhyme scheme which leaves out one line, that which ends with *clematis*, and a peak scheme which starts out with four points, recedes to one, and then swings back to full volume, even exceeding it before it comes to rest again in the final, crucial line.

Nora Wydenbruck's translation reads as follows:

Die Zeit hat mit Glockengeläut den Tag begraben,
schwarzes Gewölk die Sonne davongetragen.
Wird die Sonnenblume zu uns sich wenden, die Winde
nieder sich neigen? Die schwankende Ranke
Stütze erheischen?
Kalt
Zweig der Zypresse sich senken
auf unser Haupt?
Wenn des Eisvogels Flügel
einmal aufblitze im Glanz und verlöscht, verharrt dennoch das Licht
auf dem stäten Punkt der kreisenden Welt.

[1] This passage may, however, have been included in a pirated printing which I never managed to lay an eye on.

We ask the question of semantic adequacy first. *Die Winde*, the morning-glory, has replaced *clematis.* Since the clematis is known as a garden plant in German-speaking countries, the change seems uncalled-for. Moreover, on the second semantic level, that of associations, a serious loss has occurred: the wild morning-glory which would come to mind when *Winde* is mentioned, is white or pinkish, and the color symbolism that seems to go with *clematis*, is lost completely. *Tendril and spray / Clutch and cling* has been reduced to '(Will) the swaying spray / ask for support?' *Yew* has been replaced by *Zypresse* (cypress), the typical churchyard tree of the south. However, the image of a branch of cypress bending down is not right: the branches of the cypress reach straight up, whereas the yew squats close to the ground. *Auf unser Haupt* 'upon our head' seems gratuitous. In the last line, the pattern of *answered* and *is silent* is lost; 'when the kingfisher's wing / flashes up once in a glow and is extinguished' shifts the weight to entirely different imagery. In *the light is still*, the ambiguity of *still*, one of the major problems in translating the *Quartets*, is resolved in favor of *still* ~ 'yet' and not of ~ 'steady, quiet', as in the last line.

As far as the form is concerned, the basic structure of the metre is imitated, though the first two lines contain one peak too many, as does the next to the last. The rhyme scheme is neglected, resulting in the loss of the unique position of *clematis*. The first two lines contain assonance, but this alternative to rhyme is not pursued further. Sound patterns—in particular alliterations—have not been transferred; instead, new alignments have been established in *Wenden—Winde, Die schwankende Ranke, Zweig der Zypresse* and *nieder sich neigen*, which are not based on any concentration of any kind in the original, and which, at least in two instances, introduce new semantic entities.

Nora Wydenbruck follows the original closely in the other formal categories postulated; in particular, the peak position of *kalt* = *chill* is well preserved. No transfer from one line to another has been made, and the arrangements of the original are kept, except that *kalt* = *chill* has been dissociated from the following noun and now functions as adverb, the only way to insure monosyllabic form as needed.

On the whole, Countess Wydenbruck's translation is rather successful in preserving the arrangement of items, but falls short of perfection in matters of rhyme, rhythm, and sound, and in introducing a number of important semantic changes.

To turn now to my own attempt:

Den Tag begruben Glocke und Zeit.
Die Wolke trägt schwarz die Sonne beiseit.
Wird sich die Sonnenblume kehren zu uns, wird die Clematis
niederschweifen, sich beugen zu uns–Ranke und Zweig
Griff sein und Schlinge?
Nicht
kalte Finger der Eibe gefällt
sein auf uns? Nun da des Eisvogels Schwinge
wiedergab Licht zu Licht und stumm ward, ist stille das Licht
am stillen Punkte der kreisenden Welt.

Clutch and cling has been replaced by nouns. *Nicht* (not) has been introduced for merely formal reasons, against the original text. *Curled* has been replaced by a term usually reserved for pointed weapons and the like. *Answered* as a term of speaking is replaced by the less precise *wiedergab* 'returned', which, however, is retained in the same semantic area by subsequent *stumm ward* (became silent). *After* plus past is rendered by *now that* plus past plus present of the main clause. The decision with respect to *still* has been made in favor of *still* ~ *at rest* even in the line next to the last.

Metrical organization and rhyme scheme have been preserved intact (with assonance replacing rhyme in the third line). Alliterations have been kept only for *bell . . . buried, light to light* and–if this is to be counted–*silent . . . still.* A new pair exists in *Finger . . . gefällt.*

In arrangement, no semantic equivalent of *chill* was kept in central peak position; *nicht* rather corresponds to the original in vowel quality and in a shared general semantic property of negative value. The object was placed first in the first line. Distribution in lines and broken lines was kept. *Schwarz* in the second line was removed from normal attributive position; the whole construction is more artificial than that of the original.

Generally speaking, the Winter version reflects the original more clearly in overt form; in semantic properties, an attempt has been made to stay with the original whenever possible; formal considerations led to semantic choice adjustments in three cases. In the organization of the arrangement, the major deviations are the displacement of *chill* and a verb-to-noun shift. The Wydenbruck version, on the other hand, deviates in more semantic points, is closer to the original in its arrangement in at least one crucial point, but achieves this goal only by foregoing a matching of the very significant rhyme pattern.

Detachment is, of course, difficult but I would guess that the defects in my own version are perhaps less serious. Neither translation is adequate in poetic qualities; the Wydenbruck text is just a little bit too explanatory, interpretative; the Winter version is too terse. Nonetheless, both versions are respectable attempts to solve a probably impossible problem in translation.

Against these attempts, I propose now to contrast a case of an inadequate attempt–interestingly enough, an attempt which resulted in achieving what the two Eliot translations did not: a genuine poem.

Über allen Gipfeln
ist Ruh,
in allen Wipfeln
spürest du

kaum einen Hauch.
Die Vögelein schweigen im Walde.
Warte nur: balde
ruhest du auch.

This famous poem by Goethe was translated in 1840 by M. Ju. Lermontov, one of the foremost Romantic poets of Russia.

The translation reads:

Gornye veršiny
Spjat vo t'me nočnoj;
Tixie doliny
Polny svežej mgloj;
Ne pylit doroga,
Ne drožat listy . . .
Podoždi nemnogo,
Otdoxneš' i ty.

In order to clarify my point, I offer first a line by line rendering of Goethe's poem, then of Lermontov's translation.

Line-by-line:

Above all mountain tops
is quietness,
in all tree-tops
you sense
hardly a breath.
The birds are silent in the woods.
Only wait: Soon
you will rest, too.

2) Lermontov's version.

The mountain tops
sleep in the darkness of night;
the quiet valleys
are full of fresh mist;

no dust rises from the road,
the leaves do not stir . . .
Wait a little,
you, too, will rest.

Both original and replica are eight-line poems; both have rhyme. Goethe's is of a pattern *ababcddc;* Lermontov's pattern, similar but not identical, is *ababcdcd.* As for the content, Goethe speaks of mountains and tree tops which lie quiet, and of the birds that have ceased to sing, and then the promise of rest for the weary. Lermontov closes on the same note, and also mentions the leaves not stirring; but between the mountains at the beginning and the trees at the close, he inserts a contrasting image, valleys filled with mist, and introduces the road no longer busy. The birds are not mentioned at all.

The content then, has undergone substantial change. The general topic—rest after a noisy day, rest after a busy life—is preserved, but apart from that only a partial matching of motifs takes place.

Formally, there is the slight change in rhyme-scheme which I have already mentioned. More significant is the change in metre: the sway of Goethe's varying rhythms is replaced by regular trochaic lines with three peaks each.

With such changes in overall structure, we may forego an investigation of the finer points in formal correspondence. Except for the last two lines, there is practically no agreement between them.

As a translation, then, Lermontov's work is not satisfactory. We noted already, that as a Russian poem in its own right, it commands high respect. But what caused Lermontov to deviate so far from the original?

In terms of content rendering and distribution the only lines which can be called good translation are the last two.

If we consider them the nucleus of the translation, we find that in them the three-beat trochaic pattern is established. The first line of the poem which in close translation should be,

nad vsemi veršinami

did not fit the pattern. So the instrumental-plus-preposition construction was replaced by a nominative; then, since the pair *Gipfeln–Wipfeln* was easily available in the common alignment of *veršiny* and *doliny* 'mountains and valleys', a pattern of fixed points emerged which forced the translator to depart from the original. Because Lermontov knew his craft, a new poem resulted; not a translation, but a 'variation on a theme by Goethe'. As a translation then, *Gornye veršiny* is a failure; but as a Russian poem, it can and will stand.

Where does all this leave us? We have seen that to translate is to attempt the intrinsically impossible. We have seen that it is not entirely a matter of competence or incompetence of the craftsman that decides the outcome; that the great, commanding structures of the languages of the original and of the replica set the limit of what can be done. This may be very little; but essentially a translation always has ancillary functions: it may be a guide to the original creation, and it may be the stimulus for another creation, just as great as the original, but quite different from it. The exact lines of the original may be lost, and we may have to label the new product a failure in what it set out to be. But we can be satisfied that the bronze statue, the woodcarving, the painting has somehow, by some process hard to analyze, become, not the replica, but the pendant of the original marble sculpture.

PETER ARNOTT

Greek Drama and the Modern Stage

PETER ARNOTT *is both classicist and producer of his own translations of Greek plays. His writings include* An Introduction to Greek Drama *and a forthcoming* The Medea *and* Cyclops *of Euripides and* The Frogs *of Aristophanes.*

It is a sobering thought that, although we are brought up to revere the Greek plays as masterpieces of dramatic construction, and although scholarship is constantly reappraising their content, form and *milieu,* we rarely have an opportunity to see them on the stage. In England, where for centuries school boys were reared on Sophocles—even, as we learn from *Tom Brown's Schooldays,* flogged into writing like Sophocles—there seems to have been no public representation of Greek tragedy until the late years of the nineteenth century. Then came the dawning realization that it might be beneficial to see the plays as well as read them—though still only as an *explication de texte.* At this time we see the foundation of the Oxford University Dramatic Society, under the awesome and unlikely auspices of Dr. Jowett, with a constitution providing for the performance of a Greek tragedy in the original every three years; we see similar performances inaugurated in Cambridge, and the construction of a pocket-sized Greek theater, high priest's throne and all, in the grounds of Bradfield College. But these productions were for the connoisseur only, with the theater wrapped in a cloud of scholarship and gasping vainly for air. Oxford has long since forgotten its constitution, but the triennial performances at Cambridge still occur, piously attended by delegations of classicists who occasionally lift their eyes from the texts in their hands to observe the action going forward on the stage. Scholarship still reigns supreme. Here one may hear Greek beautifully spoken in the authentic accents of Erasmus, and watch such anomalies as an *Agamemnon* stretched out to the excruciating length of three hours, and a *Bacchae* with the orgiastic rites of Dionysus represented by the demure undergraduates of Newnham and Girton. Bradfield, fortunate in a succession of talented teacher-directors, remains as one of the few places where performances in the Greek are given with true theatrical vitality—an accomplishment worthy of even higher praise when one realizes that many of the performers have no Greek, but are drilled in their parts parrot-fashion.

These performances, however, for all their specialized interest, served to awaken enthusiasm for the dramatic possibilities of Greek drama. Soon came Gilbert Murray's translations, the first serious attempt to bring the Greek masterpieces before the public in an assimilable form; and since this time commercial managements have shown themselves more willing to venture on such revivals, though with the proviso that the experiment is linked to a successful box-office name or a company with an assured following. Such productions, however, concern themselves with only a small proportion of the Greek plays that we have. The corpus of Greek drama, already abridged by the scholars of antiquity, has been further reduced by the modern theater. Even Cambridge and Bradfield, who could afford to be adventurous, limit their repertoire severely. For many years at Bradfield only three plays were considered worthy of performance—*Agamemnon*, *Antigone* and *Alcestis*—and to propose another was to profane the dignity of the theater. Cambridge prefers those few plays commonly read in schools. In London, on and off Broadway, and, alas, in many of the universities, we find many an *Oedipus Rex*, many an *Antigone*—a great favourite, this, with girls' schools—an occasional *Trojan Women* or *Medea*, but rarely a *Seven Against Thebes, Ajax, Ion, Iphigeneia at Aulis* or *Phoenician Women*. Aeschylus, half of Sophocles and the greater part of Euripides are for the most part entirely neglected. There are of course exceptions. Jean-Louis Barrault has offered the complete *Oresteia* in Paris, an experiment which has been repeated in this country and will shortly occupy the Old Vic Company in London. Sir Donald Wolfit, and more recently Sir John Gielgud, have offered *Oedipus at Colonus. Philoctetes* has had an off-Broadway showing, and in Greece itself the festivals at Epidauros and Athens have within a few years of their inauguration brought several of the less familiar works to a delighted, though necessarily limited, audience. In comedy, it hardly needs to be said, the commercial theater offers only *Lysistrata*, an even surer box-office draw since the publicity surrounding Dudley Fitts's translation.

The main hope still lies with the universities. Classical scholars are slowly coming to realize that performance, and a working knowledge of stage conditions, are essential to the appreciation of a play—a fact which has been recognized by Shakespearian scholars for some time. Actor and director may often, by a process akin to mysticism in religion, attain to an intuitive appreciation of a difficult line or passage which defies analysis on paper. One recalls here Allardyce Nicoll's story of the actor who gave an explicit rendering of a line in *King John* which had puzzled the professor for years, but was completely unable to explain why he had delivered the line as he had.

For practical purposes, however, we must still rely largely on reading for our knowledge of Greek tragedy. It follows that translation is aimed primarily at the reading public. This attitude is perhaps summed up by the reviewer of the new Chicago University Press series, who comments that the reader is at last put into the hands of translators who are poets as well as scholars. While sharing his enthusiasm, I would point out merely that the words 'actor', 'audience', 'director' do not appear to enter his head: he is thinking automatically in terms of readers, not of spectators, and in this he is not alone. And here is our problem. The responsibility of the literary translator, though arduous, is limited in its terms of reference. His task is to give as faithful a rendering as possible of the original text, to present to English readers a version in their own language as close as possible to what the poet actually wrote. The word 'faithful' has of course a wide application. It implies rendering not only the matter but the manner of the play–style as well as content. It implies rendering not only the words but their emotive content–in Jackson Knight's phrase, the 'associative penumbra'. More often than not this will involve expansion of the Greek. One iambic line will become two, perhaps, in English–sometimes even more. The folly of line-for-line translations has been amply demonstrated by the Loeb series. Such a translator can afford some slight discursiveness, for he is writing for a reader who is in no hurry. His public can scan his work at leisure, linger over certain phrases, turn back to re-read a passage if the thought or structure becomes too complex to be assimilated at first sight. And in the last resort the translator can rely on footnotes or appendices to supply his readers with associations which would have come automatically to the Greek audience but which the modern mind has lost.

In the theater, however, we are confronted by a different set of problems which affect both actor and audience alike. Reviving a play–any play over a generation old–is in itself an act of translation, concerning itself not merely with words but with that great imponderable 'dramatic effect'. Language and style are no longer all-important. The play becomes merely 'the script', a starting-point for the work of actor and director. The translator, or indeed the original author, who surrenders his typescripts to the assembled company and watches them leaf through the pages and underline their own parts experiences at once a very proper sense of humiliation. There are many factors to take into account with which the literary translator need not concern himself, and in working with Greek drama some factors assume major importance.

I have spoken of reviving a classical play as translation in a wider sense, translation from one theatrical language into another. Convention has been termed, in a happy phrase, the grammar of theater, and one country and age does not necessarily understand the grammar of another. The director who offered an archaeologically correct reconstruction of a Greek tragic performance—even if this were possible—would not be translating at all, but merely offering a museum piece for the delectation of the initiated. The performance must have a theatrical validity to justify its existence, and this inevitably means compromise between the old methods and the new, and the finding of equivalences by means of which the play will be made as valid for an audience in New York in 1959 as for the Athenians of the fifth century B.C. We are surely entitled to assume that any work worthy of revival at all will permit such treatment.

How does this affect the text? Is the director entitled to demand any other changes beside that from one language to another? One important consideration suggests that he is. The impact of the Greek performance was primarily aural. This is perhaps difficult to realize fully without seeing a production in one of the ancient theaters. The Greek actor was dwarfed by his surroundings. He performed before vast audiences, to most of whom he would have appeared as little more than a moving dot against the scenic background. Professor Webster calculates that to a spectator in the back row of the Theater of Dionysus in Athens the actor would have appeared about ¾″ high. There was no scope here for subtlety of gesture—little scope, indeed, for gesture at all—and it is safe to conclude from the scanty available evidence that the actor's movements were highly stylized and limited to those that were broad and easily comprehensible. He made his main effect through his voice. Thus we find, in ancient critiques of actors, that voice production and delivery are always commented upon, gesture only rarely. The Athenian audiences were sensitive to any imperfection. For proof of this we need only turn to the Aristophanic joke about the tragic actor Hegelochus, who, while playing the title role in Euripides' *Orestes*, failed to indicate a necessary elision, and what should have emerged as 'After the storm I see a calm' came out instead as 'After the storm I see a cat.' To us this seems a minor point of delivery, but the contemporary audience howled in derision and the comic poets were still gleefully retailing the joke years afterwards. So, with his voice the main item in his professional repertoire, the actor went to great pains to train it. This he did as strenuously as any opera singer. Here we may adduce—for stage and assembly were closely allied—the traditional stories of the training of Demosthenes, who rehearsed speeches with his mouth full of pebbles to correct a slight impediment, recited tragic verses while running uphill and took breath-control exercises from a prominent actor. We also have Antiphon's account of the chorus-member who poisoned himself with medicines intended to improve his voice.

Rhetorical training and rhetorical drama went hand in hand, and the actor was fully equipped to deal with the long speeches, the rolling periods in which the dramatists wrote. Unfortunately, this is rarely true of the modern actor, particularly in the United States, where rhetoric has long been out of fashion. The actor today is trained to express himself in short, clipped sentences—under the pernicious influence of the Method school, clipped almost to non-existence—and has real difficulty in adjusting himself to the style of a bygone day. This weakness arises largely from the fact that contemporary theater is no longer aural, but visual in its impact. In smaller theaters, with greater emphasis on realistic portrayal and illusionistic techniques, importance has shifted from the lines themselves to the stance and gestures accompanying those lines, or to the intervening action. Bereft of the power of rhetoric and mastery of its techniques, actors are often incapable of dealing with the sustained force of a Sophoclean monologue or a passage of Euripidean invective. I have myself found actors literally gasping for breath in such passages, and having to relearn a number of vanished skills before they can master them. One realizes again the tremendous burden placed on the Greek actor, and no longer finds so naive the remark of the scholiast on *Prometheus Bound*: 'At this point the chorus sings to give the actor a rest.'

If actors have lost the ability to deliver rhetoric, audiences have largely lost the ability to appreciate it. Although the eye can follow an elaborate periodic sentence from beginning to conclusion on the printed page, and comprehend all its ramifications, the ear is no longer attuned to such things in the theater. One of the charges most frequently levelled against Greek drama by the public is that it is too verbose, and this perhaps is something to be taken into consideration in preparing stage versions. The impact of a printed play may be absorbed at leisure; the impact of a stage performance is immediate. The audience cannot go back to re-read what has gone before. A point once missed cannot be recaptured. Too often the audience is stunned by a welter of words. And so the writer for the theater might do well to bear in mind that he should cultivate clarity at all costs, even if this means oversimplifying his original. Better a lost nuance than a bored audience. A translator may complain that by chopping an elaborate Sophoclean cadence into short, concise sentences he is losing the effect of the original; but to leave the audience in doubt as to what is being said is to sacrifice a good deal of the original also. This, then, would seem to be the main point of divergence between the translator for a reading public and the translator for the stage. The former may be expansive, the latter must be pungent, and concentrate on the primary meaning of his words.

Let us consider here one particular instance of the problems involved in transposing a play from a formal, rhetorical theater to one which is neither—the long passages of *stichomythia* which so often perplex modern directors of Greek plays. In the Greek theater, the stichomythic form was almost a necessity for sustained passages of tragic dialogue. We must remember again that the actors stood at a great distance from their audience, and were masked. Nor was there, so far as we can see, much attempt at vocal impersonation. Old men, young men, women, all would deliver their lines in the same way. In such circumstances, if the audience is to be sure who is speaking at any given time, the dramatist must give them some assistance. Such assistance is precisely what the stichomythic form provides. With the form of the dialogue predetermined, the audience can make the necessary transition from one speaker to the other. The lines are tossed rhythmically back and forth, in the manner of players knocking up at tennis. At the end of the iambic line the speaker changes; all is made simple.

This problem does not, of course, arise in comedy. Comic lines, as we know, were delivered with greater freedom. The form was less rigid, and in any case the dialogue was punctuated by laughs. Thus interjections, and lines divided between two or even three characters are frequent, and Aristophanic dialogue approximates much more closely to that of modern drama. But in tragedy, to divide a line between a number of speakers was to invite confusion.

The stichomythic form imposed its own requirements on the dramatist. Often, to retain the regular alternation of lines, questions and responses had to be inserted which would be redundant in ordinary dialogue. An example occurs in *Medea,* where Aigeus is relating to Medea the message of the Delphic oracle:

MEDEA:
Then tell me, if you may, what Phoebus said.
AIGEUS:
Not to loosen the wineskin's hanging foot–
MEDEA:
Until you had arrived somewhere, or done something?
AIGEUS:
Until I reached my ancestral hearth again.

Medea's interjection here is not dictated by any burning interest in Aigeus' story. As the subsequent lines make clear, she is preoccupied with her own troubles. It is a purely formal requirement. Aigeus' information cannot be compressed into one line, and practical considerations require adherence to the stichomythic form.

The crowning example of the difficulties of this technique occur in the fragments of Euripides' *Hypsipyle.* The heroine is conversing with Amphiaraus, on his way to besiege Thebes:

AMPHIARAUS:
My wife compelled me to march, against my will.
HYPSIPYLE:
From honest motives, or with hope of profit?
AMPHIARAUS:
She was given a necklace by Polyneices . . .
HYPSIPYLE:
Where did it come from? [The rest of the line is lost.]
AMPHIARAUS:
The famous Cadmus once married Harmonia. . . .
HYPSIPYLE:
He was one, I have heard, whom the gods loved.

AMPHIARAUS:
To her Aphrodite gave a lovely necklace. . . .
HYPSIPYLE:
Yes, gods are generous to their own relations!

The modern reader is left wondering why the silly woman does not let Amphiaraus get on with his story, or why the wise prophet does not lose his temper.

On the modern stage such devices are no longer necessary or desirable. The actor achieves more intimate contact with his audience. He usually goes unmasked, and the audience can see as well as hear him speak. Women's parts are taken by women, and not as in the Greek theater, by men; and the modern actor will offer far more in the way of vocal characterization than did his Greek predecessor. So here again the two types of translator will diverge. The literary translator will often feel that he must be faithful to the formal qualities of his original and reproduce the stichomythia in its entirety. The stage translator will sense that such artificial dialogue will be too slow for the taste of a modern audience, and abridge the lines, even omit the more redundant, to give a more natural effect.

In presenting the choruses this problem of pace confronts us again. Greek choruses, if we except some of the more otiose compositions of Euripides, are tautly constructed, interlocking with jigsaw puzzle complexity, relying heavily on imagery designed to awaken a wealth of association in the minds of the Greek audience. Inevitably the literary translator feels the need to expand if he is to do his original justice. Compare any translation of, for example, the 'Insolence breeds the tyrant' chorus in *Oedipus Rex* with the succinctness of the Greek. What Sophocles can say in two words the translator needs a sentence to convey in English. What happens in performance? The director has two choices. He can have the choruses either sung or declaimed. If they are to be sung, special problems at once confront the translator. He must assume the role of librettist, and libretto-writing makes its own demands. Certain collocations of syllables must be avoided. He must virtually confine himself to monosyllables if the sung words are to be understood. Once again, he is forced to simplify. If the chorus is to be declaimed, simplification seems to be called for again, though for different reasons. Translations which read admirably on paper often seem dull and ponderous in performance, when deprived of the music which would give them grace and lightness. For stage purposes, it is fatal to allow the demands of language to enlarge the part of the chorus beyond due measure.

Another possibility, and one which I have myself used in comedy, is to employ a weapon from the director's own armoury and render some of the imagery into visual terms. In the second half of the *Frogs* the two tragedians, Aeschylus and Euripides, clash in debate. Their meeting is described by the chorus in the language of the tournament and wrestling-ground. The Greek is neat and pithy, a *tour de force* of verbal farce. Translation can only render the full effect by expanding until the joke becomes intolerably heavy-handed. In production I have concentrated on the spirit rather than the letter of the joke. The actual translation is as simple and concise as it can be, and the ludicrous contrast between high tragedy and sporting terminology is brought out by setting the debate scene in a boxing ring. Aeschylus and Euripides occupy opposite corners. Dionysus, when giving advice to the contestants, descends into the ring in the manner of a referee. In the choral interludes between the long speeches the tragedians retire to their corners, drink water and are fanned with towels. Aristophanes, I dare hope, would have approved. So far I have not ventured to apply this technique to tragedy, but it seems that work could usefully be done in this direction, and that metaphor could be made more meaningful to the audience by accepting the modern theater's greater reliance on visual effect.

I may appear to be suggesting that the stage translator's

main prerogative is that of cutting. In all translation something must be sacrificed, and I should like to discuss two specific instances where cutting unnecessary in a reading translation becomes necessary on the stage. Both are taken from *Medea:* the first from the great quarrel scene between Medea and Jason. Medea makes her speech of condemnation, adducing everything she has done for Jason, and accusing him of treating her shamefully in return. At the conclusion of her tirade we have a two-line interjection by the chorus:

Tempers run high, and cannot soon be soothed
When those who have once loved begin to quarrel.

Jason takes up the argument and defends his own conduct. Far from betraying Medea, he has given her great advantages by bringing her to Greece in the first place. He will continue his kindness by giving her money, and introductions to his friends, so that she can support herself in exile. Once again, at the conclusion of his speech, the chorus interposes a comment:

Jason, you have made a pretty speech
But I will be bold and say what I think:
It was criminal to desert your wife.

These choral comments, like so many in Euripides, are platitudinous. They add nothing to what has gone before; they tell us nothing new; rather, they detract from the effect of the speeches by capping them with so uninspired an utterance. Why then were they ever written at all? I suggest that the main reason is the one we found in discussing stichomythia—to assist the audience in following the flow of argument from one speaker to another. The main speeches are so distinguished to allow the audience to adjust their focus from Medea to Jason and back to Jason again, and, incidentally, to give the actors a brief breathing space. Thus these choral interjections appear as a technical device redundant in the modern theater. In present-day performance they tend to slow up the action, and even give a sense of the ridiculous. Thus, while the literary translator must leave them in, the stage translator can claim that he is offering no less faithful a translation by leaving them out.

Secondly, what are we to do with a passage such as the Ino chorus in *Medea?* Medea has sent her children indoors and follows them sword in hand. For the first time the children's voices are heard, off-stage, screaming. The blow is struck, and the chorus sings:

One woman, one woman only
I have heard of before this time
Who laid hands on her darling children—
The heaven-demented Ino
Whom Hera made mad, and drove abroad.
And because of the children's dying
The wretched mother drowned,
Leaping from cliff to water
To join her two sons in death.
What worse could the world still hold?
Oh women, how many sorrows begin
In your bed; what a count of ills
You have brought to mankind already.

Euripides introduces the Ino motif at this point to build up suspense. He parallels Medea's murder of her children with a similar story which would be familiar to the audience. The chorus implies that Medea must share Ino's fate—surely there can be no escape for her now, except death. For a moment the audience is swayed into believing this also, with the result that the magical escape in the snake-drawn chariot comes with far greater surprise.

But what effect will this have on a modern audience? Few have ever heard of Ino; few indeed have heard of Medea and Jason, before they see the play. A reading translation can clarify the point by the introduction of a discreet footnote, but the theater has no footnotes. The introduction at this point of yet another strange name, drawn from the remoter regions of Greek mythology, will only confuse them. Their reaction will not be the one Euripides intended—'However will Medea get away?' but rather 'Here comes that damned chorus, butting in again.' Thus, while a literary translator must include the verses, the stage translator will be perfectly within his rights in expunging them and maintaining the tension by introducing Jason immediately.

The question of the appreciation of allusions brings us to comedy, and to that most parochial and at the same time most enduring of comedians, Aristophanes. His themes are eternally topical. We still have grandiose political machinations, as in *Birds*, the vexed questions of women's rights and the communist state, as in *Ecclesiazousae*, and bogus philosophers, as in *Clouds*. Aristophanes' treatment of these themes, however, is so topical to the Athens of his own day that the problems of transferring them to our own stage seem well-nigh insuperable. Who now will laugh at jokes about Theramenes, Cleisthenes, Cleocritus and the rest of the Aristophanic rogues' gallery? The problem assumes its most virulent form in a play like the *Frogs*, which is not only thick with topicalities about Greek plays and personalities most of which are known to us only by name, but has for two of its leading characters Greek playwrights with whose lives, characters and works the original audience would have been intimately familiar. The play is read at some time or other by most students of literature and the drama; but are we still entitled to put it on the stage? How can the audience be expected to have the necessary background without a copious array of footnotes?

Various bold expedients have been attempted. Dudley Fitts, in the introduction to his translation, mentions that he toyed with the idea of substituting quotations from Shakespeare and Dryden for those of Aeschylus and Euripides. Others have taken this even further. Stage versions have been offered in which the Greek tragedians were replaced by Shakespeare and Shaw. One wonders, however, if such attempts really achieve their purpose. Is a modern audience as familiar with specific quotations from Shakespeare and Shaw–let alone Dryden–as the Greeks were with their own dramatists? One can never be sure that in substituting modern topicalities for the ancient the audience will not be even worse baffled.

Perhaps it is safer to let the text stand, and employ a technique I shall call 'writing the footnotes into the translation.' Let me give one concrete example of this. Early in the *Frogs* Dionysus explains the purpose of his projected journey to the Underworld. He dwells on the beginning of his passion for the works of Euripides; and it is important to realize that so far Euripides' name has not been mentioned. 'One day' he says 'as I was sitting on board ship reading the *Andromeda*, a great desire came knocking at my heart.' To the Greek audience the title *Andromeda* would at once connote Euripides, but to a modern audience the name means precisely nothing. The literary translator can append a footnote, explaining that *Andromeda* was a tragedy by Euripides, now lost, and that it had a romantic, melodramatic plot involving the heroine's rescue from a sea-monster by the aerobatic hero. What can the stage translator do? Fitts makes a major concession to the audience by translating 'That play by Euripides, *Andromeda*.' To my mind this is still not enough; it does not convey what sort of play this was–and this is important, for it involves Aristophanes' whole attitude to Euripides and looks forward to some of the main criticisms made in the second half of the play. Euripides must be established in the audience's mind as a writer of this new, exotic type of tragedy which relies heavily on visual excitement and stirring situations. Thus I render not merely 'that play by Euripides, *Andromeda*' but 'that play by Euripides, *The Perils of Andromeda*', hoping that the audience will make a mental association with *The Perils of Pauline*, or, even if they do not, that the title will be self-explanatory. The same technique is used with the other titles of Euripidean plays as they occur. It is not enough simply to mention *Telephus, Peleus* or *Meleager*; the stage translator must also explain. Thus *Telephus* becomes *The Beggar Prince; Peleus, Murderer at Large; Aeolus, The Incestuous Marriage*; and from these the audience may form at least a rough idea of the sort of writer Euripides was, or rather the sort of writer Aristophanes pictures him as being.

What of the topical personalities who rarely appear, but are mentioned so often–Theramenes the vacillating politician, Cleisthenes the homosexual, and others? It would be tempting in some cases to supply modern parallels, but the law forbids. Thus I render these topicalities into general terms. Where Aristophanes speaks of Theramenes, the translation speaks only of 'a certain politician', and the audience is left to supply a suitable name. Sometimes I have adopted the Gilbertian trick of talking of 'you know who, and what's his name, and–well, never mind.' Although it is now impossible to specify, the audience should be left in no doubt that a topical reference is intended.

I have attempted to show in these few examples that the work of the stage translator begins where that of the literary translator leaves off. Aeschylus, Sophocles, Euripides and Aristophanes could write plays that read well and acted well. We, their humble followers, must so often content ourselves with versions that show only one aspect of their genius; but when the version is to be acted, let it at least be the dramatic aspect.

ROBERT W. CORRIGAN

Translating for Actors

ROBERT W. CORRIGAN, *editor and founder of the* Tulane Drama Review, *is editing the complete plays of Chekhov in new translations as well as a collection of Greek plays.*

We are just now in this country discovering the plays of such European playwrights as Ionesco, Beckett, Genet, Adamov, and Ghelderode. With a prudishness that is about par for the course, we tend to reject these plays and label their authors opprobriously as *avant-garde.* But somehow—in spite of our rejection—the plays keep reasserting themselves; they have a mysterious hold on our sensibilities. For all their apparent unintelligibility and simplicity, they possess a vitality we have missed in our theater. But what is the source of this vitality?

At first glance, it is the non-didactic quality which differentiates the work of these playwrights from those stereotyped forms to which we are so accustomed; there are no clear, packaged 'morals' or 'inspiring' attitudes. But we soon discover that underlying this lack of didacticism is a more central fact: each of these writers is revolting against the tyranny of words in the modern theater. The dialogue is not a monologue apportioned out to several characters; there is none of the planted line and heavy-handed cross-reference to which we are so accustomed; there are a multitude of symbols, but these symbols mean nothing in particular and yet suggest many things. In each of these plays the characters lead their own lives, talk their own thoughts. Their speeches impinge on each other and glance away. Finally, in all of these plays there is an insistence upon the gestures of pantomime as the theater's most appropriate and valuable means of expression; an insistence that the mimetic gesture precedes the spoken word and that the gesture is the true expression of what we feel, while words only describe what we feel. In fact, these writers assert that in objectifying the feeling in order to describe it, words kill the very feeling they would describe.

It is no wonder, then, that these playwrights feel a great affinity to the mimes—Etienne Decroux, Marcel Marceau, and Jacques Tati; no wonder that they turn for inspiration to the early films of Charlie Chaplin, Buster Keaton, the Keystone Cops, Laurel and Hardy, and the Marx Brothers; no wonder, finally, that they are all under the influence of Jacques Copeau and Antonin Artaud. It is only with the recent translation into English of Artaud's book, *The Theater and Its Double* (the earlier and more seminal work of Copeau has not as yet been translated), that most of us have been able to discover what the aesthetic of this whole *avant-garde* theater movement is.

Artaud's basic premise was that in the theater it is a mistake to assume that 'In the beginning was the word.' And our theater does make just that assumption. For most of us, critics as well as playwrights, the Word is everything; there is no possibility of expression without it; the theater is thought of as a branch of literature, and even if we admit a difference between the text spoken on the stage and the text read by the eyes, we have still not managed to separate it from the idea of a *performed text.* Artaud and the playwrights who have followed him maintain that our modern psychologically oriented theater is denying the theater's historical nature. For them the stage is a concrete physical place which must speak its own language—a language that goes deeper than spoken language, a language that speaks directly to our senses rather than primarily to the mind as with the language of words.

This is the most significant thing about the *avant-garde* theater—it is a theater of gesture. 'In the beginning was the Gesture!' Gesture is not a decorative addition that accompanies words; it is rather the source, cause, and director of language, and insofar as language is dramatic, it is gestural. It is this insistence upon restoring the gestural basis to theater that has resulted in the renascence of pantomime in such plays as *The Chairs, Waiting for Godot, Ping-Pong, Endgame, The Balcony,* and *Escurial.* Those of you who have seen any of these plays in production know how different this pantomime is from pantomime as most moderns conceive of it. For most of us, pantomime is a series of gestures which represent words or sentences—a game of charades. But this is not the pantomime of history. For the great mimists, Artaud points out, gestures represent ideas, attitudes of mind, aspects of nature which are realized in an effective, concrete way, by constantly evoking objects or natural details much as Oriental language represents night by a tree on which a bird that has closed one eye is beginning to close the other.

The famous director, Meyerhold, was striving for the same thing in his attempt to restore vitality to the Russian theater at the turn of the century. With the exception of Chekhov—and the affinity of Chekhov to the *avant-garde* is greater than one might at first think—most of the playwrights of that time were trying to transform literature for reading into literature for the theater. Meyerhold correctly saw that these playwrights were in fact novelists who thought that by reducing the number of descriptive passages and enlivening the story by increasing the characters' dialogue, a play would result. Then this novelist-playwright would invite his reader to pass from the library into the auditorium. As Meyerhold put it in his essay, 'Farce':

> Does the novelist need the services of mime? Of course not. The readers themselves can come onto the stage, assume parts, and read aloud to the audience the

dialogue of their favorite novelist. This is called 'a harmoniously performed play.' A name is quickly given to the reader-transformed-into-actor, and a new term, 'an intelligent actor,' is coined. The same dead silence reigns in the auditorium as in the library. The public is dozing. Such immobility and solemnity is appropriate only in a library.

There has been a bit of intentional overstatement in all of this. Obviously, it is not a matter of suppressing speech in the theater. It is not that language is not important in the theater, it is rather a matter of changing its role. Since the theater is really concerned only with the way feelings and passions conflict with one another, and man with man, in life—Mr. Arrowsmith hit it perfectly when he used the term 'turbulence'—the language of the theater must be considered as something other than a means of conducting human characters to their external ends. To change the role of speech in theater is to make use of it in a concrete and spatial sense, combining it with everything else in the theater. In short, language in the theater must always be gestural: it must grow out of the gesture, must always act and never be descriptive. The theater is dead the moment there is a substitution of statement for dramatic process.

This may seem far removed from the problems of translation, and yet I think not. If we are clearly so incapable in our time of giving an idea of Aeschylus, Sophocles, or Shakespeare that is truly expressive of what they were trying to achieve in the theater, it is very likely because we have lost the sense of their theater's physics. It is because the directly human and active aspect of their way of speaking and moving, their whole scenic rhythm, escapes us. It is not enough to have the texts of their plays, for none of these great tragedians is the theater itself. The theater is always a matter of scenic materialization in space. Call it an inferior art if you will, but as Artaud insists, 'theater resides in a certain way of furnishing and animating the air of the stage, by a conflagration of feelings and human sensations at a given point, creating situations that are expressed in concrete gestures.'

Keeping this in mind, we must take one more step before we can deal with the specific problems of translating for the theater. And for this part of the journey we will need a new Vergil—so Antonin Artaud gives way to Mr. R. P. Blackmur, that fine gentleman and critic who has guided so many in modern criticism. I refer specifically to his essay, 'Language as Gesture.'[1]

In this essay Blackmur takes us into those realms where language becomes gestural. He sees beyond the simple distinction that language is made of words and gesture is made of motion, to the reverse distinction: 'Words are made of motion, made of action or response, at whatever remove; and gesture is made of language—made of the language beneath or beyond or alongside of the language of words.' Working from this premise it is possible for Mr. Blackmur to consider that notion which is so important for anyone writing for the theater: 'When the language of words most succeeds it *becomes* gesture in its words.' He sees that gesture is not only native to language, but that it precedes it, and must be, as it were, carried into language whenever the context is imaginative or dramatic. Without a gestural quality in language there can be no drama. This is so since 'the great part of our knowledge of life and nature—perhaps all our knowledge of their play and interplay [their drama]—comes to us as gesture, and we are masters of the skill of that knowledge before we can ever make a rhyme or a pun, or even a simple sentence.' Blackmur then goes on to define what he means by gesture in language, and I quote his definition because I believe it will be helpful to the rest of my argument. It reads:

[1] Published in *Accent* in 1943 and then reprinted in a book with the same title in 1952.

> Gesture, in language, is the outward and dramatic play of inward and imaged meaning. It is that play of meaningfulness among words which cannot be defined in the formulas in the dictionary, but which is defined in their use together; gesture is that meaningfulness which is moving, in every sense of that word: what moves the words and what moves us.

When we can capture *that* quality in words we will then be writing (or translating) for actors. And in the theater you write only for actors—never for readers. Even the most cursory glance at the history of the theater shows that whenever playwrights cease writing for actors the theater loses its vitality and loses its literature, too. Certainly, Shakespeare provides us with our strongest evidence on this point—but Aeschylus, Sophocles, Euripides, or Molière would do just as well. Shakespeare is the greatest *dramatist* in the English language and his plays are great works of literature, but he was not writing literature; he was primarily writing for actors; and, as we know, he was writing for specific actors. And this is the source of the plays' enduring vitality. Furthermore, I would even maintain that he would never have created some of the scenes he did if he had not known the actors who were to play them. And from what we know of the Greek festivals and the French theater of the seventeenth century, it is probably safe to assume that Sophocles had his Burbage and Molière was his own Will Kemp.

Now, the art of writing for actors has been almost totally neglected. The idea that plays are written to be performed appears to disturb many people. This attitude is, I think, largely a reaction to the acting practices of the nineteenth century, which so often proved to be little more than the sleight-of-hand of technique. Throughout the history of the theater this kind of magic can be found. The most guilty men were usually actors; often they were what are called 'great actors.' These virtuoso players cannot be wholly blamed, for, with some major exceptions, during the past 150 years actors have been given everything to act except plays: pamphlets, tracts, novels, newspaper articles, and even epic poems. This forced actors—who are animals with a strong sense of self-preservation and considerable ingenuity—to abandon literary texts altogether in favor of exciting and suspenseful situations that gave them the opportunity to exhibit their skill. This was very poor art, but extremely good business.

Although today we tend to measure an actor by his ability to achieve the fullness of the dramatist's intention, we nevertheless regard with suspicion any play that seems to have been written primarily for actors. This is too bad, for the actor is the playwright's most valuable means of expression. The actor's power lies in his humanity, not—as we so often suppose—in his mind, his body, his face, or even his voice. Only in the theater can the artist call on men as men to communicate, to express, and to interpret. I have never understood why the actor's art is so often discounted because of its transience. Surely the emotional force of the actor's performance—that quality which moves an audience—resides in the fact that it possesses a mortality of its own, that it is gone into the past as irrevocably as any human action.

It is for this reason that the actor's concern is to achieve, not truth, but a rightness. To perfect this rightness is his job. Movement, the costumes, make-up, even the words are subsidiary. Thus what the actor demands from a play is not words in dialogue form, but a stimulus to his imagination. It is at this point that the playwright and his actors first come together, and it is important to remember that in every way the theater is a coming together. This is true of a performance and it is true of the making of that performance. It is a playwright's vanity to claim creation because he is the first link in the chain of a production. His play would be no play if it remained words on paper.

It is for this reason that the playwright—and also the

translator—cannot really be concerned with 'good prose' or with 'good verse' in the usual sense of those terms. The structure is action; not what is said or how it is said but *when*. For example, the use of soliloquies, choral passages, stichomythia, indirect dialogue and pauses, to mention but a few of the structural uses of dramatic language. By this method it is possible to control from within the text of the play the speed and exact rhythm which are usually imposed by the director. Only by realizing the play's theatrical dynamic in this way, can the actors see the dramatic shape of an individual part within a scene and not be forced to rely on an intuitive sense which is often false and sometimes leads to distortion.

The basic, the unalterable, factor of drama is the moment 'when,' and the dramatist's first concern must be with this moment of action. If he does not, as so often is the case, it will be imposed by the director or the actors. In other words, the dramatist must create not only the dialogue, but what is done and *when*.

Recently, playwrights and critics alike have been greatly concerned with the question of style in writing for the theater. Invariably, such inquiries deal with the form of the spoken word. This is a mistake, for words are not the starting point. The great hope for our theater is that today our new playwrights are finally sensing this. We must concern ourselves first with the gestures that supply the motives behind the words. This calls to mind that old and only partly humorous adage of the theater: Never pay attention to the playwright's stage directions. (In this regard it is interesting to note, and I think it is to my point, that there are no stage directions other than entrances and exits in the plays of the Greeks, or Shakespeare, or Molière. The motive, meaning, and gestures were in the words themselves.) In the modern theater those stage directions, however, are the dramatist's first means of communication with his actors. They must never presume to take the place of the director's 'blocking' by telling the actor where to move or how to sit. Nor must they instruct the actor how to read the lines—'pensively,' 'bitterly,' 'joyfully.' (One is reminded at this point of Eugene O'Neill, whose 'flat' language had practically no emotive quality. As a result it was necessary for him to prefix nearly every speech with a stage direction to indicate how the actor should read words which had no emotional power of their own.) They must augment the words to be spoken. The stage directions are guidelines of motive and action throughout the individual parts, and when realized in performance they are as much part of the play as the words the actors speak.

By this time the reader may be wondering if I am aware that my subject is translation and not playwriting. I am, believe me; but I feel very strongly that no one can translate for the theater—just as no one can write for it—unless he knows what writing for the theater is and how it differs from literature. In fact, I would go so far as to say that good translations of plays will never come from those who have not had at least some training in the practice of theater. Without such training the tendency will be to translate words and their meanings. This practice will never produce performable translations, and this is, after all, the purpose of doing the job in the first place.

This leads us to our final consideration. Granted that translating for actors is a different undertaking, what are its specific problems and techniques?

The first law in translating for the theater is that everything must be speakable. It is necessary at all times for the translator to hear the actor speaking in his mind's ear. He must be conscious of the gestures of the voice that speaks—the rhythm, the cadence, the interval. He must also be conscious of the look, the feel, and the movement of the actor while he is speaking. He must, in short, render what might be called the whole gesture of the scene. To do this it is important to know what words do and mean, but it is more important to know what they cannot do at those crucial moments when the actor needs to use a vocal or physical gesture. Only in this way can the translator hear the words in such a way that they play upon each other in harmony, in conflict, and in pattern—and hence as dramatic. I suppose what I am saying is that it is necessary almost to direct the play, act the play, and see the play while translating it.

I first became interested in translating for the theater out of practical necessity. Several years ago I was asked to direct a production of Chekhov's *Uncle Vanya.* I had a superb cast and decided to use what is generally regarded as the best translation of Chekhov. The initial reading rehearsals were miserable. At first I thought this was the usual thing and the actors would get over their stiffness. After all, the translation made logical sense. But soon—I had the good, but unusual, fortune to have three months in which to do the show—the actors unconsciously began revising the speeches. They sounded better; there was a flow. Now, traditionally, Chekhov plays are thought of as moody, complex, soulful, vague, and impossible to perform successfully on the American stage. But my actors were giving evidence that this was not necessarily so. It was then that I recalled Chekhov's troubles with Stanislavski and how the playwright always insisted that the great director-actor was complicating what was very simple.[2] And I realized too that the translations were not expressing this sim-

[2] In fact, I would go so far as to say that Stanislavski and the tradition of The Moscow Art Theater have probably done more to distort our ideas about Chekhov than any other person or group. Which suggests that the translator should at all times be a critic. It is no accident, it seems to me, that the best translations in the oft-mentioned 'Chicago' Greek tragedies were done by the two best critics of Greek tragedy in our time. And in saying this, I suddenly realize that I have just created a kind of Craig-ian Übermarionette: The translator is writer, director, actor, audience, and now he is the critic, too. What do we need a theater for? If translators will all unite, the theater can be made obsolete in a fortnight and all our problems will be solved.

plicity upon which Chekhov insisted. Instead of the text's 'But what for?' the translation had 'though what his provocation may be I can't imagine.' Or 'There is another thing too—you take a drop of vodka now,' when all Chekhov wrote was: 'And you drink too.' Or finally, 'as if the field of art were not large enough to accommodate both new and old without the necessity of jostling;' he wrote: 'but there's room for all.'

Then, the light dawned. The meaning and complexity of his plays—and they are extremely dense—has to be achieved indirectly. When Chekhov wrote,

> The demand is made that the hero and the heroine (of a play) should be dramatically effective. But in life people do not shoot themselves, or hang themselves, or fall in love, or deliver themselves of clever sayings every minute. They spend most of their time eating, drinking, running after women, or men, or talking nonsense. It is therefore necessary that this should be shown on the stage. A play ought to be written in which the people should come and go, dine, talk of the weather, or play cards, not because the author wants it but because that is what happens in real life. Life on the stage should be as it really is and the people, too, should be as they are and not stilted.

he was trying to tell us that his dramatic actions are all enclosed by a very simple and inconsequential frame. The surfaces of life are apparently reproduced with all their natural and familiar inanity. There is very little that is dramatic in the events themselves. What makes these episodes powerful theater is the way they are combined, the sequences, the underlying associations and complications, the contrasts and ironies. It is in this way that the profound meanings are created. But if this is true of his dramaturgy, it must be equally true of the speech. It was then that I saw that the translation must be easy and natural on the surface. The inner meanings and profundities should appear—and would only appear as theater rather than statement—through the interaction of surface simplicities and not through complex or vague lines, not through what Stark Young has called a 'muggy, symbolic, swing-on-to-your-atmosphere sort of tone.'

Perhaps I can make my point with one example. In the third act of *Uncle Vanya* there is a long speech by Professor Serebryakov, that stuffy pedant who has spent a lifetime rehashing other people's ideas about the 'isms' of literature, and who now projects his own inadequacy and unconscious sense of failure onto those about him with acts of cruelty. In this speech he announces his plan to sell the estate that Vanya has worked so hard to keep productive. I take what seems to me the best of the translations of this speech:

> *Here is* maman. *I will begin, friends* (a pause). *I have invited you, gentlemen, to announce that the Inspector-General is coming. But let us lay aside jesting. It is a serious matter. I have called you together to ask for your advice and help, and, knowing your invariable kindness, I hope to receive it. I am a studious, bookish man, and have never had anything to do with practical life. I cannot dispense with the assistance of those who understand it, and I beg you, Ivan Petrovitch, and you, Ilya Ilyitch, and you,* maman. . . . *The point is that* manet omnes una nox—*that is, that we are all mortal. I am old and ill, and so I think it is high time to settle my worldly affairs so far as they concern my family. My life is over. I am not thinking of myself, but I have a young wife and an unmarried daughter* (a pause). *It is impossible for me to go on living in the country. We are not made for country life. But to live in town on the income we derive from this estate is impossible. If we sell the forest, for instance, that's an exceptional measure which we can-*

> *not repeat every year. We must take some steps which would guarantee us a permanent and more or less definite income. I have thought of such a measure, and have the honour of submitting it to your consideration. Omitting details I will put it before you in rough outline. Our estate yields on an average not more than two per cent on its capital value. I propose to sell it. If we invest the money in suitable securities, we should get from four to five per cent, and I think we might even have a few thousand roubles to spare for buying a small villa in Finland.*

In the first place, even Houdini couldn't cut through some of those constructions and no actor could say the lines convincingly. But more important, the translation misses the whole tone and meaning of the situation. Here is a bad professor giving a lecture or a talk to the Rotary Club. All the mannerisms of the podium—the bad jokes, the phrases, the outline method, the pedantic attempts not to be pedantic—are cut out or submerged in the wrong kind of verbiage. Also, the translation misses the rhetorical quality of the speech—the dramatic way the speaker sees himself. As T. S. Eliot has pointed out in his essay, 'Rhetoric and Poetic Drama,' this kind of rhetoricizing is common to us all and can be of great help to the modern dramatist in that it permits the audience to see a character not only as the other characters see him, but as the character consciously dramatizes himself. Rather the speech should read:

> *Here is mother. Ladies and gentlemen, let us begin. I have asked you to gather here, my friends, to inform you that the inspector-general is coming.* (laughs) *All joking aside, however, I wish to discuss a very important matter. I must ask you for your aid and advice, and realizing your unbounded kindness, I believe I can count on both. I am a scholar and bound to my library, and I am not familiar with practical affairs.*

I am unable, I find, to dispense with the help of well-informed people such as you, Ivan, and you, Ilya, and you mother. The truth is, manet omnes una nox, *that is to say, our lives rest in the hands of God, and as I am old and ill, I realize that the time has come for me to dispose of my property in the interests of my family. My life is nearly finished, and I am not thinking of myself, but I must consider my young wife and daughter.* (a pause) *I cannot go on living in the country; we were just not meant for country life. And yet, we cannot afford to live in town on the income from this estate. We might sell the forests, but that would be an expedient to which we could not resort every year. We must work out some method of guaranteeing ourselves a permanent, and . . . ah, more or less fixed annual income. With this object in view, a plan has occurred to me which I now have the honor of proposing to you for your consideration. I shall give you only a rough outline of it, omitting all the bothersome and trivial details. Our estate does not yield, on an average, more than two per cent on the investment. I propose to sell it. If then we invest our capital in bonds and other suitable securities, it will bring us four to five per cent, and we should probably have a surplus of several thousand roubles, with which we could buy a small house in Finland. . . .*

It is only when the sense of speakability is achieved that we have theater. I am sure that this is one of the things Hamlet meant when he advised the players: 'Speak the speech, I pray you. . . . trippingly on the tongue.' To achieve this I think translators fail to use an important source—namely, the actors themselves. I have directed all of my translations of Chekhov and time and time again the actors have made or suggested changes that have improved the translation a great deal. First, two examples of minor changes made by actors which didn't do much more than improve the flow of the words. Originally, I had 'It is too stifling.' The actor changed it to 'The day is too hot.' Or changing 'will they remember us in a kindly spirit?' to 'will they remember us with grateful hearts?' But actors can also make changes that alter the whole dynamic of a scene. When I directed *The Three Sisters,* I tried without success for three weeks to get the final scene of the third act to build properly–in fact merely to build at all. My three sisters were fine actresses and all had had good professional training and experience. I knew the build had to begin in one of Irina's speeches, but nothing happened. Then one night she took the speech her way and the whole scene came to life; we achieved what we wanted. It was only afterwards that I realized she had changed one of the lines and it was this change that made the speech and hence the rest of the scene dramatic. Originally, the line read, 'Oh, I'm so miserable! I can't work, I won't work! I've had enough of it, enough!' The actress changed it to: 'I'm miserable (*pause*). I've had enough, enough, enough. I can't, I won't, I will not work,' and in this way she got a structure that could be vocally built. Obviously, I am not suggesting that irresponsible changes be made or changes that alter the meaning of a speech. But an actor–in having to say the line–may be of great service to the translator in making the text more actable.

In addition to making the text speakable, the translator must also be prepared to lose things. Clearly, all translations are necessarily imperfect. As Eric Bentley said, 'If life begins on the other side of despair, the translator's life begins on the other side of impossibility!' This is particularly true of Chekhov since his plays are so finely textured and depend on many peculiarly Russian traits. For example, there is the watchman's rattle in the second act of *Uncle Vanya.* This is a perfectly realistic touch, but it also functions as a symbol for the action. It is used at that crucial time at the end of the act when Yelena and Sonya have just had an honest talk with each other and because of it, are capable of some feeling. The windows are open, it has been raining—and everything is clean and refreshed. Yelena thinks she can play the piano again. As Sonya goes to get permission, the watchman's rattle is heard, Yelena has to shut the window, and Serebryakov says 'no.' Their whole life of feeling has been protected by a watchman to the point that they have no feelings left. But in production when the rattle is used, the audience—instead of seeing its significance—thinks the pipes in the auditorium are rattling. The same kind of thing is true of the many topical allusions in *The Three Sisters*. The only way you can make these understandable is to write footnotes or a program note. Heaven forbid that we should do either. If the plays are done properly, however, these effects will have an impact on the audience's senses if not their understanding.

But there are some things that are lost that need not be. For instance, in all of the published translations of *Uncle Vanya* the shooting is botched. The typical translation reads:

> *Let me go, Helen! Let me go!* (Looking for Serebryakov)
> *Where is he? Oh, here he is!* (Fires at him) *Missed! Missed again!* (Furiously) *Damnation—damnation take it*
> . . . (Flings revolver on the floor and sinks onto a chair, exhausted).

Not one translator has seen that in the Russian Vanya does not fire the gun, but he *says* 'Bang!' He has become so incapable of action that even when his whole life is at stake he cannot act but substitutes words. Here is a case where the meaning of the play has been drastically changed by the translator's failure to see that Chekhov's conception of that ghastly moment is truer than our more simple-minded logic.

The last point I want to make is that in addition to being written for actors, translations must be good English. I do not wish to get involved in the controversy over free or literal versions, but obviously the translator must not feel he has to have a word for word correspondence. If you translate literally into French, 'For crying out loud' you will not have translated it. I think Bentley is right when he says:

> Accuracy must not be bought at the expense of bad English. Since we cannot have everything, we would rather surrender accuracy than style. This, I think, is the first principle of translating, though it is not yet accepted in academic circles. The clinching argument in favor of this principle is that, finally, bad English cannot be accurate translation—unless the original is in bad German, bad French, or what have you.

But in making it good English one must always try to do it in the playwright's way. Where he uses repetitions we must use them too and not discount him as wordy. After all, in Macbeth's 'Tomorrow and tomorrow and tomorrow,' it is not at all the meaning the words have that counts, but the meaning that repetition in a given situation makes them take on. The same with all the other gestures of language—puns, rhymes, alliteration. Or, when a playwright wrongly paraphrases another author or a song, the translator should not correct the author's mistake. Chekhov, for instance, constantly has his characters quote Shakespeare—but the quotation is usually wrong. The meaning is in the wrongness. But Chekhov's well-intentioned translators have always felt that poor Anton Pavelovich didn't know English very well and so they helped out by correcting his faulty efforts. Finally, it is important to remember that duration *per se* in stage speech is a part of its meaning, and stage time is based upon the breath. This means that the translator must always, whenever he can, try to keep the same number of words in each sentence.

Let me close by saying that if we always remember that the language of the stage must appear as necessity, as a result of a series of compressions, collisions, scenic frictions, and evolutions, then it will be right, for it will be gestural. 'Language as gesture,' as Mr. Blackmur revealed, 'creates meaning as conscience creates judgment, by feeling the pang, the inner bite, of things forced together,' and this is the conflict we call dramatic, the conflict most at home in the theater.

JOSEPH KERMAN

Translation for Music

JOSEPH KERMAN *is a musicologist and critic, author of* The Elizabethan Madrigal *and* Opera as Drama, *who teaches at the University of California at Berkeley.*

Our relation to works of art removed from us by time or culture is so vast and so obvious a problem that we can perhaps never understand fully the many types of mediation we employ. Yet mediation is essential. Links have to be found or forged or hypostatized in order to inform or even to ground sympathy. Literary translation presents the case in the most self-conscious form, but something analogous has to take place in music and all the other arts.

In the visual arts, what I am calling mediation is unproblematic in this respect at least, that it confines itself to the spectator. One does not translate the work of art, for a cathedral is *there* in so much more vivid a way than a poem or a fugue is. The spectator has the full, vague, confidential task of adjusting his own sympathy to the work of art.

Literary works in the vernacular are left alone, like cathedrals. It is recognized that not everything is preserved on the page; but just how Chaucer sounded is not apparently a matter of primary concern. On the other hand, what his words mean to a contemporary reader is subject to incessant private mediation. This mediation is certainly not the same process as the appreciation of concrete visual symbols, but it has the same order of difficulty and anxiety. Criticism may assist. With literature in other languages, unless we learn the languages, the words are not merely arcane, but meaningless. We translate, seizing the excuse to mediate the work of art itself by interpreting it according to another, more familiar sensibility. For the reader, a job has been half done.

With music, the sound *is* a matter of primary concern. Yet up to the present age of recordings, all we have had that is tangible is a notation for sounds, and a generation's memory. Every serious musical performance, then, is a musician's mediation operating directly and crucially upon the work of art: "an interpretation," we say. Though such interpretation is sharply limited in scope, our concept and our love of music depend very much on powerful performance styles: the Solesmes plainchant, Casals' Bach, Schnabel's Beethoven, Robert Craft's Webern. Since there are many more performances than translations, there are of course also many more trivial exercises which we want to shut out of our ears as interference. We become habituated to small mediating minds at work.

Another kind of mediation, musical transcription, would seem to be intrinsically more interesting than performance, though it is much less common, and as commonly abused. Transcription may be said to begin when, for instance, Bach is played *verbatim* on a foreign instrument like an electronic synthesizer, or a piano. Great piano virtuosos of the nineteenth century doubled octaves and filled in harmonies and generally adjusted Bach's notes to the ethos of the piano that they knew. Stokowski reconceived Bach for modern orchestra. One can also go further and add or change notes, harmonies, phrases, contexts–thus a sixteenth-century organist, Claudio Merulo, published the works of a then famous older madrigalist, Philippe Verdelot, corrected to modern taste; Bach rewrote one of Palestrina's Masses for chorus and baroque orchestra, complete with trumpets and drums; Mozart copied out some Bach fugues for strings, joining them to preludes of his own composition. There are nineteenth-century examples, and in our own time, notably Stravinsky's re-creations of Pergolesi, Tchaikovsky, Gesualdo, and Bach. Stravinsky has recently written about the genesis of *Pulcinella:*

> I knew Pergolesi only by the *Stabat Mater* and *La Serva Padrona,* and though I had just seen a production of the latter in Barcelona, Diaghilev knew I wasn't in the least excited by it. I did promise to look, however, and to give him my opinion.
>
> I looked, and I fell in love . . . *Pulcinella* was my discovery of the past, the epiphany through which the whole of my late work became possible. It was a backward look, of course—the first of many love affairs in that direction—but it was a look in the mirror, too. . . . People . . . cried "sacrilege": "The classics are ours. Leave the classics alone." To them all my answer was and is the same: You "respect," but I love.[1]

A phrase of R. P. Blackmur's comes to mind: "Criticism, I take it, is the formal discourse of an amateur. When there is enough love and enough knowledge represented in the discourse it is a self-sufficient but by no means an isolated art . . ." Stravinsky's transcription of Pergolesi is the closest thing in music to a serious translation in literature, and as such, deserves to be treated as criticism of a high type. So Stravinsky thinks:

> I believe, with Auden, that the only critical exercise of value must take place in and by means of art, i.e., in pastiche or parody; *Le Baiser de la fée* and *Pulcinella* are music criticisms of this sort, though more than that, too.

Like art itself, criticism may or may not strike a response; there are many people who are left cold by "pas-

[1] Igor Stravinsky and Robert Craft, *Expositions and Developments* (Doubleday, New York, 1962), p. 127; the next quotation is from p. 124.

tiche or parody." Personally, I never "saw" Pergolesi until I heard *Pulcinella.*

II

These large thoughts are hazarded as a *context* for the topic I am to treat, translation for music—that is, translation of the words in vocal music. This context should serve to stultify the topic. For while there does exist something in music to discuss on a plane with literary translation, it certainly isn't translation for music, which musicians have always regarded as a disagreeable makeshift. Reasonably enough, musicians are infatuated with their own characteristic mediative act, performance. They seldom interest themselves in literary values, let alone in the delicate matter of mediating such values. Evidently, here is no atmosphere for serious artistic activity. Fortunately for this essay, however, W. H. Auden and Chester Kallman have recently set about translating operas from another point of view, closer to that of the literary translator, regarding the final poem as a work of art, as integral rather than *ersatz.* As a result *The Magic Flute* in their version wears a plucky smile instead of a hangdog look; it is instantly lovable in a way that no previous translation has been.[2] Unhappily it seems blithely to destroy half of Mozart's own intentions. But as I know no other translations with any comparable graces, I take this one to knock around for ideas about a possible *craft* of translation for music.

III

The axiom is devastating; Auden and Kallman put it in words of one syllable: "The goal of the translator, however

[2] Originally written for the NBC Opera Theatre, the translation was published by Random House in 1956. I discussed Auden and Kallman's very striking interpretation of the play as a whole in *The Hudson Review,* Summer 1957.

unattainable, must be to make audiences believe that the words they are hearing are the words which the composer actually set."[3] I should separate out three requirements for this belief:

Plausibility of language: if other criteria are to be given weight, you cannot hope for elegance, lucidity, or force of language; merely for plausibility. This is of course a function of the poetic convention that is established. But this must be a live convention, not some preposterous poetic license invoked tacitly to support lines like *Oh, how to see her I am yearning!/ Oh, how to free her I am burning!* or *I know not if 'tis joy or pain/ That overwhelms my reeling brain.* If Auden's version were merely plausible—but it is a great deal more—it would already stand nearly alone in a field which poets have, understandably, avoided. But if this work is to be done, poets are needed, precisely because their craft allows them to create infinitely wider ranges of plausibility than the rest of us know about. This range provides a reserve—which should be spent not first of all in refining literary quality, but in the precarious service of further demands.

Plausibility of declamation: again, no more than plausibility can be hoped for. Hope to persuade the audience that the composer might reasonably have set your words, not that he set them beautifully. And again, plausible declamation is a relative matter depending on the musical convention, for musical styles set up their own imaginative consistencies of verbal treatment, even unlikely ones (as we know from *The Rake's Progress*). Once the convention is grasped, however, the translator ought to bind himself to it fanatically. For an audience, nothing

[3] From the translators' preface to *The Magic Flute*. They have also written elsewhere on the subject: Chester Kallman, "Opera in Translation," *Center*, I No. 1 (1954), pp. 11–13, and W. H. Auden in collaboration with Kallman, "Translating Opera Libretti," in *The Dyer's Hand* (Random House, New York, 1962), pp. 483–99.

destroys the illusion that "the words they are hearing are the words which the composer actually set" so instantly as clumsy declamation at a sensitive juncture. One bad slip and the whole convention totters. The idea of having words sung instead of spoken seems suddenly monstrous.

Momentary meanings, syntax, verse form, etc., should be kept or simulated when (*and only when*) *they are important to the musical conception.* I crowd all these considerations together because admittedly none is a *sine qua non,* as I consider plausible language and plausible declamation to be. Yet unless they are honored in translation, musicians will always complain. To illustrate for the moment generally and simply: suppose a sudden rich harmony occurs in the music, prompted by and joined to an emotional phrase like *Ich fühl* in the original language. I wish the English phrase to be not only decent in itself and well declaimed, but also roughly parallel in meaning. *Heart* or *rich* or *marvel* will do as well as *feel,* often enough (and luckily enough); but unless the word is somehow emotional, the harmony will seem limp because unmotivated. Or to take a syntactical example: where a musical climax is spurred or supported by mounting tension in the sentence structure, something parallel should occur in the translation. To bring a preposition at the climax will be weak in itself and false to the composer's total gesture. As to verse form, rhymes are never important intrinsically, but only in situations where they have been used in a significant way, such as for example to cement parallel cadence structures. It is obvious that a crowd of possibilities as vast as a composer's imagination can turn into necessities here.

Auden has not often felt himself committed to considerations of this kind. But ideally the translator should penetrate into the musical conception, take a position on just what is and what isn't important in the total complex of word and tone, and then struggle to keep or simulate factors that he finds important. He is free to scrap the rest, even if it means changing notes or rhythms. "A too-literal translation of the original text may sometimes prove a falsification," said Auden, and then later: "it is often better to put the actual words out of mind and concentrate on writing as good an English lyric as possible." It will be better only in cases where the setting is so neutral that the sense of individual words and word order has only a superficial relationship to the music. Papageno's strophic songs are such cases. But where Mozart is writing at full tilt, melody, harmony, phraseology, accompaniment and all the rest are bound in with momentary verbal meanings. If falsification is to be avoided, a good deal of careful respect for the original words is required after all.

The two poets have gone at *The Magic Flute* like literary translators. I scarcely blame them; that is the only way to do it with any joy. Unfortunately, or fortunately, the music remains as a rigid control. A literary translation is made for someone who does not read the original, or else (in the grimmest case imaginable) for someone who reads the original and the translation a piece at a time, successively. But in a musical translation, the music is steadily in your ears, not merely in the back of your mind. Imagine reading Pope's *Iliad* while Homer is chanting the original hexameters synchronized exactly with the English, line by line.

Let me give just a few notes on how my three requirements confront the translator in one specific instance, Tamino's Air in *The Magic Flute.*

Dies Bildnis ist bezaubernd schön,
Wie noch kein Auge je gesehn!
Ich fühl es, wie dies Götterbild
Mein Herz mit neuer Regung füllt.

Dies Etwas kann ich zwar nicht nennen,
Doch fühl' ich's hier wie Feuer Brennen;
Soll dies Empfindung Liebe sein?
Ja, ja! die Liebe ist's allein.

O wenn ich sie nur finden könnte!
O wenn sie doch schon vor mir stände!
Ich würde—würde—warm und rein—
Was würde ich? [ich würde] sie voll Entzücken
An diesen heissen Busen drücken,
Und ewig wäre sie dann mein.

True image of enchanting grace!
O rare perfection's dwelling-place
Where beauty is with virtue shown
More noble than itself alone.

Is she the dream to which I waken,
The pursuit where I am overtaken,
Body and mind and heart and soul?
She is! To love her is my goal.

How do I speak as though I knew her,
When I must find her first and woo her?
O tell me, image, grant a sign—
Am I her choice?

She will be won—O sweet occasion!—
By gentle force and warm persuasion,
And with her love will answer mine.

Mozart's poem is wretched (in case you hadn't known). As poetry Auden's is immensely better. Obviously, he determined to take a strong line about sentimentality: *Herz, Busen, fühl, Entzücken* and even much of the first person singular have been neatly paraphrased away. But the question is, what has the poetic tone to do with the music? a great deal, and the translator ought not to remove the offending mush, but keep it—refined, if he wishes, to a seemly emotionalism such as Mozart presumably read through the mush. What Auden has done is write the lyric that we should have preferred Mozart to have set. But if Mozart had had Auden's lyric—*O sweet occasion!*—the music would have come out differently; and the music is *there*, as a rigid control. The music can be "interpreted," but it can no more be translated than a cathedral.

So I would have to start over:

Sweet vision of enchanting grace,
O rare perfection's dwelling-place!
I marvel: at this heavenly sight
My heart is moved to strange delight.

This nameless feeling quite evades me,
But a sweet contentedness pervades me;
Can it be love that wakes in me?
It is! I love her: that must be.

How may I seek her to confess my love?
How may she answer when I tell my love?
I'll seek her—seek her—far and near—
but how, indeed?
I'll seek her hand; I will behold her;
And in my arms with joy enfold her;
So dearly won, she will be mine.

Such literary refinement as this can claim it can thank Auden for; the elegance and simplicity of his first couplet seems to me reproachless, and I very much wished to keep it. *Ist* in Mozart, and especially *of* in Auden, deftly undercut the second beat. The word *image,* however, falsely convicts Mozart of false declamation—and in a sufficiently conspicuous context. *Image* is a pyrrhic word, which quantitatively, might stretch to a spondee but not to a trochee; *picture* or *portrait* or *vision* are examples of roughly spondaic words which might be stretched either to iambs or trochees. The first two seem drab for Mozart's ecstatic opening 6th-leap. Of course in meaning *vision* is flabby by comparison with *image.* But as between plausible declamation in an exposed position, and precision of meaning, the choice is or should be forced.

True vision would make no particular sense. *Sweet vision* injects a little warmth right away, and also catches

Larghetto
Sweet vi-sion of en-chant-ing
Dies Bildnis ist be-zau-bernd
p
grace, O rare per-fec-tion's dwelling place! I mar-vel, I
schön, Wie noch kein Au-ge je ge-sehn! Ich fühl' es, ich

mar-vel: at this heav'n-ly sight My heart is
fühl' es, wie dies Göt-ter-bild Mein Herz mit

moved to strange de - light, My heart is
neu-er Re - gung füllt, Mein Herz mit

moved to strange de - light.
neu - er Re - gung füllt.

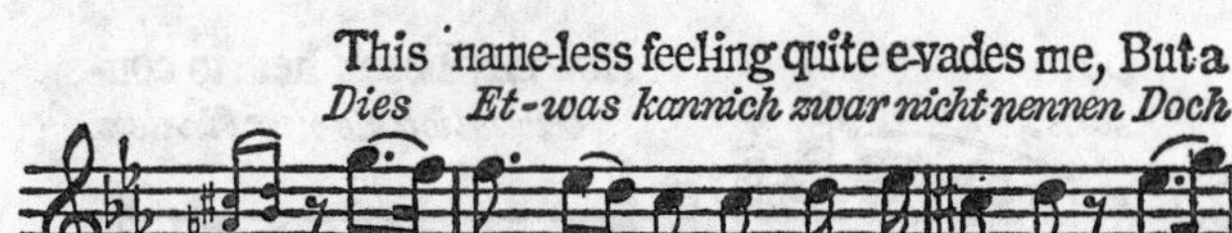
This name-less feeling quite e-vades me, But a
Dies Et-was kann ich zwar nicht nennen Doch

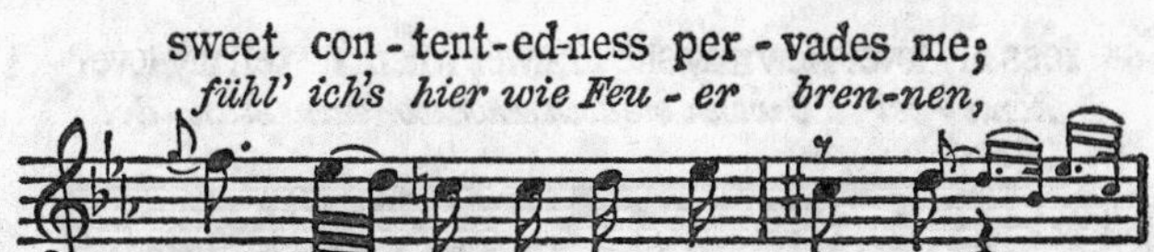
sweet con-tent-ed-ness per-vades me;
fühl' ich's hier wie Feu-er bren-nen,

Can it be love that wakes in me,
Soll die Em-pfin-dung Lie-be sein,

Can it be love that wakes in me?
Soll die Em-pfin-dung Lie-be sein?

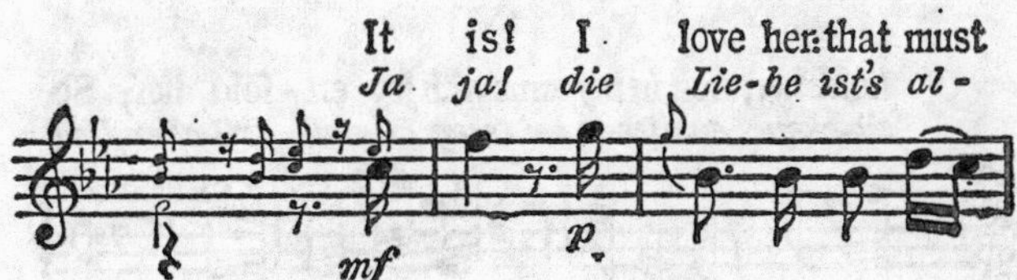
It is! I love her: that must
Ja ja! die Lie-be ist's al-
mf
p

be, I love her, I love her, I love her: that must
lein, die Lie-be, die Lie-be, die Lie-be ist's al-
sfp
f
p

be. How may I seek her to con-
lein. O wenn ich sie nur fin-den
f p
cresc.

fess my love? How may she an-swer when I tell my love?
könn - te! O wenn sie doch schon vor mir stän - de!
I'll seek her, seek her far and
Ich wür-de, wür-de warm und

near.. but how, in-deed? I'll seek her hand, I will be
rein.. was würde ich? ich wür-de sie voll Ent-
G.P.

hold her, And in my arms with joy en - fold her; So
zü-cken An dies-en hei - ssen Bu-sen drü-cken, Und
cresc.
f

dear-ly won she will be mine, So dear - ly won she will be mine,
e-wig wä-re sie dann mein, Und e - wig wä-re sie dann mein,
p
etc.

the spitting *s B* of *Dies Bildnis.* A subtle detail, perhaps: in Mozart the clash of consonants plays in to the breathless exclamation, and in a curious way echoes or justifies the panting 32nd-note upbeats of the orchestral preface.

Auden's equally elegant second couplet is unfortunately far too cold. Tamino cannot speculate, he must register strange emotional stirrings. Not to speak of the German verse, why else would the music indulge those exquisite inverting chromatic inflections, the surprising 7th-leap, the cadential appoggiaturas, and the diminished 7th interrupting the cadence? At the start, the repetition of words on the musical sequence should not only be kept, but if possible also motivated: Tamino half stammers, something he would not be expected to do expatiating upon aesthetic value. He stammers because the unexpected chromatics overwhelm him; they should be linked, if not to *feel,* at least to something like my sense of wonder. At the end, likewise, an affective word such as *delight* makes sense of the romantic cadence; Auden's *alone* does not. Like it or not, *heart* or something as obviously sentimental ought to be preserved here. For *heavenly sight* there is less excuse; but it does pick up the high note, and the musical contour masks some of the triteness.

In the next stanza, Auden's Tamino talks like Tom Rakewell; the music, to be sure, is rather neutral and courtly. I too allowed myself a slightly dandified *quite* and the double rhyme *evades me—pervades me.* The recurrence of *sweet* seems blameless; *sweet contentedness,* while considerably cooler than *Feuer brennen,* keeps a modicum of warmth in the verse. The last half of the stanza in my version is flat as a pancake, notably *that must be,* but even the least elegant of variations seems to wreck the passage. Auden's run-on line 7 goes against Mozart's *Zwischenspiele,* the first of which acts as strong punctuation, and the second of which comments serenely on the fresh insight: *Liebe.*

Faced with a sloppy final stanza, Mozart paid little or no attention to poetic form. Anyhow, his hero is getting excited. But faced with the first "couplet," translators have always improved upon him by supplying a rhyme. This seems to me undesirably pat; I myself ran into a half rhyme which I like well enough. With line 11 in view, *how* was deliberately reiterated, and *seek* deliberately planted, in spite of the double *k* sounded with *confess*. The extra syllables at the end of these lines seemed no violation, here as elsewhere.

Now, this line 11 is the only one in the piece which declamation actually controls. For once the line has no melodic integrity. There is a particular urgency, then, in the declamation sounding entirely natural; if not, the listener won't even be left with purely musical consolations. Auden had the charming (and scenically useful) idea of making Tamino question the portrait at this point, and then receive a silent answer in the evocative *Generalpause*. However, his climactic question *am I her choice* could never conceivably be declaimed to the notes that Mozart molded to *was würde ich*. *Her choice* comes out gobbled, *choice* so weak as to provoke a mirthful denial. A case could be made out for altering Mozart's notes here—only I should not care to do so, not with Mozart. Instead, my attempt, which also changes the original sense somewhat, contrives to keep the original conceit of an unexplained stammer word (*würde*) answered by itself in the next line, after the *Generalpause*. *I'll seek her/ I'll seek her hand* is trickier than the German, and admittedly *but how, indeed* makes only the most approximate sense. But hopefully it sounds like an involuntary interruption, as does the music, and echoes appropriately the *hows* in the previous lines, and declaims itself tolerably well (unlike *am I her choice*, or *what would I then, ah what would I*, or *what would I do*, as variously translated before).

The stammer word should be repeated when the melodic 4th figure recurs a step lower. Especially in declamatory writing of this kind, such a sequence makes no sense except as the outcome of verbal repetition. *Far and near* is fitted to Mozart's G-flat; *far* sets up (or at any rate, can support) overtones of distress to match a diminished-7th harmony that is the most intense and disturbed in the entire composition.

A foolish *non sequitur, I will behold her,* goes by more smoothly than you might expect, and is correct at least to this extent: it provides verbal intensification to the musical repetition, which is what Mozart needed in this case and what he achieved with *Entzücken.* The climax of thought and music develops surprisingly fast here; one should avoid the temptation to let Tamino's fantasy blossom too early. For once, at the line *And in my arms with joy enfold her* the inversion strikes me as plausible and right, because ostensibly forced on the verse by the emotional crescendo both of the music and of the word sequence culminating in *enfold her* (*drücken:* the most vivid, physical word on Mozart's V/IV chord). Auden depersonalizes the fantasy while still artfully managing the climactic surge. But, however squeamish, I did feel a need at least for *arms, joy, enfold. . . .*

The final line cools again, more than in the German. Mozart's first musical setting of the line seems to me to emanate a curious and affecting stillness; *so dearly won,* I venture to hope, may be heard in support of this sense, which is more precious than the subsequent coarser tone of the cadential repetitions (where *dearly won* may sometimes be replaced by *always.* In Auden's final line, *with* cannot really bear the responsibility of one and a half beats plus a turn). My last and least of concerns, at this point, was the rhyme, which Mozart pretty well obscured by his free handling of line 11. Naturally I should have preferred to rhyme the very last word with *near,* or perhaps with *delight,* or even half-rhymed it with *enfold her*—but I could not. It seemed a small loss.

IV

I have to favor, in short, a literal method of translation for music, what Auden and Kallman would probably call a too-literal method, though I say it is selectively literal, depending on the quality of the music from point to point. Music is the primary art here. Its little delicacies ought not to be ironed away, even by the smoothest literary hand.

The simpler issue, as between word-for-word rendering and a more or less independent lyric, was drawn as soon as there was modern music to translate. In 1588 a London musician called Nicholas Yonge published a large group of Italian madrigals under the title *Musica Transalpina,* the poems translated with labored precision. Sometimes the literalness was wasted trouble, though often—with madrigals as with Mozart—the words matched the music closely. Presently a well-known literary man, Thomas Watson, issued a similar collection of music translated according to the other principle: *Italian Madrigals Englished Not to the Sense of the Original Ditty* . . . Watson's independent lyrics go so far as to include some elegies for Sir Philip Sidney. They generally obscure musical details in the original.

Yonge was really right, but he refused to join cudgels, apologizing later for his madrigals: "Perhaps they speak not English so well as they sing Italian; and (alas) how could they, being as yet but late sojourners in England?" I expect he would rather have been able to do what Watson had done. Given the quality of many madrigal lyrics and of most opera librettos, poets like Watson and Auden are generally able to create something finer than the original verse; this sustains them, and delights us. It is not easy to complain at a poet writing poetry.

The alternative is a musician doing clumsy work outside his talent, finding pale correct words to counterfeit another musician's idea. Or else we can envisage massive musical recomposition (transcription) in the service of new poetry, such as Auden has provided. But in a transcription, as Beethoven once remarked,

> not only would whole passages have to be entirely omitted or altered, but some would have to . . . be added; and there one finds the nasty stumbling block, *to overcome which one must either be the composer himself* or at any rate possess the same *skill and inventiveness*—I have arranged only one of my sonatas for string quartet . . . and I am quite convinced that nobody else could do the same thing with ease.[4]

There is a practical limit beyond which musicians will not go in this matter. Even Wagner, who was critically concerned with the relationship of words and music, stopped short at the staggering prospect of transcription. An examination of the Paris version of *Tannhäuser* shows that Wagner adjusted music to fit the new French words only when things were easy. In the declamatory passages, such as Tannhäuser's Rome Narrative, rhythms were altered liberally; but in the lyric sections, such as Elizabeth's Prayer, Wagner left the music alone to the tender mercies of his poets. The result included a good number of stupidities and instances of false declamation which a French audience would have resented, if the Jockey Club had allowed them to hear what was going on. Seeing even Wagner content with this makeshift, in a situation where he had everything at stake, we should not be surprised at the general lack of responsible foreign versions of operas and other vocal compositions.

There is one opera that has always seemed to me to lie well within the practical limit: *Pelléas et Mélisande*, because it is almost exclusively declamatory in style. The words are no difficulty; make a good translation of Maeter-

[4] *The Letters of Beethoven*, translated and edited by Emily Anderson (St Martin's Press, New York, 1961), No. 59.

linck, then recompose the vocal line from the ground up to fit it. The issue of recasting lyric utterance, which Wagner shirked, scarcely presents itself, and the orchestra does not have to be touched. All that is required is "skill and inventiveness," in a modest proportion, and a less modest proportion of nerve. Of the two alternatives to Auden's way that I have suggested, transcription seems to be the more promising, and in this exceptional case, even feasible.

But not so attractive as singing, conducting, or listening to the original; that is why translation for music has no brilliant tradition and can have none. I have not spoken of the arguments in favor of "opera in English," most of which are vulgarian, because I do not think that they have much to do with the case. Without reasonable rewards in artistic satisfaction, no species of mediative work is likely to flourish, whatever its abstract virtues or vices. Difficulty, unattainability—that is really less of a problem. The combination of expertise, sensitivity, industry and grit needed to produce responsible translations for music is at least imaginable. What is hard to imagine is an incentive, in the artistic sense, that can be taken seriously.

SIDNEY MONAS

Boian and Iaroslavna: Some Lyrical Assumptions in Russian Literature

SIDNEY MONAS, *novelist, historian, and translator, is the author of numerous translations from Russian and German. His* Third Section: Police and Society under Nicholas I *was published by Harvard University Press.*

One cannot legislate or even effectively normalize good translations any more than one can poetry itself. There must always be room for the unexpected, to which no rules apply, both in the mind of the translator and in the receptivity of his audience. Too many learned articles on translation veer from the lurid tradition of the police memoir ('Some Bad Translations I Have Known') into the closely related and even more dismal atmosphere of the marriage manual ('How to Make Your Translation an Artistic Success'). What I propose to deal with here are certain attitudes, situations, relationships, which have historical and cultural weight, which are in Russian differently laden than they are in English, and to which the English translator must first accommodate his sense and then his language. He may survive literal mistranslation more easily than emotive misconstruction.

The lyrical assumptions I wish to discuss have a remarkable persistence and ubiquity in Russian literature. They are not the assumptions of a single author, or even of the nineteenth century alone. I would like to begin by illustrating some of them from a late twelfth century work, the *Tale of Igor's Campaign*, the sole surviving example of the secular heroic literature of the Kievan period.[1] Here are the opening lines, the invocation:

> *Would it be amiss, brothers, to begin in the old style telling those hard stories of the campaign of Igor, of Igor Sviatoslavich?*
>
> *But let us rather begin true to the facts of our time, and not by Boian's invention.*
>
> *When Boian the seer wished to create a song, he would spread wings in thought and would be in the trees; and would be as a gray wolf on the ground and as an eagle, blue-gray, among the clouds.*
>
> *For whenever he thought, as he said of himself, of the struggles of old, he would loose ten falcons on a flight of swans.*
>
> *'And the swan the falcon seizes begins to sing first.'*

[1] It was discovered by a Russian antiquarian late in the eighteenth century. He had a copy made for Catherine II., and himself published a small edition. The original text was lost in the Moscow fire of 1812, the copied versions did not entirely agree with each other, and both contained copyist's mistakes. No other text was discovered, or even a comparable text from the same period, so that many of the words and allusions remained (and some still remain) obscure. Full of the MacPherson-Ossian scandal, scholars began to dispute the authenticity of the text, some regarding it as an eighteenth century forgery. Pushkin attempted to resolve this controversy by the application of rare good sense: there was no one in Russia in the eighteenth century, he pointed out, who could write that well. Today, the authenticity of the Igor Tale has been established beyond reasonable doubt. I have used the remarkable scholarly reconstruction of the text by Roman Jakobson, Jakobson's excellent translation into modern Russian prose, and the rather painfully academic translation by S. H. Cross into English, all to be found in the volume published as the *Annuaire de l'institut de philologie et d'histoire orientales et slaves,* tome VIII (1945–1947), *La Geste du Prince Igor* (New York, 1948). I have also made use of the great German translation by Rainer Maria Rilke, to be found in *Russian Epic Studies* (ed. by Roman Jakobson and E. J. Simmons, American Folklore Society, Philadelphia, 1949), pp. 186–198.

But in truth, brothers, Boian did not loose ten falcons on a flight of swans; he laid his magic fingers on the living strings. And these hymned praise to the princes—to old Iaroslav, to Mstislav the Bold who struck down Rededa before the Cherkess hosts, to the fair Roman Sviatoslavich.

And so, brothers, let us pass from Vladimir of old to the present, to Igor; to Igor, who tempered his mind with strength and sharpened his heart with valor. Filled with a warlike spirit, he advanced his bold hosts against the Polovtsian land for the defense of the land of Russia.[2]

The Tale begins with a remarkable question, which is by no means purely rhetorical. 'Would it be amiss?' And the answer is both yes and no. It would not be amiss because Igor is a hero entirely worthy in his personal qualities to be sung by Boian, the legendary bard of Kievan Russia's heroic days. It would be amiss because the outcome of the campaign has nothing to do with Igor's personal qualities—it is a disaster. This is a hard story for hard times; therefore, the style of Boian is out of place. The style must be 'true to the facts of our time.' The metaphor of the ten falcons and the flight of swans was probably a stock epithet; with a kind of marvelous and dignified regret, the author divests the metaphor of its magic. It was the poet's fingers on the strings; but the author does not say 'only' his fingers, and they remain, after all, *magic* fingers. This magic is merely more wistful and more homely.

The old magic is never very far away, but lurks in the background, there to be invoked. The Russian language to this day keeps a wider channel open to the primitive animism of its distant past. Boian is on the ground '*as* a gray wolf,' not '*like* a gray wolf,' through the instrument of metamorphosis. In many heroic folk songs of a much later date, it can be established only from the context

[2] These are strophes one to seven of the Jakobson text.

whether a metaphor is intended, or a literal metamorphosis.[3] Of course, in modern Russian it would be a metaphor; but the metaphor is closer to its primitive origins than it would be in English. To take another example, Russian like many European languages retains a strong feeling for the gender of nouns. The days of the week are personified according to their endings; Friday is feminine and Thursday masculine, and a whole iconography depends on these attributes. In Russian families, the dropping of a fork at dinner presages the arrival of a female guest, and of a knife a male; because 'fork' is feminine and 'knife' masculine. This presents a simple, but often not easily soluble, problem for translators. Pasternak's first well-known book of poems, for example, is called *My Sister Life* (life is feminine in Russian–and death, too) which does not jar in English, though perhaps it loses some of its dash. But in German 'life' is neuter, and in Czech, which, like Russian, retains a vivid animism, the translator goes wild because 'life' is masculine.[4] That Russian is an agglutinative language invests it with further 'magical' possibilities that often pose a problem of tone or intensity, if not of meaning, for the translator. 'Snow' for example (*sneg,* masculine) can be turned into a 'snow-maiden' (*snegurochka,* feminine) by the addition of a few simple suffixes (including a diminutive and a feminine ending) without any joints awkwardly perceptible to the ear or eye.

As for Boian the seer being a wolf–turning yourself into a wolf used to be the essence of magic. The word for 'seer' in the Igor Tale is *veshchii,* but it is almost synonymous with an older pagan word, *volkhv,* distinguished by only one letter from the word for wolf, *volkh.* The language lends itself so easily to magic that the effort at realism is

[3] See the article by R. Jakobson and M. Szeftel, 'The Vseslav Epos,' *Russian Epic Studies* (Philadelphia, 1949), pp. 13–86.

[4] I owe these particular examples to R. Jakobson, 'On Linguistic Aspects of Translation,' in *On Translation* (ed. R. Brower, Cambridge, Mass., 1959), pp. 232–239.

all the more remarkable and dramatic. It is, after all, only *in thought* that Boian becomes a wolf or an eagle.

In the passage that follows the one I have translated, the assembled host of Igor is described standing under an evil omen, an eclipse, a darkening of the sky. We have passed 'from Vladimir of old to the present.'[5] Boian, who appeared before us in the preceding passage with such living force, is now invoked to speak from the background. This is how Boian, grandson of the god Volos (the Russian Apollo), would sing of Igor, grandson of Oleg: 'Horses whinny along the Sula; Kiev rings with shouts and horns hallo in Novgorod.' That is, even Boian would be 'true to the facts of our time'; even Boian would strike a more realistic note.[6]

When one considers the twelfth century date of the Igor Tale, and compares it to, say, the *Chanson de Roland*, which is not much earlier in time, and which probably shares the Norse and Greek influences that are dimly evident in the Russian work, many of its qualities appear as doubly remarkable. It is not, of course, 'realistic' in the sense that we associate with the rise of democracy and the industrial revolution; there are the animistic nature passages (to which I will return presently); there is Boian, and his magic fingers. In spite of obscure allusions, however, the action is described with remarkable clarity and in soberly unmagical terms. Igor in combat is not swathed in the numerical hyperbole that distinguishes the *Chanson*. Every time Roland's sword Durandel swishes through the air, a vast number of Saracens bite the dust. Igor, brave as he is, has no such luck. What he does and

[5] This marvellous transition—and for that matter, the entire work—is incredibly botched in the only readily available translation into English, that of B. G. Guerney, in his *A Treasury of Russian Literature* (New York, 1943). Guerney adds lines, or subtracts them at will, and omits the entire passage of Sviatoslav's dream.

[6] A passage entirely omitted by Guerney.

what happens to him is entirely clear and rational. And the movement, from beginning to end of the Igor Tale, though complex, is a single whole; it does not break down into set scenes and asides. Even the switch-backs–Sviatoslav's dream and Iaroslavna's lament–emerge out of the narrative and are part of an overall flow. And Sviatoslav's dream, compared with Charlemagne's, is quite realistic as a dream–though it may also be taken as prophetic. Neither Igor nor his enemy, the Polovtsian khan, dominate the action; they are only life-size–or perhaps even a bit smaller than life-size, as they would be in a realistic novel. The dominating figures are not the warriors at all, neither the Christian Russians nor the pagan Polovtsy, but 'the land of Russia' and the 'Polovtsian land', and these are animated entities that move and breathe and have life. There is also the goddess Obida, the strange figure of calamity in the image of a swan, who dips her wings in the Black Sea. Adjectives are scarce in the Igor Tale, and the landscape as well as the people who inhabit it are known through their movements. The movements in the landscape are no less rich and varied and precisely definitive than the movements of the people. It is here that the remarkable qualities of Russian verbs are utilized to the full, and it is with the verbs that the translator must be at his wariest.

The Russian verb is not very good at expressing *relationships* in time. For example, the English sentence: 'By the time I shall have been there, he will not yet have arrived,' would be very difficult to translate accurately into Russian. On the other hand, Russian verb forms possess unmatched resources for rendering the precise nature of a movement, its frequency and duration, in a compressed way. A Russian friend of mine, as a joke, once composed a participle, a single word, which has to be rendered in English as 'He who makes a practice of making fresh starts on projects involving a limited amount of beating.' This practically unpronounceable word is a monster, granted—*perezapobivyvyvushchii*—but there it is.[7]

It has been said of Tolstoy that he could endow even animals with individuality. Perhaps the most memorable example of this is the scene of the hunt in *War and Peace* in which not only the rabbit, but each of the hounds pursuing it, has a distinct character. The artistic means used to accomplish this is the precise use of verbs and verb-forms which say a great deal in little space, permitting accuracy of perception without slowing down the pace of the story. Aylmer Maude's rendering of this scene into English is a kind of *tour de force* of translation. Nothing quite like it had ever been done in English; it is a touchstone of his merit as a translator.

The growing, emerging character of Natasha with all its sudden and mysterious flips and turns is again rendered primarily through a precise description of her movements. Tolstoy piles on the participles; one participial construction after another. To a Russian ear, this excessive use of participles, uncommon in the colloquial, sounds a bit awkward, and Tolstoy is occasionally accused of lacking style. The real point is that when it came to a choice between elegance and precision, Tolstoy chose precision every time. And so, in his own curious twelfth century way, did the author of the Igor Tale.

A style that is true to the facts of our time: Pushkin's youthful polemics against the Lovers of Russian Letters were entirely in the spirit of the twelfth century poet, though at first glance it seems as though it was the 'Lovers' who were defending the twelfth century. They stood on the dignity of the old Slavonic, a courtly and pious language; Pushkin loved foreign words, puns, neologisms, translations from French idiom, and the vernacular. And the first canto of *Onegin*, so gay and innocent-seeming today, was a real shocker when it first appeared in 1825,

[7] I owe this example to Vera Sandomirska Dunham, of Wayne University.

the beginning of a 'novel in verse,' free, spontaneous, impious to the conventions, intimate and familiar, full of details of the everyday and the near-at-hand, and at the same time fresh and undeluded, full of that dignity and assurance that finds itself free to dispense with pomp and formality.

'My uncle, of the most upright rules . . .' it begins. A young rake is thinking of his uncle who did all the right, fashionable things, but who is nevertheless dying; thinking of the fortune he is going to inherit; and thinking, 'to attend a sick man day and night—what a bore!' Familiar thoughts, frivolous, unabashed—and at a time when the very foundations of the state and the social order were believed to rest on filial piety, quite shocking to the 'patriarchs'. They were outraged, of course, not by Pushkin, but by his exposure of their own experience. Pushkin insists on identifying himself with his hero not because he is like Evgenii, whom he quite sees beyond, but because he wishes to draw his reader close to a too familiar and therefore obscure pattern of life. Look, he says, this is where Onegin went and what he did; no doubt you've been there too and done the same; *I* have. Our familiar capital city is really a remarkable place; *but*—and here the aside is an allusion to Pushkin's trouble with the censors, the Emperor, and the political police of St. Petersburg —'the northern climate is bad for my health.'

Onegin's character has two fundamental aspects. On the one hand he is young, fresh, eager for experience, unwilling to be imposed upon by any routine other than his own. On the other hand, his own routine has been molded to an artificial European mode—the pose of the Byronic hero —which is not wrong because it is European, but deadly because it is artificial. It serves to keep him at a certain distance from the high-society milieu in which he lives; the show of spleen actually intensifies his flair for and success with 'the tender passion'; but it does not open out into daily life, either into the humdrum or the abiding or the multitudinous. It lacks the smell of cabbage soup, which, for Pushkin, was the essence of poetry. After a night of social whirl, Onegin rides home in his carriage oblivious to the daily round of the great rococo European city under the northern lights. He does not hear the feet of milkmaids scrunching the snow or see the German baker opening his *vasisdas,* the porthole through which he passes loaves to customers. Alas, the *vasisdas* has disappeared from all the English translations I know, and it is of the essence of Pushkin, the odd foreign phrase which the perfectly controlled flow of the Russian form accommodates so easily.

The iambic tetrameter and the *ottava rima* sustained over incredible length is suitable only in Russian to the vast range of tone and subject that one finds in *Onegin* —Russian, with its almost infinitely flexible word order (even more so than English), its great abundance of rhyme, and its easy assimilation of foreignisms. Pushkin throws in everything: lyrical asides, descriptions, conversations, catalogues of names, and atrocious puns. Struck by the incongruity of a 'modern' road in a backwoods Russian province, he attaches as a footnote a lengthy quote from a poem by his friend Viazemsky in which the latter speaks of MacAdam and MacEva! Through skillful use of enjambment, he manages the most dramatic shifts in tone. He plays with diction, with levels of tone conveyed through diction, in a way that might well have driven the Lovers of Russian Letters frantic.

What is the poor English translator to do, with very different linguistic resources at his disposal? He has only to look at Byron's *Don Juan* to see how impossible it is —like a drunk walking a tightrope. And yet, without sustained meter and a complicated rhyme scheme, the poem loses its backbone, collapses into a banal jelly. The complex Italian mold is necessary to structure the tremendous disparities, the breath-taking shifts, the vigor, the lyricism, the playfulness, the vast restlessness of the Russian life it contains. Vladimir Nabokov, whose linguistic abilities are prodigious, and whose all too rare translations from the Russian have been by far the best of their kind, wrote in an article a few years ago of the woes of translating *Onegin.* His devotion to the great poet is complete. He will not be satisfied with less than the exact meaning and effect, and if this cannot be rendered in English verse, he will have 'footnotes skyscraper high' to explain.[8] For years he has tracked Pushkin through the waste of minor eighteenth century French writers and French translators (in whom Pushkin was steeped) and discovered instance after instance of literal translation or adaptation from French idiom. His fertile imagination has provided him with English equivalents. But he runs the risk of turning *Onegin* into a period piece, of conveying the flavor of Pushkin's time at the expense of the particular excitement Pushkin created *in* his time. Translations of the Igor Tale into an 'epic' English derived largely from Butcher and Lang clearly won't do; Nabokov's derivations for *Onegin,* on the other hand, are fantastically scrupulous, but by just this literal faithfulness to an idiom that no longer commands the same lyrical assumptions they seem to me to run the risk of pedantry.[9] Of course, the translation has not yet appeared, and it may well be quite different in effect from the obsessive kind of article Nabokov has been writing *about* it. I certainly do not wish to prejudge it. In his own way, there can be no doubt that Nabokov too is being 'true to the facts of our time.'

Pushkin was as much concerned with an appropriate audience as he was with an appropriate style. It was part of the same problem. The courtly style was not appropriate to a writer who needed to earn a living by writing. Through his cold and beautiful wife, Pushkin found himself partly a captive of the court, where his 'six hundred

[8] V. Nabokov, 'Problems of Translation: *Onegin* in English,' *Partisan Review* (XXII, 1955) pp. 496–512.

[9] Nabokov is nimble and may escape, but see his article, 'The Servile Path,' in *On Translation,* pp. 97–110.

years of nobility,' of which he was passionately proud, were derided by powerful parvenus with German names. Behind these vulgar sophisticates loomed the power of the throne and the political police. Pushkin (tragically, in the long run) bent every effort to remove himself from their shadow. On the other hand, both his high sense of literary calling and his self esteem as a nobleman were offended by the venality of Russian journalism, the most successful practitioner of which was an unscrupulous Pole named Bulgarin, known to be an agent of the political police. Bulgarin, sniffing out a potential competitor in Pushkin, attacked him in print, on the one hand for being an aristocratic snob, on the other for pretending to an aristocratic family-tree that Pushkin, one of the 'middle class of the nobility,' really had no authentic claim to. Pushkin replied in a poem called 'My Genealogy.' Bulgarin is referred to as 'Figliarin,' a pun on his name, meaning in Russian, 'juggler' or 'buffoon.' The refrain line of the poem, with some variations, repeats 'I am a bourgeois,' or 'I am a Russian bourgeois.' But the word in Russian –*meshchanin*–is invested with more contempt than our 'bourgeois.' It is the essence of mediocrity, not only intellectual (as in English) but moral as well. Bourgeois Street in St. Petersburg was the red light district. Pushkin deliberately sets out to rescue the word. He relates how his ancestors fell from favor by refusing to bootlick or flatter, while newcomers curried power–'and *thus* I am a Russian bourgeois.' But he goes beyond that. 'I am Pushkin,' he writes, 'I am great in my own right.' He depends on his talent alone, not on a family tree. 'I am a bourgeois among the nobility, but Figliarin is a nobleman on Bourgeois Street.'

Pasternak, who at many points in *Doctor Zhivago* invokes Pushkin, called his own work a 'novel in prose,' which has struck many English readers as redundant. What else would a novel be written in? Of course, Pasternak means to emphasize both the similarity and the difference between *Zhivago* and *Onegin*. Structurally, even for a novel, *Zhivago* is almost formless. What holds it together is not *ottava rima* or even a prose equivalent, but an interlacing of symbols that take their meaning in part from Russian experience, in part from the novel itself. Pasternak says of the landscape of the Revolution and Civil War that it assumed the appearance of modern art. Familiar objects and people, wrenched from their familiar context and weirdly juxtaposed by the force of calamity, appear in a new light and display a significance previously obscure. What gives the novel its final coherence–a novel the main theme of which is the importance of poetry in human life–is the sequence of poems at the end. These echo in vocabulary and theme many passages of the novel, and these echoes and knots are, alas, left undone in the inept English version by Guerney which accompanies the, on the whole, impressive translation of the prose. A literary vocabulary where the original is even eccentrically colloquial, and use of the passive voice and many words where the original is compact and active, compound the formlessness of the verse and the abandonment of rhyme.

Between 1934 and 1956, 'socialist realism' enforced by all the means at the disposal of a totalitarian state made it quite impossible for writers to remain true to the facts of their time. That was an entire generation: there were grounds to fear that, except perhaps in an occasional surviving old fox like Pasternak, a great tradition had been killed. But in the summer of 1956, I was startled to see, in a fine anthology, a poem by a young poet–Vassily Goncharov–entitled 'I Hate.'

I hate the retouchers,
Nothing more terrible than
Their work
Hiding truth from the light
For money.
A child weeps

But the sly scalpel
Always breaks through,
And this boy
For joy to the world
Suddenly smiles.
Here is a dwarf—
Never grew up—
All very simple—
He stands higher
Than a poet's honor!
Here is the brute
Face of a scoundrel.
The scalpel is ready—
And on the portrait,
A family smile.
I hate the retouchers
Of the daily light—
Ready with a mask
For the whole planet.

And we?
We laugh and weep—
Wards of light.
More familial
For us the planet
Without extra trimmings.
Thou shalt not retouch the earth!
Leave earth as earth. . . .
You know truth.
Like a heart,
It is always with you.[10]

The poem carries its own force, and the translator can pick it out from the poem itself; but whether through learning or through intuition he must on some level be aware of a great tradition behind it.

[10] *Den' Poezii,* (Moscow, 1956) p. 48.

The real protagonist of the Igor Tale (to come back to that) is 'the land of Russia.' As Igor's hosts advance, the Russian landscape is bright with birds. As they enter Polovtsian territory, the landscape darkens, and we hear of Div, the demon-bird of darkness. When the Russians are defeated, and Igor is forced 'to exchange his golden saddle for the wooden saddle of a slave,' the Russian land responds as a person. 'In sorrow the steppe-grass wilted low, and the trees hung down in grief.' It is curious, since the 'darkness' and 'uncleanness' of the Polovtsy derives from the fact that they are pagan, whereas the Russians are Christian and had been, at the time of the poem, for two hundred years–yet they are spoken of in the poem as 'grandsons of Dazhbog' (the old Russian Zeus) and there is not a single Christian obeisance. The landscape dominates the story; whereas in the *Chanson de Roland* it is entirely incidental.

The Russian feeling for landscape and nature, for 'the land of Russia' persists to this day and produces something rather different from the alienated landscape that appears in European literature from *Don Quixote* to the present. It is not merely an oddity of the half pagan Igor Tale. Even the tremendous internalization of Christianity that took place under the impact of the Mongol occupation in the fourteenth and fifteenth centuries did not destroy it. Dostoevsky's favorite book in the Gospels was the Book of John–and Pasternak's, too; he constantly plays on it throughout *Doctor Zhivago*. The Johannine element has always been particularly strong in Russian Christianity. Of the four gospels, it is the Book of John that most strongly emphasizes the world as the creation of God, the life of nature as a paradigm for the life of man.

Nature is not alien to man in Russian literature, but his great home. Even Mayakovsky, the poet of the revolution, addressed 'brother planets' and 'comrade stars.' Turgenev's haunting landscapes are not, as they have sometimes been interpreted, symbolic representations of the psychic state of his characters, but rather the other way round. They are, in Santayana's terms, 'naturalist' rather than 'symbolist.'[11] In Russian fairy tales and folklore the personifications of nature, the river and woodland demons, the talking animals, are at worst cleverly mischievous; sometimes, to people, fatally mischievous—but never truly wicked or evil. The most powerful and dignified is the bear; the most formidable, *Moroz Krasnynos* ('the red-nosed frost') who is a great demon, but who remains morally neutral. The Russian Holy Grail is not an artifact, but an animal: *Zhar Ptitsa,* the fire-bird.

If one has read much in Russian literature, the Russian landscape, when one actually sees it, strikes one as incredibly drab, dreary and monotonous. One can understand why the adjective *krasny* means both 'red' and 'beautiful' or 'fine.' One is grateful for any bit of dash or color that relieves the grays and browns. The landscape lacks 'natural' coherence; yet it is not like Texas or North Dakota in that it has been inhabited by a people with a continuing (if changing) tradition, that has survived and absorbed all its many catastrophes from time immemorial. The fate of nature is the fate of man. There is a rhythm of life to which nature and man respond in the same way. The human and natural landscapes hold each other together, just as in Pasternak's Siberia, 'marriage and friendship linked village to village and town to town.' In one of his most beautiful early poems, 'The Weeping Garden,' Pasternak evokes the emotive state of a garden in the rain and sums it up with the question: 'Am I alone? or is there a witness?' Then he asks the same question of himself.

11 'That things have their poetry, not because of what we make them symbols of, but because of their own movement and life, is what Lucretius proves once for all to mankind.' George Santayana, *Three Philosophical Poets* (New York, Anchor Books, 1954), p. 38. And on 'symbolists': 'For they play with things luxuriously, making them symbols for their thoughts, instead of mending their thoughts intelligently, to render them symbols for things.' *Ibid.,* p. 57.

This is not the 'pathetic fallacy'—the assumption that a human state of mind kindles a response in nature—nor quite its reverse, but rather the working through of something common in both man and nature.

The 'land of Russia' was held together in Kievan times by the *rod*, the clan of princes descended from Rurik of whom the senior was Prince of Kiev. But all the princes were brothers (or cousins; there is no distinction in Russian) and the unity of the 'land of Russia' depended on their acting together as a clan. It is part of the calamity that overtakes Igor that they are no longer capable of doing so. When the swan-like Obida dips her wings in the sea, she shakes up discord among them, and they take up arms against each other instead of against the Polovtsy:

> *Then brother said to brother: this is mine, and that, too—and the princes began to say of a small thing that it was great, and strife flared among them. And the pagans plunged from all sides victoriously into the Russian land. . . .*

Rod is not only the clan, but a god, the god of the hearth and the family, over which he presides with his female assistants, the *rozhanitsy*. From *rod* the adjective *rodnoi* is derived, and its appearance on a printed page should be a warning-signal to the translator, for not only does its translation depend on context (there is no precise English equivalent), but it is one of the most heavily-laden and passionate words in the Russian language. It means not only 'native,' 'familial,' 'kindred,' 'pertaining to the family,' in the literal sense, but someone or something with whom real intimacy is possible; it pertains to an inner affinity that is a prerequisite for real communication. Its antonym *chuzhoi* conversely means not only 'foreign,' 'strange,' 'alien'—there is an entirely different adjective for the *merely* foreign—but inwardly incompatible. The greatest calamity is the transformation of something that has been assumed as *rodnoi* into something *chuzhoi*. In Russian love poetry it is more terrible than physical betrayal. In the poem by Vassily Goncharov, the portrait by a socialist realist painter (of Stalin or Beria, it scarcely matters) is described as appearing with a '*dusha rodnaia.*' *Dusha* means 'soul' or 'spirit' or 'heart,' but can also mean that which reveals the spirit, the expression, which I translated as 'smile.' *Rodnaia,* however, is loaded with bitter irony that I'm afraid my phrase 'a family smile' does not entirely convey, but it is at least better than the literal translation, 'a kindred spirit.'[12]

After the description of the princes' bickering and Sviatoslav's vain attempt to rally them, we come to the most remarkable and beautiful part of the Igor Tale, the point at which tragedy turns into something that is after all a minor triumph:

> *Far as the Danube sing the spears.*
>
> *Then I hear Iaroslavna's voice, like a solitary dove mourning since dawn. I will fly, she says, like a dove down along the Don! I will dip my beaver sleeve in the Kaial River; I will wash the bloody wounds of my Prince's awesome body.*
>
> *Iaroslavna weeps since dawn on the walls in Putivl and says: 'O Wind, Wind–Lord, why blow so strong? Why carry the Khan's arrows against my beloved's army on your soft wings? Is it not enough that you blow high under clouds and shake ships on the blue sea? Why, Lord, have you scattered my delight across the steppe?*
>
> *Iaroslavna weeps on the walls since dawn in Putivl-town, and says: 'Dniepr, Son of Slovuta, you broke through stone mountains into the Polovtsian land. Fondly you carried Sviatoslav's boats into the camp of Kobiak; tenderly carry my husband back to me,*

[12] For the foregoing, I owe a good deal to Vera Dunham, who discussed with me the *rodnoi-chuzhoi* dichotomy. At the time she was writing an article on recent Soviet lyric poetry, and I believe it was scheduled to appear in the journal, *Soviet Survey.*

Lord, that I no longer send him tears down to the sea at dawn.

Iaroslavna weeps since dawn in Putivl on the walls and says: 'O bright and thrice-bright sun! You are warm and beautiful to all. Lord, why do you press your light, burning, on the warriors of my beloved, so thirst has parched their bows in the waterless land and weariness locked their quivers?

How different is the appearance of Iaroslavna from that of Alda at the end of the *Chanson de Roland!* She is not the *fair* Iaroslavna; there is not a word of description; no attempt is made to engage our erotic sympathies. She is Igor's wife, mourning her husband, and appealing directly to the elements, speaking to them almost as she would to her husband.

The imagery that follows her lament is spectacularly dramatic. 'Half the night long the sea rose in swells; waterspouts drifted like clouds.' We are not told that Iaroslavna made a magic, but that 'God shows Prince Igor the way out of the Polovtsian land back to the land of Russia, to his father's golden throne.' Nevertheless, the image of Iaroslavna lamenting on the walls of Putivl dominates the entire breathless account of Igor's escape and return to Kiev. We cannot help feeling that it is Iaroslavna who has after all retrieved something from calamity. While the princes responded to Igor's defeat by taking arms against each other and adding to Russia's woes, Iaroslavna's response was entirely in harmony with the grief of the land itself. (I should point out that in the original she mourns in the image of a cuckoo; I have transmogrified her into a dove, since 'cuckoo' clearly has all the wrong connotations in English.)

Iaroslavna on the walls in Putivl-town may seem a far cry from Pushkin's Tatiana, Turgenev's heroines, Tolstoy's Natasha, Dostoevsky's Sonia and Grushenka, but she is invested with the same basic feeling. Eros and Aphrodite are not active here, but Mokosh', the earth goddess, the fertile and long-suffering. We recall that Dostoevsky does not think it important to tell us whether Sonia ever sleeps with Raskolnikov; we do know, however, that she follows him to Siberia and looks after him and that she is known as '*matiushka*' among the convicts.

The most popular of the real-life heroines of the nineteenth century Russian intelligentsia were the wives of the Decembrists, who insisted on following their husbands to Siberia, giving up all the privileges of noblewomen in order to attend their husbands' needs and share their fate. They were immortalized by Nekrasov's poem, 'Russian Women'; that at least two of these women were French deflates Nekrasov a bit, but does not fundamentally affect the point I wish to make here.

One of these heroines wrote home to friends who were wondering at her powers of self-sacrifice (and there is nothing of Marie Antoinette playing milkmaid in this letter) that she herself found nothing remarkable in what she had done: 'Every year thousands of peasant women follow their husbands into convict exile in Siberia.'[13] The peasant woman was the model heroine, just as the peasant (or at least the imagined peasant) was the model of much the Russian intellectual aspired to. In a world in which a frivolous, artificial, 'false' European culture was associated with a grimly repressive state that did not even speak the same language as its people (in *War and Peace* both the state and high society speak French) the peasant was seen as the repository, the living source, of an integral native tradition. The peasant male, subject as he was to all the pressures of servitude, the military order of the state and grim labor on a scanty soil, might easily succumb to drunkenness and riot. It was the peasant woman—the model of the strong, integral heroine of Russian literature,

[13] Mme. Volkonskaia, as quoted by M. Gernet, *Istoriia russkoi tiur'my* (1st. ed., Moscow-Leningrad, 1946) II, p. 182.

with her capacity to suffer and endure—who held the family and the clan together.

She is a maternal, not an erotic figure. Neither sexual vitality nor its containment in maidenly purity are her attributes. In Russian icons, even Mary appears not as the Virgin, but as either the Queen of Heaven or the Mother of God. Her great virtue is *compassion*—the capacity and the will to share the sufferings of others. (This is to be distinguished from 'pity' which is never without a certain condescension.) She does not make moral judgments. In an ancient Russian story, Mary accompanies Jesus in the Harrowing of Hell, and intercedes for the sinners. The woman merely recognizes, intuitively, the man's inmost moral qualities no matter how deeply they lie hidden beneath the surface of his riot—as Grushenka recognizes Dmitry Karamazov. In the works of both Turgenev and Dostoevsky, a woman's recognition and compassion are the best hopes a man has for his moral salvation. Tolstoy makes it quite clear that he regards the real meaning of Natasha's girlish eroticism, the confused stirrings of life in her which invest her with such irresistible charm, to consist in the fact that they finally mold her into something very close to the condition of a Russian peasant woman.

There are, of course, numerous and impressive erotic passages in Pushkin and Tolstoy. (Pushkin even wrote a mildly erotic and utterly blasphemous poem on the virgin birth, 'The Gabrieliad.') Their main import is elsewhere, however; and the relative 'chastity' of Russian literature has often been remarked by Western critics, though certainly 'chastity' is not the right word. D. H. Lawrence (himself almost a Russian novelist in so many ways) could not abide this Russian disregard of the sexual, this excessive 'spiritualization,' and fulminated against it in many of his letters and articles. It should not, however, be mistaken for prudery, and there is nothing like the fingertip-feeling of Henry James, even in Turgenev. There are no insurmountable inhibitions about dealing with erotic experience directly; it simply is not regarded with the same decisive awe.

There has been a tendency in English translations to soften and prettify scenes and statements which in the Russian are presented quite bluntly. Constance Garnett's Tolstoy and Dostoevsky are prettier than the original, quainter, with more grace notes in the margins. Russians are often furious with her, not so much because of the seriousness of her mistakes (she made many, but surely their gravity has been exaggerated) as because of the fact that some of the peculiarities of her own style—in particular, its occasional quaintness—have been taken by the English reading public as peculiarities of Russian literature. At least she had a style of sorts. More recent translations, superior in literal accuracy, smell to me not like Garnett's of the Victorian parlor, but of dehydrated potatoes and the welfare state. In poetry, the distortion has been far more serious, though difficult to separate from the sheer ineptitude and lack of skill of the translations. Pushkin has suffered the greatest atrocities. Of the great Russian poets, it is perhaps Nekrasov, however, who stands the least chance of assuming a viable shape in English. This is not so much because of the difficulties of his meter (those endless hexameters!), alliteration and multisyllabic rhymes (pointing to these features makes the English reader think of Swinburne, who is as remote from Nekrasov as Byron is from Pushkin) as it is the very essence of his sensibility, which is profoundly 'feminine' in the Russian sense; that is, *compassionate,* alive with the felt suffering of others. This is, it seems to me, the overall distinctive quality of Russian literature as a whole—it is feminine as Iaroslavna mourning on the walls in Putivl.

WILLIAM ARROWSMITH

The Lively Conventions of Translation

WILLIAM ARROWSMITH *is the translator of five plays of Euripides, and the* Satyricon *of Petronius; he has published versions of Aristophanes'* Birds *and* Clouds, *and his translation of Marcus Aurelius'* Meditations *will appear shortly.*

When we speak of a 'literary convention', convention means less actual agreement than some shared assent, either conscious or unconscious. It looks like habit which creates the expectation that the habit will be continued; habit grown tacit, an inarticulate assent to a 'promise' that somehow sprang up and whose existence dismisses the questions that might otherwise trouble its status, its absurd artificiality and its pleasure in the effects of its pretence. Wherever we look in literature, convention is with us; and nowhere is it–or ought it to be–more prominent than in the act of translation. And yet what more startling convention could there be than this assent on which translation rests, this fiction of the impossible or downright absurd? Hektor the Trojan speaks Greek, and we accept it; and then in translation we also accept Hektor the Greek-speaking Trojan who speaks English. This fact of absurdity, this indispensable pretence, is the central lively convention of all translation.

But translation has other conventions too. We translate, for instance, into the literary 'conventions' of our own age, and although these conventions are not absolute–since the central convention allows the translator a certain strangeness, an oddness playing now and then over the language or erupting in the unassimilable artifacts of a culture not our own—they are something we disregard at our peril. And there are all the various conventions of culture too, both of the language from which we translate and our own; and these compose a necessity whose boundaries must be discovered or explored, unless we give up translation for simple 'adaptation'. There are even conventions which we may have borrowed from other translators without being aware of the indebtedness; an obvious instance would be the assumption—or convention—that the only proper form for translating a choral ode from Greek tragedy is 'free verse'. And if we have our own conventions, the original has its specific conventions too, such as the chorus and *stichomythia* in Greek drama. And the more conventions there are the more ticklish translation becomes. In some cases, the conventions may become so numerous that the only way of handling them with decent loyalty is to adopt a 'language of conventions', renouncing the effort to render the smaller verbal units of the original, and translating from the original's convention into a different but analogous convention of your own language. Such attempts are almost always denounced as treacheries, either because the necessity that sparks them is not appreciated or because the argument of necessity is so frequently abused. But true necessity requires the risks of loyal improvisation and there are times—far more frequent than most scholars suppose—when the worst possible treachery is the simple-minded faith in 'accuracy' and literal loyalty to the original. More pertinent is the fact that literalism fails precisely because it conflicts with a convention whose demands it *cannot* satisfy except by becoming less literal. Only by recourse to living conventions can the difficulties be mitigated or solved.

In translating Greek comedy the conventions, whether Greek or comic or English, with which the translator must cope are so numerous as to be downright bewildering. His responsibility to his Greek text may be shaped by his responsibility to English; and that responsibility will in turn be conditioned by the kind of stage for which he is translating and even by the skills or lack of skills of the actors who will—if he is lucky—interpret it. And even supposing that the linguistic problems were easily solved, how will he solve the cultural incompatibilities between societies separated not only by custom and language but also by time? If you translate from one modern language to another, the problems are ticklish enough, but the problems of sustaining the crucial convention of ancient Greek comedy in contemporary cultural terms are as formidable as translating fiction into fact. The very convention itself—the translation of an ancient classic into contemporary language and concepts—is already under the maximum possible strain. How does the translator sustain the tact that can keep so preposterous a convention from shattering into a thousand pieces?

It is initially the hard facts of culture that most torment the translator of Greek comedy, since comedy everywhere touches common culture and the peculiar habits and commodities that compose it. Tragedy—even Euripidean tragedy—keeps a decent distance from common life, but comedy dumps into the translator's lap an intolerable profusion of *things*—odd bits of clothing, alien cuisine, unidentifiable objects, pots and pans and utensils of bewildering variety and function, unfamiliar currency, etc. What, for instance, is good idiomatic English for *chitōn,*[1] or worse, *chitōnion,*[2] or still worse, a *spolas?*[3] How do we translate a currency made of talents, minas, drachmas and obols? What the devil can a translator do with a culture in which women, for esthetic reasons, depilate their pubic hairs, or with a comedian who can build a whole recognition-scene on the fact? What is reasonable English

[1] A woolen undershirt; frock; kirtle.
[2] Diminutive of *chitōn,* i.e. a *little* woolen undershirt.
[3] A buff jerkin!

for the 'Old-New Day' in *Clouds,* or that famous effeminate kneading-trough which must also have the same gender as Kleonymos? How can you effectively translate jokes based on distinctions of gender or case in a language which fails to observe either? Before such apparent impossibilities, all translators are equal—though some are more equal than others. But the crucial requirement is tact: first, the tact of discretion by which the translator distinguishes between what is difficult and what is impossible; and second, the tact of skill with which he improvises before impossibility. Nothing more effectively dooms a translation than the failure of the translator to improvise when confronted with transparent impossibility, or the converse, the habit of improvising before what is merely difficult. In the first case, we get an intolerable literalism that threatens our central convention, while in the second, the true trials of the translator are sloughed off in the name of a spurious freedom.

If we return to those questions which I imagined the translator of comedy asking, it will be apparent that most of them are perplexing difficulties rather than impossibilities. And in the case of money and clothing, the difficulties are more apparent than real. In each case the criterion is whether or not a particular crux can be brought within the framework of our central convention or a subsidiary convention—for instance, a convention of character or rhetoric. If it can, it is a difficulty merely; if it cannot, it is either an impossibility or its difficulty is such that it requires the translator to accomplish the almost impossible, that is, to create a new convention quite literally from nothing. For clearly no convention can possibly cope with a situation in which the laws of the original language are at total odds with the translator's own language. If Aristophanes makes puns out of the resemblances between a vocative and a feminine termination, these puns cannot possibly be carried over into English; and in such cases the translator must of necessity improvise or fail to translate at all. His improvisations, if responsible, will naturally aim at an analogous effect, but following the thrust, rather than the words or grammar, of the original.

Mere difficulty, as opposed to impossibility, can often be successfully resolved within the framework of the central convention; and if handled with tact and craft, it will in turn support the convention by which it is resolved. Here everything depends upon the effectiveness with which the central convention is sustained and shaped and the translator's success in securing that assent without which he cannot work at all. Given a strong convention, strongly sustained, such difficulties as alien currency and clothing become comparatively trivial. But not entirely so. After all, if convention allows the translator of Italian to speak of *lire* rather than dollars, there is no reason why the Greek should not have his drachmas. *Lire* may be more familiar to modern ears, but a little shaping and emphasis by the translator, even an intruded gloss where required, will make of drachmas and obols a perfectly acceptable convention, since monetary contexts are almost second nature.

But once we establish the right of Greeks to deal in drachmas, we make it correspondingly easier for our audiences to accept still stranger conventions. A spectator who can take obols in his stride is better prepared to appreciate, say, the odd preference of the Greek male for a *mons Veneris* shorn of its shrubs. And it is only by making demands upon a convention that a translator can extend it and shape it. It is a perilous labor, and a crafty one too, for a jarred or broken convention spells the end of illusion. But surely the central convention itself allows, even expects, a certain strangeness, an exotic flavor: we do not require our Greeks to bear English names, and we disbelieve in them when they wear business suits or codpieces or swear by Jesus Christ. It is this fact, the initial permissiveness, the licensing of essential and nonessential oddities (as well as the prohibition of *total* cultural translation), which the translator enjoys by virtue of his central convention. If he is wise, he exploits it to the fullest possible advantage, deftly, gently, tactfully extending wherever possible the range of his illusion so that permitted strangenesses shore up less permitted strangenesses in a steadily rising arc of earned freedom. This freedom is, of course, limited, but it is the only meaningful freedom there is in translation. Translation is not an heroic activity nor are translators heroes, but their necessities, triumphs and failures are similar. The translator's necessity is convention, and like most human necessities, it is ambiguous, both a blessing and a curse. What matters is how it is met and used, and whether or not the translator can earn freedom rather than slavery in accepting it. Courage in translation is patience and tact and skill, taking in order to give, sustaining complex crossed loyalties, plus a great deal of sharp practice and hankypanky in the dirty business of good language. Translation is the skill of honorable deception, which is why it is not a mug's game.

But how far should the translator of comedy go in the direction of total cultural translation? If we dislike the literal *Lysistrata* of the Bohn translator, with its hideous deformities of English idiom, do we really want a Sexual Summit Conference presided over by a committee of Russian and American womanhood? Or a *Knights* with a demagogue called McKleon? Or is the answer a compromise in which the translator draws a line and says: at this point no further concessions will be made, either to the conventions of my own culture, society and age, or to the linguistic and social idiosyncrasies of Greek culture? As I see it, such a line could be drawn, but should not be. For although the Greek may impose a stern necessity upon the translator, and although he must, if he is to translate at all, negotiate with the conventions of his audience and contemporary theatrical form and practice, these are conventions and necessities whose limits have not been ascertained.

On the side of Greek, the translator's advantage is not only the relative freedom which the central convention allows him, but our very ignorance of Greek culture and language. For language requires precision, and if we cannot tell the exact shade or freshness of a Greek metaphor or the degree of inflection in a pivotal word, this very inability is the translator's ticket to improvise, provided that the improvisation be, in terms of the Greek, a defensible one. On the English side, his advantages are the very amorphousness of our own theatrical conventions as well as their richness, and similarly the richness and amorphousness of the culture that supports our richly impoverished theater. Never before, I think, has the translator enjoyed such extraordinary freedom, such an *embarras de choix* in the matter of exploitable conventions. But this very multiplicity of available conventions means that the force of any one, its ability to command instant assent, is attenuated; and this in turn means that the translator's difficulties are complicated. My point, however, is not to assess the translator's troubles, but to show how he forges his advantage from his two enveloping necessities, tactfully searching for English and theatrical conventions which, properly introduced and sustained, might housebreak the oddity of much Greek experience and culture, and how at the same time he tactfully uses the freedom granted to him because he translates Greek, ancient Greek, to validate and, if possible, enlarge his English conventions. By so doing, he holds the possibility, however modest, of reshaping his own theater.

But I was speaking of total cultural translation and the lengths to which the translator should go. *Tot homines, tot opiniones.* So far as Greek comedy is concerned, it seems to me that the translator should avoid like the very devil any attempt at total 'transfer', just as he should avoid any word or phrase whose excessively local or temporal applications might threaten the stability of his convention. The Greek characters in Ezra Pound's shabby *Women of*

Trachis, for instance, manage to persuade us that they are neither Greek nor American nor English by employing a bastard argot never spoken by anybody but Pound, and in consequence, the whole convention founders. Similarly I think the translator should avoid underscoring the obvious by heavy-handed topicality where a hint will do the trick. Kleon is not quite McCarthy, though he suggests him, and Nikias, for all his ponderous piety and cautious incompetence, is not quite Eisenhower. Nor is Athens America, though Aristophanes' Athens must suggest America. It is not, of course, that topicality is wrong of itself; indeed, translators sometimes talk as though topicality were risky because it condemned their translations to early obsolescence—as though the translator had any right to refuse the risks that Aristophanes took and overcame. What is wrong is the heavy and insistent topicality which asserts that Athens not merely resembles America but *is* America; for this emphasis destroys completely the only real advantage the translator enjoys—his happy and ticklish position between two disparate cultures and ages, his license to an allowed absurdity. What he wants is basically a simile, not an identity. Once he asserts that Athens *is* America, his title to an occasional but crucial strangeness vanishes; he must follow his idiot metaphor logically to all of its absurd conclusions. But surely it is the sustained suggestion of similarity that is the source of everything: on it rests the translator's best hope of generalizing his experience. Who, for example, could possibly watch a well-translated and well-performed *Knights* and not see, all the more powerfully for its being left allusive and anachronistic, both the face of McCarthy and the history of human demagogy superimposed upon Kleon? And it is surely a sound theatrical economy to leave some of the work to your audience. Yet those who drastically dub into Aristophanes' lines our own social bugaboos and catchphrases deprive his plays of their generalizing power by the sheer weight of simpleminded insistence.

Greek comedy was performed in masks and this fact, combined with the enormous size of the Greek theater, made the actor dependent upon gross physical gesture and a formal rhetoric—less formal than that of tragedy, but formal indeed when compared with the language of contemporary comedy. Hence, the translator is immediately confronted with the task of compensating for the loss of a whole dimension of expressive power, since the loss of physical gesture in our own theater is more or less irreparable, and to this fact the translator must bow. But although naturalism may be the dominant mode in contemporary theater, it is not the only mode; among audiences familiar with traditional repertory (among which we must surely count the possible audience for Greek comedy), there is still, however tenuous, an awareness of the traditions and conventions of English comic rhetoric. Moreover, by virtue of translating a Greek play, the translator, as we have seen, enjoys a special position, and a title to a little unconventionality; that is, he has a right to rhetoric, even though his need for rhetoric is not absolute. No translator of an Aristophanic comedy could possibly translate a page of trimeter dialogue without realizing that his dialogue must be essentially colloquial; that it cannot afford the full flood of traditional rhetoric. Indeed, the essential condition for Aristophanic dialogue is precisely a balance between the colloquial and rhetorical modes, since the incongruity between different modes—fustian and slapstick, cant and wisecrack, lyric and obscenity, poetry and doggerel—is the source of Aristophanic wit.

And the translator may even be encouraged if he believes, as I do, that the basic naturalism and distrust of rhetoric which our contemporary theater exhibits is a slander against contemporary speech: our ordinary prose habits may be firmly unpoetical but they are not therefore unrhetorical. If so, his strategy will be clear. He needs a rhetoric but not a consistent rhetoric; and he requires a rhetoric *beyond* what the Greek text may literally permit him, since he knows that his text has been impoverished by the loss of the language of gesture. Between the rhetorical and the colloquial modes, he must take care that natural *enjambement* is possible. The rhetorical must rise naturally from the colloquial and cede to it in closing, just as the meter must be flexible enough to sustain the illusion of colloquial speech and yet be able to adapt itself to the formal parody of tragedy or traditional 'eloquence.' And it must also be adapted to making good poetry in its own right when the thrust of Aristophanes' language suddenly turns unmistakably passionate or memorable.

Thus my own choice of a five-beat line—rather than Lattimore's supple six-beater—was based on the belief that the stylization required could best be achieved by a meter capable of modulating, without jar or difficulty, back to the norm of English dramatic verse, the blank. It offered a base that *looked* reassuringly conventional and so flexible that it could be converted at need into a line traditional enough to support both fustian and dignified statement. At its most humdrum such a line was indistinguishable from prose; worked up, patterned with regular stresses or set off in an incongruous prosy context, it could be 'traditionalized' into tragic cant or realized as poetry. Moreover, if the loose five-beater were carefully handled, it might also, I thought, insensibly establish its own convention to the ear, its own pauses, movement and variations; and once this convention were established, the line would acquire that wonderful flexibility that comes of being bound by the expectations of familiarity. A convention makes a promise, and depending on whether the promise is merely kept, postponed, anticipated, overfilled or flagrantly broken, the translator can contrive wit, satisfaction, resolution, gratitude, surprise or shock. The very wit, the verbal play and rhetorical incongruities upon which Aristophanic comedy depend, are helpless without conventional rapport. And though it may be true that contemporary audiences lack that finesse of ear which makes possible this complicity in convention, the translator has no choice. If his comedy requires a convention, and the convention needed is non-existent or moribund, it must be invented or re-created. If you want rapport, you must first speak a possible language of rapport. Or so I saw it.

There were also practical considerations. It seemed to me that actors experienced great difficulty in getting their mouths around a line that exceeded five stresses and speaking it as a natural poetry, just as they experienced difficulty in reading blank verse without a Shakespearean emphasis. The natural solution was therefore a loose five-stress line, so constructed that it would be impossible, except when useful, to speak it with a ranting inflation or Shakespearean cadence. Once this step was taken, it seemed natural to go further. Thus I have everywhere broken down the staccato pattern of formal *stichomythia* on the grounds that this convention, however powerful in Greek, could not be domesticated into the contemporary theater without intolerable awkwardness. Both of these strategies were practical concessions to the conventions (and therefore to the necessities) of our own theater, but the first concession —the flexible five-stress line—seemed to promise advantages which more than outweighed the real loss of formal *stichomythia.*

Consider a fairly simple example of the rhetorical problems involved and the relevance of rhetorical conventions. In Aristophanes' *Birds,* the herald from Earth comes rushing in to hail the successful Pisthetairos with a long string of superlatives:

> *ō Pisthetair', ō makari', ō sophōtate,*
> *ō kleinotat', ō sophōtat', ō glaphurōtate,*
> *ō trismakari', ō katakeleuson . . .*

> *O Pisthetairos, O Blest, O Wisest,*
> *O Most Glorious, O Wisest, O Most Refined,*
> *O Thrice-Blest, O—give the word . . .*

Despite the flat literal translation, the Greek here is extravagant and fulsome heraldese, whose fun is not merely the pompous ratatat of the continuous superlatives and the giveaway repetition of *sophōtate*, but the herald's inability to halt the momentum of his own professional rhetoric. He can't untangle himself from the coils of his own superlatives, and he typically and grotesquely stops only by asking Pisthetairos, in a command phrased as still another superlative, to intervene. Clearly translation of this passage requires a comic English equivalent both of the rhetoric and its cant and the sudden colloquial pause which, as so often in Aristophanes, brings the rhetoric tumbling down in comic ruin.

Consider a few examples of possible solutions. First, the extremely literal version of the great Victorian translator, B. B. Rogers:

> *O Pisthetairus, O thou wisest, best,*
> *thou wisest, deepest, happiest of mankind,*
> *most glorious, most—O give the word . . .*

The failure is obvious and radical, typical of the deep losses of literal translation. By transcribing the Greek rather than translating it, Rogers has completely lost the comedy. The herald's language is not really fulsome and it has renounced the sound of the Greek superlatives without the slightest compensation in English; worse still, the incongruity between the herald's 'high style' and his collapse into colloquialism is unfelt because there is nothing high about his language and nothing clearly colloquial about his collapse. Rhetorically speaking, the whole passage takes place on a single humdrum plane; it is flat, dull and unfunny. No actor could possibly realize the lines because the words are not working at the power of the Greek. They have not been translated.

Second, the solution of Dudley Fitts:

> *O Pisthetairos, O blessedest! O sagaciousest!*

O Superlativest! O Sagaciousest! O Perspicaciousest!
O Thrice Blessedest! O And so forth!

The sensitivity to the requirements of the passage is instantly visible, Fitts makes fine comic rhetoric by simply inventing a humorous series of ungrammatical English superlatives. The sound of the Greek superlatives is comically matched in English because the similar ungrammatical endings draw attention to themselves and the fulsomeness of the words to which they are attached. Better still, the adjectives are chosen for their inflation and their position in a series: *sagaciousest* is precise comic English for *sophōtate* (as opposed to Rogers' dull *wisest*), and O *Sagaciousest! O Perspicaciousest!* marches miraculously with the ascending fulsome absurdity of the Greek's *ō sophōtat', ō glaphurōtate.* If there is a weakness in this version, it is the O *And so Forth!* with which Fitts closes, to my ear and understanding of the Greek too bland and bored to earn the wanted incongruity. But the whole version is remarkably close to the Greek and also theatrically viable.

The third version, and probably the most radical of the three, is my own:

Pisthetairos! O Paragon! O Pink!
Thou Apogee of Genius! O Phoenix of Fame!
O . . . Apogee of Genius! O Flower of Finesse!
O happy happy Chap! O Blest! O Most!
O Best!
—oh balls.

Whatever its virtues or inadequacies, this version provides a simple and compact instance of translating by convention rather than by words. Confronted with a series of overblown Greek superlatives, I thought the most effective translation could be achieved through an equivalent—though different—English rhetoric of comic exaggeration. I wanted, that is, not superlatives but supersuperlatives, immediately identifiable as such, and arranged in a marked comic crescendo. But compared with the Greek, normal English superlatives are colorless and weak. However, if English lacks the fine *-otatos* flourish of the Greek superlative, it compensates for it, both in literature and colloquial speech, by its richness of metaphorical superlatives and the ease with which it yokes two nouns together in the service of a single exaggeration. Accordingly, I constructed a series of absurd rhetorical superlatives for each adjective of the Greek, counting on the conventions of conventional stage-comedy for support, and attempting to make up for the loss of the sound of the Greek superlatives by heavy alliteration and assonance. I tried to truss the rhetorical conventional tone with metrical emphasis as well: thus the first three lines are—like the lines which precede them—basically five-stress lines, while the last line and a half is pompous blank verse, intended to score the climax and its crash. The final adjective in the Greek is *trismakari'* (thrice-blest), and to the Greek ear this is a superlative so outrageous, so fulsome, that it cannot be capped; having said it, all the herald can do is to collapse into repetition or silence. For this reason I have deliberately expanded the English equivalent, beginning low and trying to end on a breathless staccato high. And for the same reason I have, at the expense of what the Greek literally says, ended the herald's high-notes with a low colloquial anticlimax.

In view of the economy and neatness of Fitts' solution, my own may seem unnecessarily extravagant. But frequently Aristophanes leaves the translator no choice: he must translate by convention or not translate at all. And nowhere is this more true than when he is dealing with Aristophanes' spoofs of professional jargon, scientific cant and officialese. Greek jargon and officialese, after all, are not ours, and a literal translation of an alien jabberwocky may sound quaint, obscure or even profound. In *The Birds,* for instance, Aristophanes uses the astronomer, city-planner and geometrician Meton to make a delightful burlesque of scientific jargon and humbug. Asked by Pisthetairos who he is and what he wants in Cloudcuckooland, Meton replies literally as follows:

> *I have come to survey the plains of your air and to parcel them out into lots. . . . You see, the spaces of the air have precisely the shape of a celestial oven. Now with this bent ruler, I draw a line from top to bottom; from one of its points I describe a circle within the compass, and with this straight ruler I set to work to square the circle. In its center will be the marketplace into which the streets, all straight, will lead, converging on this center like a star which, although orbicular, sends forth its rays in a straight line from all sides.*

Now this is low-pressure jargon at low linguistic pressure, but the pressure is not Aristophanes' doing. His parody of a city-planner's geometry is based upon what we might call a relatively immature professional jargon; compared to our glorious modern proliferations, the Greek seems remarkably chaste. And yet the pedantry with which Meton speaks is surely a genuine jargon, as offensive and amusing—in small doses—to the Greek ear as the vernacular of modern sociology is to ours. In such a situation the translator *must* heighten the Greek and jargonize it in terms of our own jargon conventions until he achieves the putative effect of the Greek. My own version of the scene reads as follows:

METON:

My purpose here
is a geodetic survey of your collective atmosphere
and the allocation of all this aerial area
into cubic acres.
Now attend.

Taken in extenso
our welkin resembles a vast and cosmical oven
or common potbellied stove worked by convection,
though vaster. Now then, with the flue as my base
and twirling the callipers thus, I quickly obtain
the azimuth, whence by calibrating the arc subscribed–
you follow me?

PISTHETAIROS:

No, I don't follow you.

METON:

No matter. Now then, by training the theodolite
here on the vectored zenith at the apex A,
I deftly square the circle whose inward conflux
or C, I designate as the center or axial hub
of your Cloudcuckooland.

This may be too extreme an expansion, but I am convinced that the strategy behind it is sound; even at the cost of intruding a gloss (as I have done here with Meton's 'cosmical oven'), anachronizing (as with azimuth, theodolite and *in extenso*), or jargonizing, the thrust of the Greek rather than its words must be followed in order for translation to take place.

And this counsel is especially appropriate to the theater. Consider the minor problem of the entrance of the martial braggart Lamachos in *Acharnians*. To an Athenian audience Lamachos carried his own meaning; everyone knew him or knew of him, and therefore when he appears, he appears without introduction. But a modern audience has no such knowledge, and Lamachos' appearance is so brief that unless the translator instantly, through the right convention, identifies his type, the scene is lost. Luckily, however, the old convention of the Miles Gloriosus is still viable, and in his translation Mr. Douglass Parker makes splendid use of it, intruding an exaggerated stage-direction and then following this up with four lines of fine martial hullabaloo:

[Two long trumpet fanfares. Lamachos strides out, in full armor, a long cloak and a considerable amount of ordnance, including a shield, a sword and two lances, all grossly exaggerated. Most noteworthy is the helmet, capped by three enormous brilliantly-dyed horsehair crests. He is the shortest man on stage.]

LAMACHOS:

Who cried HAVOC? *Who waked this ghastly, grim-be-visaged Gorgon from her shield?*

—I distinctly heard a clamor

Portending internecine struggle, slaughter and decimation.

. . . .

You BLOODY FOOLS,

WHAT HAVE YOU DONE WITH THE WAR?

In this instance, no particular violence has been done to the Greek because the convention has been established in the stage-direction. But other appearances make real trouble which can be coped with only by improvisation or expansion. Intruded glosses can help, of course, but at times translation must take place at the cost of scrupulous accuracy and loyalty to the text. After all, the translator of Aristophanes is translating for actors as well as readers—or he hopes he is—and if he refuses to take loyal liberties with his text, the director is almost certain to, with unpredictable results.

In my opinion dialects in Aristophanes and dialectal humor should always be translated by convention rather than realistically. Across the Aristophanic stage walks an army of Greek dialects: Spartan heralds, Megarian peddlers, Boeotian farmers, a mock-Persian, a Scythian policeman who talks barbaric Greek, and the immortal Triballos who speaks pure Neanderthal. So far as can be gathered—which is not very far—Aristophanes' Greek dialects are realistic, though I think the base is conventional, a familiar Athenian imitation-language of outlandish

Greek. But on the assumption that Aristophanes' dialects are all directly realistic, translators have commonly attempted a similar realism within the context of their own language. Thus in Starkie we get an almost indecipherable Scots or brogue or Shakespeareanized Somersetshire, each dialect presented with exhaustive—and defeating—accuracy. In Rogers' *Thesmophoriazousae* the Scythian policeman talks what I take to be the actual pidgin-English of a Dutchman, and Triballos speaks an exact transliteration of the Greek jabberwocky. All this seems to me completely wrong-headed; at least dialectal realism fails for me to be funny in any way, and I assume that Aristophanes intended these dialects to be comic. But realism fails because it destroys the central illusion. When a putative Spartan walks on the stage talking like a Welsh nationalist or an Outer Hebridean, the incongruity is so glaring and the jar so severe that the crucial convention founders; we withdraw assent. Worse yet, the attempt to get scrupulous realism invariably drives out the conventional rhetoric which should support the device; the demands of realistic dialect *preclude* loyalty to the Greek since the possibilities of most dialects are so severely limited in actual usage. What then should the translator do? Surely his only hope of success lies in adopting a *conventional* comic dialect—not Southern speech, but minstrel-Southern; or Minnesota Dane in its stereotyped form, variety-hall Yiddish, *broad* Brooklynese, etc. But never the real thing; always its conventionally comic appearance. At this point, of course, British and Americans part company; British dialect conventions (comedian cockney, stage-bumpkin Somerset) are not ours, and an American translator of Aristophanes must content himself with American conventions. Thus Dudley Fitts' solution for the Spartan dialects in *Lysistrata* seems to me completely sound; because the dialect is conventional minstrel-Southern and not realistic, it can be accepted as convention even despite the anachronism—or perhaps because of it. It is a traditional 'comic' convention and we accept it as such. What does one do with the Scythian policeman of *Thesmophoriazousae?* My own solution was to make him talk Katzenjammer-kids German, trusting to the stolid absurdities of the convention to convey what is required for the Scythian: atrociously comic Greek and a sensibility so dense that all of Euripides' sophisticated stratagems fail to penetrate it. And so too with Triballos' jabberwocky. After all, every language has its own good nonsense-sounds, and if you do what most translators do and simply transliterate the Greek into English, the results are not apt to make good English nonsense.

Obscenity also requires translation by convention, not in order to minimize it or bowdlerize it, but to earn it as humor and wit. Obviously the translator of Aristophanes has a license to be obscene; this is what audiences expect of Aristophanes and, in my opinion, they should not be disappointed. But Aristophanes' audience was clearly an earthy one, while ours is sprung from the thin pink earth of suburbia and points west. What will such an audience do with the splendid soliloquy on the agonies of constipation in the *Ecclesiazousae?* Or the elaborate metaphors Aristophanes uses to describe the amours of the homosexual Kleisthenes? The issue here is delicate and vexing, since as regards obscenity and frankness the comic conventions of our audiences and those of Aristophanes' audience are to some degree at odds. But I suspect that the disagreement is less sharp than it looks and the translator can, with care and craft, bridge it by working at the best limits of English convention. For instance, if we refuse on principle to bowdlerize—as I think we should—is there any means by which the constipation-soliloquy can be turned to comic advantage but kept in the full force of its obscenity? If baldly or literally translated, it is bound to fail, and the failure will fatally jar our central convention. But what if it were turned with a fine, formal, rhetorical elegance, with such neatness and craft that the audience could recognize the perfect rightness of the incongruity, the fine civilized control of the formal verse *and* the splendidly natural agony of the constipated man? Isn't this precisely the pleasure any intelligent man takes in a good limerick exquisitely turned, when he feels unmistakably the neatness and rightness of the limerick's last line coping, in fine formal incongruity, with the strong obscenity of the matter? I am not, of course, suggesting that the constipation-soliloquy be turned into a limerick, but that rhetoric and elegance conspire to produce that esthetic pleasure we take in a good limerick. Mere literal obscenity is dull and stupid; it is when form and language converge with obscenity that we get comedy and wit. Incongruity and craft make the obscene more obscene, *truly* obscene. And this is what the translator wants.

But the scholar may perhaps object: this is unaristophanic; the translator's business is to translate his text, not improve upon it. But is it unaristophanic? In technique surely it is completely typical, for although Aristophanes has a reputation—which he deserves—for strong obscenity, he seems to have thought of the slapstick smut and the four-letter words as his concession to the groundlings; his pride was his wit and true obscenity married to the high style. Think, for instance, of the smutty jokes between Sokrates and Strepsiades which surround on either side the splendid soaring lyrical ode of the approaching chorus of Clouds. Or of the exquisite alternations between smut and lyric in the *parabasis* of *The Birds*, dropping from the *tio tio tio tinx* of lyric into prosy obscenity and then rising again in the antistrophe, *tio tio tio tinx*. This is the true dialectic of Aristophanes' comic poetry, the sublime and the formal offsetting the ridiculous and colloquial, the ridiculous mocking the sublime, and all the wit concentrated in the tension and incongruity between the two. Why should this technique not be applied to the constipation-soliloquy to earn both obscenity and comic wit? It seems to me possible and mandatory, but it has yet to be written.

One example, however, may illustrate the technique of translating by apposite rhetorical conventions and the means by which the formal turn of an elegant line resolves, musically and naturally, a gross obscenity, thereby earning it as comic. In *The Clouds* the old peasant Strepsiades plans to enroll in Sokrates' Thinkery in order to learn the sophistic techniques which he needs to evade his creditors' claims. But before he has quite made up his mind, one of Sokrates' students fires his enthusiasm by describing the achievements of Sokratic science. His example is Sokrates' ingenious answer to the question: is it the gnat's mouth or his tail that causes his characteristic buzzing whine? Aristophanes' interest here is, of course, multiple. He wants not only the fun of some good obscenity and a spoof of the scientific jargon of the sophists, but a device for demonstrating the connection between scientific research and philosophical and legal immorality. Socratic (i.e. sophistic) science is as consequential, he says, as the microscopic analysis of a gnat's intestines; and applied to the law, it becomes pettifoggery and hair-splitting. And typically he allows the peasant 'shrewdness' of Strepsiades to perceive the relationship and expose it by a burst of obscene rapture:

STUDENT:

Attend.
According to Sokrates, the intestinal tract of the gnat
is of puny proportions, and through this diminutive duct
the gastric gas of the gnat is forced under pressure
down to the rump. At this point the compressed gases,
as through a narrow valve, escape with a whoosh,
thereby causing the characteristic tootle or cry
of the flatulent gnat.

STREPSIADES:

So the gnat has a bugle up its ass!
O happy happy philosophers! What bowel-wisdom!
Why, the man who has mastered the ass of the gnat
could win an acquittal in any court.

Obviously the Student's explanation of Sokrates' gnat-anatomizing required the same 'conventionalizing' treatment as the Meton-episode discussed earlier: touching up, heightening and jargonizing until it became dramatically realizable as plain professional humbug. But my major effort was expended on Strepsiades' reply, in which I wanted, if possible, to create that crucial tension between slapstick and formal control which I thought the passage required. With the first two lines there was no problem, since Strepsiades' comments are good fun, at which, I think, almost anyone might laugh. But I wanted those lines resolved with wit and force in such a way that the climax of the passage would become instantly and sharply clear. I wanted, 'Why, the man who has mastered the ass of the gnat/ could win an acquittal in any court.' to be a neat and memorable resolution, since it was crucial to Aristophanes' polemic purpose in the play as Strepsiades' slapstick enthusiasm was not.

If obscenity is taxing, the metrical requirements of Greek comedy are even more so. Aristophanes, after all, is a poet who goes through more meters in a single play than most English poets get around to in a lifetime. Moreover, the secrets of Aristophanes' pace, as well as much of his wit, lie in his mercurial shifts of tempo. Hence the translator must make use of every means at his disposal if he is to cope properly with even half of Aristophanes' meters. I do not mean that the translator is required to match Aristophanes meter for meter—there are not that many useful metrical possibilities in English, if by useful we mean a meter that any conceivable contemporary audience can appreciate by ear. And some of Aristophanes' commonest and best meters are beyond any possible ingenuity the translator can muster; I have never seen any translation of Aristophanes which managed with any success whatever to cope dramatically with his long trochaic passages or the splendid anapests of the *parabases*. And the reason is obvious: English, apart from blank verse or some loose stress-line, has *no* meter that can tolerate *sustained* dramatic punishment and formal regularity for upwards of a hundred and fifty lines at a stretch. If you try—like Rogers, Murray and others—to create a formal line, you end up with something that cannot be acted or spoken; and for this reason, most translators—myself included—replace trochees or anapests with a loose six-beat line, totally informal, whose sole virtue is that it can be played dramatically. Nonetheless, no reasonable metrical resource can be neglected, and in my opinion this means the whole repertory of English comic forms, both traditional and free.

But there seems to be a notion abroad—strengthened perhaps by the common practice of translators of Greek choral odes, especially tragic—that the only proper form for a Greek lyric is free movement. In tragedy this prejudice perhaps makes sense, since it accommodates the translator's necessary discomfort in the choral convention with an appropriate permissiveness. When a Greek poet sat down to write his choral lyrics, he clearly envisaged his odes as *songs* to be sung and danced; but because it has become *de rigueur* for choral odes to be chanted in modern productions of Greek tragedy, most translators unconsciously allow this fact to influence their choral passages and end up writing that bastard abomination, neither song nor poetry, a hypnotically cadenced chant. In this case, current theatrical practice seems to me a convention born of incompetence and preciosity, and I should like to see translators boldly flout it by writing either poetry or songs. Under poetry and song, needless to say, I include both traditional and free verse, providing always that the 'free' and 'traditional' verse alike be realized as genuine poetry in their own right. I should also like to see the traditional forms restored to dignity and given a place beside free forms. Both have their function, and tragedy needs both. There is, for instance, a variety of identifiable types among choral lyrics, and some (the 'escape' ode, the 'anxiously expectant' ode, the 'hymning' ode, etc.) seem to me ideally suited to free treatment, while others (the 'reflective' ode, the 'summation' ode, etc.) seem to require that neatness and formal rightness of resolution that traditional forms, properly handled, can provide. I think, for instance, of the stunningly lovely formal periods in Robert Fitzgerald's *Oedipus at Colonus*—in my opinion one of the very finest of modern translation of Greek tragedy—and especially the ode beginning, *Not to be born beats all philosophy*. Ideally, any tragedy requires its plateaus of perfect resolution and apparent peace, and for these the traditional forms are incomparably the appropriate choice.

If traditional periods are recommended now and then in tragedy, they are absolutely essential to comedy. It is, for instance, a fact that formal pattern, regularity and rhyme are, in English verse, almost mandatory for a certain kind of wit. Humorous poems in free forms tend to be drole, ironic, lightly satirical, wry, sardonic, nostalgic or tongue-in-cheek; they excite the marginal kind of humor, the chuckle, the amused smile, the understanding of pleased complicity. In formal comic verse, however, the very neatness of the form with its chances of rhymed emphasis and harsh contrast, the possibilities of flirtation with a familiar pattern and a recurring beat, permit starker surprises and explosive incongruities. And the completeness, the necessity for right resolution, make responses direct and immediate, releasing the outright laugh or open pleasure in formal wit. It is precisely this formal effect at which many Aristophanic choral passages aim. Not all of them by any means; nor was the nineteenth century right to adopt the Gilbert and Sullivan patter-convention at every available opportunity. Aristophanes wrote superlative lyrics, magnificent march-anapests, doggerel, patter-songs, catches and comic arias for virtuoso performance, and the translator's job is to match as frequently as possible the variety and wit of his original. But where the Greek gives the opportunity, cries out for formal play, the chance should be seized. If our actors and choruses cannot read—or sing—formal comic verse successfully, they will have to learn, for there is no reason why the translator should make concessions to unnecessary incompetence.

My example is taken again from *The Birds,* and I want, without comment and at the risk of seeming infatuated with my own strategy, to set before you Dudley Fitts' fine 'free' version and my own 'formal' version of a lyrical monody. The speaker is Pisthetairos, and he is trying to persuade the reluctant birds to reclaim their great inheritance by contrasting their ancient glory and their present misery.

Fitts:

You understand then, that years and years ago
you were great, even holy, in the eyes of men.
But now? Now you are rejects, fools,
worse than slaves, stoned
in the streets by arrogant men, hunted
down even in your sanctuaries
by trappers with nets, springes, limed
twigs, cages, decoy-
boxes;
caught, sold
wholesale, goosed, prodded
by fat fingers, denied
even the grace of wholesome frying,
but served up sleazily, choked
with cheese, smeared with oil,
sprayed with vinegar, doused
as though you were dead meat, too gamy,
in rivers of sweet slab sauce.

My own:

Such were the honors you held in the days of your soaring greatness.

But now you've been downgraded.
You're the slaves, not lords, of men.
They call you brainless or crazy.
They kill you whenever they can.

The temples are no protection:
The hunters are lying in wait
with traps and nooses and nets
and little limed twigs and bait.

And when you're taken, they sell you
as tiny hors d'oeuvres *for a lunch.*
And you're not even sold alone
but lumped and bought by the bunch.
And buyers come crowding around
and pinch your breast and your rump,
to see if your fleshes are firm
and your little bodies are plump.

And as if that wasn't enough,
they refuse to roast you whole,
but dump you down in a dish
and call you a casserôle.

They grind up cheese and spices
with some oil and other goo,
and they take this slimy gravy
and they pour it over you!

Yes, they pour it over you!

It's like a disinfectant,
and they pour it piping hot
as though your meat were putrid,
to sterilize the rot!

Yes, to sterilize the rot!

But wherever you look, and the longer and harder you look, the more it seems that our opportunities—at least in translating ancient literature—reside in the simple laborious business of exploiting neglected possibility and lively conventions. This is perhaps no great truth to come bearing home, but it is all I can offer. Like criticisms or poetry, translation is perpetually hindered and sometimes frustrated by its assumption that its limits and necessities are immediately apparent and that its practices can therefore be expressed as self-evident principles. Sometimes, too, even after years of practice, a wayward and arbitrary 'principle' will still evade the translator's attention, remaining uncorrected because it lies too deep to be acknowledged as the prejudice it is. This is natural and expectable, for it takes either genius or long experience to know the boundaries of necessity, and most of us are therefore sentenced to groping, which is not really such a bad life. Alternatively, we can ignore necessity altogether and go a-translating with Robert Graves or Ezra Pound, persuading ourselves that our author is best translated by simply usurping him and setting up shop in the shambles we make.

[illegible] we [illegible] the reader [illegible] [illegible] opportunity—at least to [illegible] a [illegible] alteration [illegible] in the simple [illegible] possibility and [illegible]. This is perhaps no great [illegible] it is all I can offer. Like [illegible] of poetry, translation is [illegible] hindered and sometimes [illegible] by the assumption that [illegible] possible [illegible] precise [illegible] expressed [illegible]. Often [illegible] sometimes [illegible] will [illegible] make the translator's [illegible] nothing [illegible] because it has [illegible] professional [illegible] for it takes [illegible] genius or [illegible] experience to [illegible] and [illegible] much [illegible] sentence [illegible] when it [illegible] really [illegible] a bad [illegible]. Alternatively, we can [illegible] necessity altogether and go [illegible] with Robert Graves [illegible] ourselves that [illegible] him [illegible].

ROGER SHATTUCK

Artificial Horizon: Translator as Navigator

ROGER SHATTUCK, *author of* The Banquet Years, *has translated Apollinaire, Daumal, and other French authors. His study of Proust, titled* Proust's Binoculars, *was published in 1963.*

I

As translator, I have made two trips in my life. In neither case did I have the least notion in advance that my travel had anything to do with translation. Yet today, in trying to grasp the slippery subject, my thoughts revert to those trips by irresistible attraction to something more palpable than meanings of meanings in literature. Egypt and Paris taught me something about the elements of distance and direction in the work of translation.

When I arrived in Cairo in June, 1951, a few weeks before the incensed mobs burned Shepheard's Hotel, Arab street urchins were still bravely hawking copies of *The Memoirs of Fanny Hill*—in the original. It was Ramadan, the Moslem lent; and since all males fasted till sundown, none of the guides would escort me to the top of the Great Pyramid in the punishing early afternoon heat. Having bumblingly bribed the two guards to look the other way, I climbed the monstrous pile alone, lost my straw hat in the wind, read fifty centuries of graffiti (again in the original) at the top, and was seized by such violent vertigo on the descent that I had to creep down backwards like a bear stuck in a tree. A knot of apprehensive people had formed to receive me back to earth, and for several years after I kept the shoes in which I had made the trip as relics of an expedition from which I should never have returned. But I had still not seen the Egypt I had come in search of.

Ten minutes after the early morning train left Cairo for Luxor and Upper Egypt, I was convinced that a railroad employee had been stationed on the roof of the car to toss alternating shovelfuls of sand and cinders through the window. As a lone tourist hopelessly out of season, I was ceremonially victimized by beggars, dragomen, money changers, hack drivers, and pimps; they had smelled no prey since the mercury rose permanently over ninety, two months earlier. At nine o'clock in the evening, starving, unclean, and cowed, I sank into a Luxor Hotel carriage that had been waiting at the station. A hot bath, a cold meal, and a bottle of wine restored me to life, and I could measure my distance from Western Civilization by the plaintive harsh nasal chant which was exchanged all night between the two mosques outside the hotel window. At sunrise, from the same window, I looked out directly on the long colonnades of the temple of Luxor and over it across the Nile to the temples and tombs of the ancient Theban necropolis, and then watched a man tirelessly dip water out of an irrigation ditch into a sunken flowerbed in the park next to the temple. In a loin cloth he would have been one of Pharaoh's gardeners.

After a day peering at the antiquities through a moiling cloud of dragomen, all of them claiming to be on familiar terms with André Gide and Jean Cocteau who had recently visited Luxor, I concluded I should never see Egypt no matter how far I travelled. Nothing had prepared me for so great a quantity of buildings and for the inscrutability of their beauty. I was totally lost in the ruins. Finally I resorted to the letter of introduction a friend had given me in Paris to the Egyptologist, Alexandre Varille, whom he called 'the most controversial figure in Egypt.' Varille received me in his book-lined study in the same hotel, a short figure with a dark massive head, sunken eyes, and no discernible age. The intensity of his speech and manner convinced me that to see and understand what was left of Ancient Egypt would require devotion and attention and not a little enchantment. When he asked me how I had happened to come, and at this season, I replied lamely about a childhood fascination with everything Egyptian and went on to say how I had tried to prepare myself by reading up on the subject. Particularly I had made an effort to study translations of heiroglyphic texts and had spent several weeks with Breasted's volumes, *Ancient Records of Egypt.* I asked him, a little shamefacedly, why these texts seemed so uninteresting, so completely devoid of profound thought, of anything but the most superficial ritual of religion, of any convincing description of human actions and feelings.

'So you were disappointed?' he asked with a chuckle. 'You don't want to believe the Egyptians had so little to say for themselves? I can't show you anything here but photographs. Tomorrow we'll go look.'

For five days we had a look on both sides of the Nile. We lengthily examined the temples, walked along the sphinx-lined ceremonial roads, descended by candle light deep into the glittering darkness of the royal tombs, and dined by moonlight on the excavation site of his associate, Clément Robichon, at Karnak. At each location Varille would begin by drawing in the sand with his ivory handled cane diagrams that linked the building in front of us to the terrain, to the gradually rising level of the Nile floodwaters, to the other buildings in the valley, and to the positions of sun, moon, and stars. His explanation of a statue or an inscription led immediately to its relationship to the other statues and inscriptions around or behind or under it. Varille's gestures reached out from small details toward the total structure of the temple, of Thebes, of the kingdoms of Upper and Lower Egypt, of the entire cosmos. He showed me a large inscription at Karnak which had recently been 'translated' in a leading archeological journal, and pointed out how a previous inscription on the same surface had been only partially obliterated or 'usurped' and still showed through. The translator had not realized that the later text has to be read in connection with the earlier text in order to gain its full dimension of meaning, a true palimpsest. Another inscription he pointed out remains meaningless unless interpreted in conjunction with the statue of a monkey across the colonnade. The monkey supplies the key to its time references, for this species of African monkey was believed (and still is, locally) to urinate with perfect regularity every three hours and thus represents a standard unit of time. There is no gratuitous detail in an Egyptian temple; nothing stands alone in this system laden with significances.

These temples had all started as small rudimentary structures. Then, as the Nile each year raised the level of the terrain by a predictible amount (measured by a well-like 'Nilometer' in the foundation of each temple), they were torn down at intervals and rebuilt by successive rulers. The kings always reused the old materials and added more. But the process, far from being a haphazard attempt to obliterate the remains of a former ruler, followed strict rules of growth so that the old structure was materially and symbolically contained within the new. Superseded inscriptions, though invisible because turned in to the wall, still formed part of the organic whole of the temple and provided the historical explanations of texts newly carved on the exposed surface. Across several centuries these temples, by a process of perpetual renovation in harmony with the political fortunes of the Pharaohs and the everlasting rhythms of the Nile and the Zodiac, grew like living creatures into enormous complex structures. Varille's explanations of this 'new past' rested on three basic principles:

1. The records of the vastly underestimated Egyptian civilization are almost all still there in the monuments

preserved by the climate of Egypt. However an irresponsible approach to excavation and restoration can destroy these records, as has already begun because of many museums' desire to expand their collections. There are more written texts contained in the tombs and temples of the Nile valley than we have recovered from ancient Greece and Rome together, yet their meaning and quality remain to be ascertained.

2. The barrier between us and the Egyptians is one of language and expression. When Champollion, the greatest of all Egyptologists, cracked the hieroglyphics on the Rosetta stone in 1821, he went only half way. Little real progress has been made since then. The knowledge of the Egyptians was expressed in their monuments and buildings through a form of total symbolism; isolating one detail in order to 'translate' it robs it of its meaning.

3. The principal knowledge expressed in these monuments as the 'symbolists' have begun to interpret it seems to be a magnificently worked out vitalist philosophy: man's environment extends literally to the stars—as if Shakespeare's cosmological metaphors were statements of fact. The scientific knowledge by which the Egyptians dressed stone with incredible accuracy, and by which they transported (often underwater) and erected enormous obelisks still standing, of which modern engineers refuse to touch any but the smallest—all this they took little pains to record. Rather they strove to express, by the transformation of an entire valley in orderly fashion, universal laws which have come down to us as surely as if they had been buried in a time capsule with the dimensions of the desert. But we have not yet deciphered them.

Varille and Robichon gradually convinced me, as they had many others, of the promise of their 'symbolist' interpretation of ancient Egypt. Their researches have nothing in common with the irresponsible fads and prophecies of the 'pyramidologists'. Traditional Egyptology has continued to resist their ideas, even though a lively public debate was carried on in Paris newspapers and reviews for about two years in the early fifties and overflowed to London. Varille's articles are eloquent by their sheer weight of observed fact.

My estimate of the symbolist position can have little importance. Yet I have gone to these lengths to present it because of a very simple lesson it taught me. My last day in Upper Egypt I was standing with Varille in the temple of Luxor where he had just showed me how the knees of all the statues in a certain part of the temple carry peculiar markings. They showed, he said, that in the enlarged configuration of a man that a temple represents, we were standing at the knees; each part is marked to indicate its position and function. 'This temple grew like a man from a seed, and every stage of its development lies partly hidden here, along with the story of Egypt and its kings and its ambitions to enter the cosmic order of living and dead. But no one in our day has grasped the whole message. The inscriptions, read alone, come out as dry descriptions of ceremonial or lists of royal exploits.' I asked him if he would ever be able to translate these writings in such a way as to convey a sense of ancient Egypt, for even Breasted had failed to do so.

'It was only about a year ago it came clear to me', he said. And he lowered his huge head to look at the figures his cane was already drawing in the sand. 'A literary translation, no matter how well it is done, will never serve. The Egyptians had no literature as we know it, no books which alone represented their civilization. They lived in mud huts and brick palaces that have not survived the centuries. But when they wrote, they wrote for eternity, in stone. This is their writing, their literature.' And the cane now swept in a circle toward the temple surrounding us. 'How do you translate a temple unless you can stand someone inside it and walk around it and point at it and talk about it? . . . There is a way, which will take time and money and people and a whole new career for me. A film. Or rather hundreds of films. In a film I can show a general view of a building, its plan, an overlay of successive plans alternated with details of the structure, inscriptions and usurped inscriptions, reused materials hidden in the walls, and the fall of the sunlight and moonlight, which often picks out the text appropriate to a particular season.' As he talked on, he described all the dramatic and expository possibilities of montage technique, its total flexibility and plasticity in time and place. He had not, he admitted, read Eisenstein but hoped to soon.

I left Egypt fired by the meaning of the revelations. Along with others not mentioned here, they shed new light on the traditional position of Greece as the sole source of Western philosophical traditions, the history of the Hebrews in Egypt, and the origins of Christian ritual. Then, the following autumn, a few hours after I lunched with him in Paris, Varille was killed in an automobile accident on his way back to Lyon. Egyptology was deprived of its most brilliant and unrepentant gadfly, whose work had scarcely begun.

The manifold problems of Egyptology all lead to the central question of understanding the antiquities we have discovered in staggering quantities. So great a distance intervenes between us and Egypt, the premises of their thinking in religion, politics, philosophy, and morality are so remote from ours, that translation becomes a basic discipline for everyone in the field. But the records to be translated lie so far outside the ordinary media we associate with translation that Varille had to abandon writing in order to find a feasible solution. When the distance between cultures exceeds any possibility of transposing units of discourse, then the first task of translation will be to find a suitable form for the text in the new 'language.' The only language we know that can begin to express three millennia of dressed stone architecture and divine kingship lies in our most complex and sensitive art form, the moving picture. We have not yet mastered its resources, and the film director has yet to claim his role as translator of certain domains of expression still barely explored.

II

Standing before the monuments of ancient Egypt, one can be little more than a witness striving for undisturbed vision of the whole. Amid the people and events of modern Paris, one cannot long hold back from becoming a participant. I shall speak less lengthily of this second trip, for it repeats to a great extent the experience of those who have resided more than a year in a large European city. I went to Paris in 1947, survived strict rationing of everything worth eating, the hottest summer in forty years, and the mass trauma of the general strike, which at its climax left the city for two hideous days without water. No clearly defined reasons took me there, and a year after arriving, I found myself resigning a desirable job with an international agency and settling down to translate Guillaume Apollinaire. I had deluded myself into thinking I knew enough French and was enough of a poet to render one of the language's most appealing and evasive poets into English. As a result, my principal credential as a translator is that of having published several of the most horrendous bloomers in translation in this century, one of them cited (namelessly) by Justin O'Brien in a recent article on translations from the French. Yet, apart from the whoppers it tricked me into, this stint of translation and a few that followed taught me something I have had to face again as a teacher of language.

A near contemporary poet in French speaks to us across a very short interval. If one thinks of Egypt, it seems like no interval at all. Despite what we sometimes conceive of as a cultural and linguistic chasm between us, Americans and Frenchmen of the 20th century look at much the same objects and make not so very different noises in order to refer to them. And these noises differ along so clearly parallel lines of structure that the transposition from one language to the other can be made with little wrenching of one's categories and operations of thought. Outside of differences in style and usage and rational discipline that arise principally from variations in education and culture, the two languages display only one major contrast built into their essential structure. This is, on the one hand, the reliance of English on the passive voice, and, on the other hand, the reliance of French on reflexive forms. Otherwise, the peculiarities in time sense, order, preposition usage, and inflection in either language can be easily grasped by a native speaker of the other language. Though a perspective can readily be found to underscore utter incompatibility (and this would be the normal point of view of an essay on translation), we are dealing with two languages incredibly close together, not so similar as good English and good Frieze perhaps, but so nearly on top of one another as to produce an annual crop of boners and fractures and bloomers on every level of linguistic practice. After all, French was not spoken in England for three hundred years to no avail.

The translator, like the language student and teacher, reckons with this proximity in terms of what are called 'false friends.' These treacherous words, which slip across the common frontier from one language to the other on forged papers and work up to very important places in students' vocabularies and translations, make up part of the price we pay for having a common frontier. There could be no false friends between a modern language and Egyptian, only larger and smaller degrees of approximated meaning. In our dealings with a closely related language, therefore, the great danger consists in regarding this intimacy as an unqualified advantage.

When I first approached certain stanzas of Apollinaire's poetry, they seemed to offer no linguistic difficulty but rather purely prosodic problems of rhythm and rhyme.

The already nostalgic modernism of these lines dates from 1905.

Soirs de Paris ivres du gin
Flambent de l'électricité
Les tramways feux verts sur l'échine
Musiquent au long des portées
De rails leur folie de machines

Drunk on gin the Paris nights
Blaze with electricity
The trolleys flashing lights behind
Sing out along their endless tracks
The folly of machinery

The translation may sound all right, but I had completely missed a buried image to which the verb *musiquent* should have alerted me. I read right over *portées,* assimilating it to *rails.* But *portées* is also the word in French for musical staff, a sense which now links the song of *musiquent* to a visual image of trolley tracks evenly ruled like music paper, and, by extension, trolleys like rolling notes.

Drunk on gin the Paris nights
Blaze with electricity
The trolleys showing greenish lights
Warble along their staves of tracks
The madness of machinery

In this revised version the *portées* metaphor is awkwardly restored and another semi-false friend, *folie,* has been changed to 'madness.' Yet the stanza still limps. Nothing is so resistant to translation as a simple suggestive style; it seems fated to become either colorless or precious.

Faced by a proximity that deprives him of elbow-room and often challenges him to a word by word version as the only authentic one, the translator is tempted to create artificial distance in order to gain freedom of action. As with most considerations in this equilibrists' field, he is right up to a point. He is right to make much of such small differences as word order, of the suppression of articles, and of the exactness of prepositions. He will grieve long over ambiguities that cannot be carried over satisfactorily or at all, and puzzle over some that crop up in English when the original calls for direct statement. What does he do with words like *conscience* and *jeu* and *esprit* in French; and *time* and *get* in English? In these cases he must be sure he knows each language independently and does not become hyponotized by its distorted mirror image in the other. For the only appeal in translation from the insoluble dilemma is to a larger unit of discourse—from word to phrase to line to sentence to stanza or paragraph to the entire work. And in this reaching out toward the larger unit, one must leave behind dictionary meanings and formal syntax, and often one has to assert a discursive distance that the face of the text does not seem to require. Free translation is often not an indulgence but a duty.

The false friend itself frequently turns out to be no such manageable unit as a word, but rather an entire thought or sentence or stanza—even a work. In these cases translation begins to resemble the kind of puzzle that used to appear frequently in the papers. In a jumbled overcrowded landscape of trees, flowers, bushes, and clouds, one is instructed to find the letters of a certain word. They lie carefully camouflaged under the shrubbery or tucked away in a cloud or snuggling around a chimney—present but blended away into the features of the landscape. The entire composition here constitutes a deliberate false friend which our eyes mistranslate because they have been deceived by conventional shapes. This is just the way I have come to feel about one of the most celebrated sentences in modern French literature, which, because translated early into English in a more or less definitive version, has never been scrutinized by a string of sceptical translators, as have equivalent lines of poetry. I refer to the opening sentence of Proust's *A la recherche du temps perdu.*

Proust wrote his novel predominantly in the imperfect tense, a condition which makes the pervading tone of sadness and illusion untranslatable into English. For we have no simple tense between the past (aorist) and the unwieldy progressive. Against the long lush undulating stretches of imperfect, the actions in Proust's story requiring the *passé simple* stand out in startlingly clear silhouette. Marcel acts comparatively rarely, but his acts assume monumental proportions when raised on this vast plateau of the imperfect–monumental, and occasionally so contrived and trivial as to carry us far into the realm of the grotesque. Through these two basic tenses, imperfect and past definite, the present weaves a thread of generalized observation and permanent 'truth' or 'law.' What, then, is one to make of the opening sentence, especially when one comes back to it after reading through the rest of the novel? For it is in the *passé composé* or present perfect. Once one begins to consider the other possible versions of the same sentence in French, it appears deliberately to avoid the characteristic tenses of the novel.

Longtemps, je me suis couché de bonne heure.

Why did Proust not clarify his meaning with a temporal preposition?

Depuis longtemps, je me couche de bonne heure.
Depuis longtemps, je me couchais de bonne heure.
Pendant longtemps, je me couchai de bonne heure.
Pendant longtemps, je me couchais de bonne heure.

There are arguments against all four. The first directs the flow of time entirely toward the present and begins to sound confessional and familiar. The second tends to anticipate a specific event coming along to break the routine suggested by the imperfect. The third suggests an unacceptable slow motion effect. The fourth—probably the least distorted and the version which is usually understood instead of the inscrutable sentence Proust actually wrote—yields too quickly to the pull of reminiscence. Is the sentence then merely conversational and temporally noncommittal? I strongly doubt it. May we say that Proust wanted to keep this opening sentence free from any exact location in time and to begin in a temporal free-zone? In part this is surely the effect, whether deliberate or no. *A la recherche* begins outside of time, or hovering above it, and it will end by climbing back up to this altitude.

But if we look closely and listen long enough, this sentence suddenly reveals a deeper secret in the heart of its verbal construction. *Longtemps:* a period of indefinite duration at any point in time, past, present, or future. Then: *je me suis couché. Passé composé.* Not a simple tense, but a compound tense composed of two other tenses or times (*temps* means both tense and time in French). The French language, like English, contains a verbal form which crosses the present with the past participle, breeds them to form what we curiously call the perfect, a past action still working its effect in the present and not yet separated from us by insignificance or temporal remoteness. We are dealing with two times then, past and present locked in a compound verb form. The circumstance allows us to perceive in this, the first verb of the novel, the double time sense and double orientation of the entire work. Marcel is in bed both literally in the past and symbolically-grammatically in the present as he tells of it—an indefinite time spanning past and present, *passé indéfini* as it is also called. Without this interpretation, the first sentence remains annoyingly vague and amorphous; with it, these eight words embody the mood and significance of the three thousand pages to follow by virtue of the fact that this sentence does not employ one of the simple tenses out of which the rest of the book emerges. We can read fully into the depths of the sentence only when we have already finished the novel and plumbed Marcel's past and present, here crossed in a syntactic equivalent of timelessness.

An educated Frenchman reads this sentence with an imprecise sense of its vast submerged meaning; no critic I know of has stopped to analyze the time dimension it opens up. An educated translator however, specifically a translator into English, will be confronted by a serious problem. Scott Moncrieff translated not the sentence Proust wrote but one of the versions Proust rejected:

For a long time I used to go to bed early.

Since Moncrieff's almost complete translation of the novel, despite numerous shortcomings and mistakes, has the enormous virtue of being homogeneous, no new version has replaced it, nor is any planned to my knowledge. As a result, no reader confined to English has ever entered the world of Proust through the proper portal. But how can the line be translated? Is it possible to put this simple sounding sentence, this oversized false friend, into English at all?

Time and time again I have gone to bed early.

It comes closer, yet our perfect tense has taken on different connotations, and *longtemps* drifts innocently beyond the reach of 'time and time again.' In order to disentangle himself from the apparently elementary nature of this sentence, a translator would probably have to resort to a cumbersome note or to a complete recasting of the structure and vocabulary. Either way the unadorned rhythm and reflexive mode of Proust's first utterance is lost.

III

It is possible however, that a solution may turn up because of the very nature of our age. For I am convinced that, with a period of intensive literary revisionism closed in both France and England (and probably America), we may be entering a new age of assimilation and translation. To some extent translation goes in cycles, and since the war we have had new versions in English of scores of literary classics from the Greeks to the Symbolists. Many more are in progress. It means that we may have time to catch up with ourselves, to rediscover the new past and to examine the breathlessness that opened the twentieth century. This large scale reckoning-up is gathering momentum under the threat of such total destruction that the spirit of innovation in the arts swings back naturally to conservatism. Whether we are in for a Dark Age or a Golden Age, one of our rare remaining avant-gardes may well be found among translators laboring long and with comparatively small reward to bring into modern English the wealth of world culture.

Upon reflection, I find this thought disturbing, as I do the systematic stockpiling in our mushrooming museums. As we develop smoother, more modern, racier translations, we come closer to the museum situation of art objects deprived of a site. As classics are translated afresh and assimilated into the present with all time-lag and linguistic shift removed from their substance, we are making them more and more into culture fragments. The ultimate in this tendency to uniformity would be a literature without an author, not many steps short of Malraux's 'Museum without walls.' We already have 'world literature' and are looking for 'machine' translations. Ours may be the age of 'Anon.' resuscitated.

For poetry, as Jackson Mathews has suggested, the solution may well be to supply two translations–an accurate and fairly literal prose version opposite the original poem, and, appearing alone, a freer 'poetic' version re-creating the tone and movement of the whole in modern idiom. This practice would recognize the fact that translations, particularly of poetry, can be either transparent or opaque, and rarely both. In the former we see through the translation to the original and use the translation as a crude lens for improving our vision; in the latter, the self-contained literary qualities of the translation absorb our attention and shut off from view the particular traits of the original. It is the standard dilemma, which too often leads to failure by compromise. Only rarely does the opaqueness of a good poetic version in the new language combine with transparency to the fundamental poetic tone and movement of the original.

The terms transparent and opaque leave us still caught in a conventional line of thought about the direction of translation. Translation means literally to move something from one place to another, and yet by long habit we use the word in the narrow linguistic sense of an original text being rendered *into* a new language. But if we think less of individual works and more of a process constantly carried on in a culture, is this the true direction of translation? Is translation assimilation, a breaking down of original tissue and reconstitution along lines consistent with a different system? To these questions we should answer a strong negative. In its truest role translation does not consist solely in reducing all foreign works to the limitations of, say, English, but equally in reshaping and enlarging English to reach meanings which it has not yet had to grapple with. As much as the work is translated into English, English should be translated to and around the work. Before being a stomach in which to break down and absorb the work, the translator must, like a starfish, turn himself and his language inside out in order fully to surround the work, still intact and asserting its form. What I am saying here applies principally to poetry, yet also to prose far more than translators usually take the time to recognize. Smooth translation can drain all life out of a text. It is often said that Dreiser reads better in French than in English, for his style has been 'improved.' Yet does it remain Dreiser? This entire domain of translation as an important means of extending and refining the language has been too much ignored in the interest of naturalness and smoothness. Many works have neither quality in the original, and the roughness of Rimbaud or Céline stands for an aggressive refusal of polished language. Rivarol, in introducing his own translation of Dante's *Inferno*, saw it all clear in the eighteenth century: 'Thus I have concluded that [translations] should serve equally the glory of the poet being translated and the progress of the language that translates.' By making that last verb intransitive (I have translated it literally), Rivarol suggests something like a reflexive–a language which translates itself to or transports itself toward the desired object. When this happens, as in the King James Bible or Amyot's *Plutarque*, the translation resists the erosion of time that would normally destroy its usefulness in fifty years.

The handy Venn diagrams used in formal logic can schematically represent this relationship between languages. Two widely separated cultures and language systems, like English and Egyptian, correspond to two circles with no point in common. (*No men are monkeys.*) To cross the space between them, or to bring some part of one into contact with the other, new tissue has to be created that participates in both systems. Varille's films, had he lived to make them, could have been this kind of tissue, reaching out to discover a different symbol system by using our own most elastic means of communication. Strictly literary translation cannot bridge the gap and produces in this case little more than inferior works in English. On the other hand two cultures or two languages so closely related as French and English might be seen as two extensively overlapping circles, with only a crescent shaped area left on each side. (*Many men are morons.*) Translation from modern French into modern English reveals itself as a problem not of remaining always within the shared area, but of exploring in English that crescent which is exclusively French. Proust's use of the *passé com-*

posé clearly falls in this area where a translator should not fear, gingerly, to tread. An extreme case could be conceived in a monosyllabic utterance to be translated into a language without monosyllables. In her fine book, *Racine and English Classicism,* Katherine Wheatley investigates this crescent in an original fashion. She develops a reverse critical method that consists in discovering essential qualities of an author by remarking their absence in misguided translations and adaptations.

In both cases I have been considering, that is, translation across a large span and translation at close quarters, the translator spends a considerable portion of his time and thinking in a limbo region belonging to neither language, neither culture. Out there, where he has left behind him one set of expressive symbols and has not yet found the corresponding and different set he is seeking, the translator must carry with him an interior device to keep him on course between the two and give him an image of the ground under him and his position in reference to it. For aircraft, exactly this instrument has been perfected and named the artificial horizon, a sensitive gyroscopic device that sits firm in the sky while the ship changes attitude around it. The pilot flying on instruments refers above all to his artificial horizon. In a process that has had very little scrutiny, the translator navigates his most crucial moments on instruments, hovering between two languages and trusting only to his linguistic artificial horizon. His flight, his leap into darkness, however brief, should enlarge both the meaning of the work he is translating and the expressive range of the language he brings to it.

It has become a commonplace of translation to say that every version of a work in a foreign language necessarily suggests a critical interpretation of the work. Far too little do we remember that the translator-navigator must also offer a commentary on his native language seen from a new vantage-point; and far too rarely do we grant him the right to violate the rules of usage that it should be part of his function to push to the limit and if necessary overstep. I am sorry that Chapman, the translator of Homer, never wrote a sonnet entitled 'On First Looking back at Shakespeare's English.' Awed by the task of raising English at last to the level of the Greek epic, Chapman might have anticipated Keats' famous last line in order to describe the mood of a translator beholding afresh the poverty and riches of his mother tongue:

Silent, upon a peak in Darien.

NOTE

Several of the ideas that are here expressed took shape during my reading of Georges Mounin's *Les Belles infidèles* (Paris, 1955). It is one of the most intelligent single works on translation I have discovered, both a sharp criticism and a stout defense.

The opening remarks on the 'symbolist school' of Egyptology may be documented in Varille's chief works, all published in Cairo: *Quelques caractéristiques du temple pharonique* (1946), *Dissertation sur une stèle pharonique* (1946), *A propos des pyramides de Snefrou* (1947), *Deux bases de Djedthotefankh à Karnak* (1950). The following non-technical texts treat the subject in general terms: Jean Cocteau, 'Louxor,' *La Table Ronde*, oct. 1949; Pierre Missac, 'L'égyptologie, la tradition ésotérique et la science,' *Critique*, déc. 1948; André Rousseaux, 'La querelle des égyptologues,' *Mercure de France*, juillet & oct. 1951; Walter Smart, 'A New Egyptology,' *The Cornhill*, Winter 1950/1951.

Part Two

THE CONTEXT OF TRANSLATION

DENVER LINDLEY

The Editor's Problem

DENVER LINDLEY, *an editor of the Viking Press, has turned several volumes from French and German into English—including four novels by Remarque and the last novel of Thomas Mann.*

The whole subject of translation, for those who are professionally involved in it, is a potpourri of hesitation, exasperation, compromise, headache and occasional thrills and satisfactions. From the editorial side of the desk, these difficulties bear a different weight and are less time-consuming than the problems that face the translator locked in private contest with the chosen text. They can, however, be nerve-wracking, and since the choice of the text, in all but the happiest instances, rests with the editor (or the House he represents) they are worth looking at.

The ideal situation is easy to picture: a book of obvious merit by an established author, a translator of proven skill whose rates are already established and who is free to undertake the job, the translation delivered on time and requiring no more than routine copy-editing procedures before going off to the printer—and, finally, successful publication. This delightful sequence of events does occur—perhaps once in a hundred times. Ordinarily there are doubts, difficulties, and delays all along the line. These constitute the stubborn facts in the face of which the hazardous business of publishing current books from abroad must be carried on.

What books will the publisher choose? Obviously, the best he can lay hands on, provided they fit into his general program. He will read advance notices, talk to European publishers, consult scouts. And the books will come in, from these sources, from agents, sometimes from the authors themselves. Or they may be suggested by the would-be translator—who too often suffers the disappointment of discovering that the translation rights have already been sold. How then to make the choice? There are two principal requirements: intrinsic merit (either in the sense of literary excellence or wide popular appeal, ideally both) and the sturdiness necessary to withstand the rigors of transplantation. This second requirement automatically rules out rather more than nine-tenths of the possible candidates. To have a reasonable success in the American market, a book must be, at least in some respect, well above average: it will almost inevitably suffer loss in translation and it must have enough vitality left to overcome the American reader's reluctance to make the effort of adjusting his mind to foreign ways and foreign scenes—not to mention the prejudice shared by many of us against translations *per se*.

If the publisher or his editor can read the language in question, he can at least make an informed guess whether any given book meets the two requirements. In most cases, it will be a gamble, but his own. If he has to rely on outside reports, his position is much shakier. Specialists in foreign literature are only in rare instances possessed of publishing experience, and yet this, from the publisher's point of view, is a necessary ingredient in the decision he has to make. He is invited to bet on a horse he has never seen on the advice of a man who knows nothing about horse-racing, though he may have a fine eye for horse-flesh. It is only fair to say that the results are sometimes brilliantly successful. The uncertainties, however, furnish part of the answer to the question: Why aren't more foreign books available in English?

Let me pursue the grimy details, details that are important to the translator as well, for they constitute the conditions in which he must exercise his profession or ply his art if he wishes to see his work in print. Suppose the choice of a book has been made, the rights have been acquired, but no obvious translator is at hand. Very likely the publisher has a file of applicants, from which he may select an unknown, testing his ability by requiring a sample translation. (In the near future he will be able to consult a list of qualified translators now being compiled by the American P.E.N.) If he is wise he will make sure that the prospective translator has read and likes the book. This is an elementary precaution. Its neglect prejudices success: an indifferent translator will produce flaccid copy; a hostile one forfeits the aid of his own unconscious and may convert this indispensable ally into a wily adversary.

What about the delicate matter of remuneration? There are more or less standard rates—so many dollars per thousand words—varying with the translator's established reputation, or lack of it. (Many people, and almost all translators, believe these rates are too low. A convincing argument can be made for this view by computing the number of hours of intensive labor required to produce a good translation.) This sum, be it large or small, must come from somewhere. In the first instance, of course, it comes from the publisher, but he in turn must make it fit into his 'formula.' This magic word represents the result of abstruse calculation of foreseeable average profits and losses; on it depends his hope of staying in business. But it assumes a text written in English. How is the extra cost to be absorbed? Shall the publisher increase the price of the book, thereby penalizing it in a competitive market or shall he offer the author a lower royalty rate—beginning, let us say, at 7½% instead of 10? The latter practice is the more general. One distinguished member of the profession put the matter with magisterial succinctness: 'I see no reason to pay an author a bonus for writing in a foreign language.' (In the case of an assured best seller, the publisher may choose to pay this 'bonus,' counting it, in effect, as a higher initial royalty.)

Here a complicating factor intrudes. English translation rights are usually sold to both a British and an American house. This permits a single translation to be used and thus reduces the cost to each publisher. But it raises the question: who commissions and supervises the translation? The American publisher is likely to feel that he can keep the matter better in hand if he does his own selecting. The British publisher, especially if he was first in the field, is likely to be adamant—for similar reasons, plus the fact that British translators are in general even worse paid than American. A subject for negotiation—with the odds a bit against the home team.

Difficulties notwithstanding, translations are produced even in this country. Overcoming the occupational hazards of insomnia, hypochondria, and alcohol, translators do from time to time deliver a completed manuscript. And then an editor reads it. He reads it first of all to see whether it is in English. On this subject he is competent to judge, whether he knows the original language or not. Having reason to believe that the author is competent in his own tongue (otherwise he would not be committed to him) he has a right to expect readable English in the translation. No degree of literal fidelity can compensate for the betrayal of a good writer by Englishing him in limp or ludicrous style.

Changes may be necessary, anything from stylistic vetting to re-translation, an exasperating and thankless job. When, as sometimes happens, a translation appears without a translator's name attached, this may not indicate callous disregard of the translator's rights but simply the fact that so much re-writing has been necessary that to attribute the result to the original translator would be, in effect, dishonest and misleading. (Translation of technical works is not considered here. In these, knowledge of the subject outweighs everything else, and editorial re-writing is the rule rather than the exception.)

This is the extreme, though alas not altogether uncommon, situation. Most translations by professional hands are readable and reasonably accurate. An editor will assume the latter unless something arouses his suspicion. Even if he is competent to check the translation line by line, time will usually not permit him to do so. He may miss egregious errors. Let me cite a few published examples: the mysterious blind man wandering about in the woods, resulting from a translator's too literal rendering of *Blindgänger*, which means a shell that has missed its mark, a dud; the unexplained explosion in a powder-factory, introduced by a translator who consulted the dictionary for *poudrerie*, and did not know that in French Canada it means a windstorm accompanied by powdered snow; the highly ingenious invention of steps leading down to the bottom of a well in a translation from the English by a man who took *stairwell* at face value.

With luck and alertness, however, the editor should be able to spot these gross errors, using the same test that the translator should apply: collision between meaning and context. Against lesser slips, not open to the test of consistency, there is no safeguard.

The question of literal accuracy has been long and fruitlessly debated. It is essentially meaningless. The translator, if only for his own convenience, will try for as much literal accuracy as is consistent with his purpose of transmitting his author's meaning as accurately as possible in a style that corresponds as closely as possible to the original. Sometimes the words do not correspond at all. For example, the title of Remarque's famous novel of World War I comes from a sentence near the end of the book: *Im Westen sei nichts Neues zu melden.* The literal translation would be: In the West there is nothing new to report. But this is not the right wording for a military dispatch. With brilliant appropriateness Wheen gives the English equivalent: All Quiet on the Western Front.

Slang or colloquialisms of all kinds are a recurrent problem. It would be a great convenience to follow George Moore's counsel and use a neutral language. Unfortunately, this often entails too great a loss, especially in the modern novel where dialogue is so extensively used for purposes of characterization. No one would recommend imitation of the British translator of Aristophanes who invented a Scotch-Irish dialect of such density that in many passages it can only be elucidated by reference to the Greek text. Some middle way is needed—and can usually be found in the use of hints and light touches rather than the heavy hand. This, like so many problems of translation, is in theory insoluble and in practice a subject for compromise, depending upon the ingenuity, taste, and, above all, the ear of the translator.

Since in a literary work these qualities of the translator are of such crucial importance, an editor will be strongly inclined to choose a person born to the English language. The richness, flexibility and splendor of our tongue offer the translator unparalleled scope for ingenuity, taste, and sense of style. But the inexhaustible resources of English are only an asset to the extent that he can command them. Too often they torment and haunt him. It is by no means an unfamiliar experience for a translator to wake up and find some word or phrase for which he has been diligently searching crystal clear in his mind—eight months after his translation has been published. However, when the season is favorable and the fates allow, it is possible, at least in theory, for a devoted translator, calling upon the resources of English, to make good the losses inherent in the process and produce a work equivalent to the original.

This possibility has seldom been realized—the shining exception is, of course, the King James Version—but it is of immediate relevance today when a renaissance of translation of the classics is in full swing.

We are now on loftier ground than before, but we can still survey it from the publisher's viewpoint. It was in fact a new development in publishing, the appearance and sudden popularity of paper-bound editions, that gave impetus to (and provided funds for) this renaissance. For fifty years before the advent of the paperback many of the great translations of the classics were labors of love, produced without aid or comfort from a publisher and without assurance that they would ever meet the public eye. Today the position is much improved, and the first fruits of this improvement are already at our disposal. There are more to come.

In commissioning these re-translations the publisher is, of course, putting his money on known winners. There is no question about the vitality of these works; they have survived the torments of translation before—some of them scores of times—and presumably they can do so again. They are imperishable, but their English dress, even when it is of the best quality, goes out of fashion. Chapman's *Homer* (alas) is little read today. Florio's *Montaigne* has been superseded. Every generation finds timeless literature a little more acceptable when it is presented in contemporary garb.

But there is, of course, another and more compelling reason for this reduplicated effort. It is the hope of producing a classic of translation, a work more nearly worthy of its great original than any of its predecessors. Translators by the dozen are ready to rise to this lure. The reason is simple enough. A translator's most essential business, and his most exciting activity, is a traffic in meaning. A moment comes in the translation of any important passage in any significant book when the author's intent hangs naked in the translator's mind. It has shed its original clothes and has not yet found new ones. The translator, a little like Edna St. Vincent Millay's Euclid, looks on meaning bare.

What is true of a single passage is, in a wider sense, true of a book and even of an author's whole work. Could there be anything more intoxicating than the belief that you, and you alone, could communicate the true meaning of Shakespeare to someone incapable of English? This service has in fact been done with a remarkable degree of success in the Schlegel-Tieck translation—the work of two hands, to be sure. How successful that is can be judged from the unshakeable conviction among many Germans, some of them well acquainted with English, that the translation excels the original. It is the reason, too, for the even odder belief held in certain quarters that Shakespeare is a German poet. Whatever one may make of these ideas, they at least go a long way to prove that some measure of greatness has in fact been communicated.

Communication—that is the purpose and the delight of translation. 'This is something I admire so much,' says the translator, 'something I find so profound, so beautiful, so piercing that I must make you understand and admire it too, even though you, through some inadvertence, have neglected to learn the language in which it is written. Let me show you how it goes.'

This is a healthy impulse, very similar, on a different level, to the urge to share a good story. It is healthier, for instance, than the solipsistic belief that you alone fully understand Shakespeare and that therefore *you* must be the author of his plays. But it is harder to carry out than the telling of an anecdote. The difficulty increases in proportion to the literary excellence of the work, the degree to which its form and content are forever wedded. At the top of the scale, all authorities agree, translation becomes impossible. (Translators are the first to assent to this proposition, if they have not already signed an affidavit that *all* translation is impossible.) Moritz Haupt put the matter quite clearly: 'Do not translate: translation is the death of understanding. The first stage is to learn to translate; the second to see that translation is impossible.' He was speaking specifically of Pindar. No one yet has proved him wrong. But neither this iron interdict nor the skeletons that litter the path to the heights will permanently discourage new aspirants. Aeschylus, Pindar, Racine, Goethe—these unscaled summits—continue to bewitch, beguile, distract and beckon. Once clearly seen, they cannot be ignored. And from time to time there will be someone who finds he has no choice but to attempt the climb.

An editor, even if he has not tried his hand at the craft of translation, cannot very well be unaware of these hopes and stirrings. With the enlargement of the market, noted above, he can actively encourage renewed attacks upon the impossible. But most of his time—insofar as he has time for this important matter—will continue to be spent in the complex guessing game of picking out contemporary books that have (he hopes) enough viability to survive on alien soil.

RICHARD HOWARD

A Professional Translator's Trade Alphabet

RICHARD HOWARD *translates professionally from the French, free-lancing for several editors. To his credit: close to a dozen specimens of the* nouveau roman, *Andre Breton's* Nadja, *and a volume of General de Gaulle's memoirs.*

ARTICLES OF FAITH: Translations of French writing are made for people who do not read French and are to be judged from this perspective. The fact that the necessary demolition work ('Miss X has preferred to translate *esprit* throughout as *spirit* when a more flexible rendering, such as "mind" or "essence" would have seen her over many hurdles') is so often done by critics and reviewers means that the publisher has not performed his task properly: all translations must be edited (we do not have, as Eric Bentley has said, a profession of thoroughly competent translators), yet I advance from my own experience that it is not possible to read a translation, even a translation properly edited, as a *work in English* if the reader knows French and is concerned with the problems and practices of equivalents between the two languages. I have often wondered at the policy of the *New York Times* Book Review Supplement, for example, which assigns all French books in English to be reviewed by translators of French, Professors of French literature or critics of French birth, though I confess that the consequent flying fur and wrist-slapping is one of the few diverting spectacles the Book Section affords. Are books by women always reviewed by women? Similarly, would it not be more interesting to know what a critic of the novel makes of, say, *Martereau* than the reactions of a well-known translator of other French fiction? After all, now that the foreign work has been made available, let us have the reactions of the native 'common reader'—or uncommon—not those of the expert on foreign words and works.

BRITISH TRANSLATIONS: Many American publishers buy British translations of French works, though I suspect much of the *cachet* of such work has by now worn thin or been shown for the amateur thing it is by those publishers who do not trouble to read what they have contracted for. Of course if an American publisher has the opportunity to split translation costs with a British publisher, total production costs are less, but then on which side of the Atlantic is the actual work to be done? Since British translators are so badly paid, the choice is almost always made in favor of expedience. Yet a number of American houses have painfully learned the amount of doctoring that must be done on British work—so extensive that it is frequently as costly as the initial difference in fees between American and British work. Revisions—aside from those necessary to accord the two languages, British and American, which have crucial divergences in technology, dialogue, and emphasis—affect the very attitude toward the process itself: as far as I can judge, the British reader prefers his translated French book *not* to sound like any English a compatriot might produce. To publish a British translation here *tout court* is usually to confuse or irritate a good many readers, and I should suppose the same applies in England with regard to American texts that have not been thoroughly edited.

CRITICISM: My barber advises his bald customers, as I have learned, that there is only one thing they can do: resign themselves, and I counsel a similar stoicism without being very good at it myself. All translators, I suspect, are nervous wrecks unless they have bastioned themselves within the citadel of academic infallibility.

Do-it-yourself: Frequently the translator, in the course of his reading, or directed by some indulgent spy, encounters work which he feels is so valuable that he will translate it 'on spec' and then attempt to market it. This practice leads to occasional disasters, of course: rights and priorities can become extremely tangled affairs. But often such a strategy is the only way to introduce a new writer difficult to 'sell' for one reason or another. For example, through Mr. Edouard Roditi and Mr. Donald Allen, the work of E. M. Cioran was brought to my attention, and from his latest volume, *La Tentation d'Exister*, my translation of his essay *On a Certain Experience of Death* was shortly published in the *Evergreen Review #4*. A subsequent essay, *Beyond the Novel*, is soon to appear in the same periodical. But because of the fiercely speculative nature of this work, it will be difficult, I wager, if not impossible, to convince any American publisher to accept a volume of Cioran's essays until they are better known here; hence I am translating a number and circulating them among the editors of my acquaintance. Cioran writes 'philosophy' the way one feels St.-John Perse writes poetry—as if no one had ever written it before, and for all his corrosive wit his spirit is a saving, a restorative one. Placing the remaining nine essays in American and British periodicals requires the patience though hardly the conduct of a saint, but it will then be much more likely that an American publisher will show an interest in such work taken as a volume. Such strategies must be marginal for the professional translator, but I suspect he has a better chance to place work close to his heart than the inspired amateur whom neither authors nor editors know. *See* Qualifications.

EDITING: Editors are to translators rather what I imagine directors are to actors, and I for one have always found their suggestions invaluable, though I have not always accepted them. So frequently a translation has to be recast, by which I mean its tone must be reconstructed, not its words, even though the former consists of the latter and the latter are not *wrong*. Problems in translation rarely result from wrong words; more frequently they are a matter of tempo, of flexibility, and of accent. This is why it is easy, as Gide somewhere remarks, to discredit a translation, to alert readers to obvious errors, but hard to appreciate and point out fundamental virtues.

FEES: I recall translating a short novel by Giraudoux for my friends, before I had any notion of becoming a professional translator. The task took many months, usually three or four hours of work a day. Years later I managed to interest a paper-back publisher in this version, and was offered the astonishingly small sum of $250 for the text. Since I preferred to see the work in print rather than in my desk drawer, I accepted the pittance. During the same period I was asked by a film producer to make a 'rough' translation of a novel by the author of *The Bridge over the River Kwai*. I was able to furnish this in four days, for which labor–in my ignorance–I asked four hundred dollars (I learned later that I could have stipulated a thousand and received it. Movieland!). The American publishers of M. Boulle asked me to 'polish' this version and paid another two hundred dollars for the pumicing, admitting they were getting off cheap. Dramatic contrasts like these abound in the translator's professional life, and I suppose the art of translation, if the phrase has any meaning, is the art of serving God and Mammon in proportions that permit survival.

GRIEVANCES: *See* All Other Articles.

HAND-TO-MOUTH: Why is so much left to chance? Why are the translator's arrangements so casual? I think because for the publisher translations are obstacles in the way of a book's publication, deterrents—and expensive ones—of the normal author-to-audience process. Significant of this attitude is the problem of payments. If you make your living by what you are paid (and when you are paid it—if for tax reasons you prefer to be paid in installments), it is often inconvenient to be paid only upon completion (and approval) of the work. Yet to arrange for an advance on a translation is not always an easy matter; it is a favor, never a spontaneous or even readily agreed-to motion on the publisher's part. Only the translator-adaptors of hit Broadway plays (the category of translator-adaptor exists because our theatrical producers have the notion that a foreign play has to be qualified for American consumption; such a notion may be correctly inspired, but the results have so far scarcely justified the genre, it seems to me) get paid on a royalty basis for their pains. In other cases, the professional translator must rely on his speed, his English, and his sense of honor.

ISOLATION: *See* Other Translators.

JACKETS: Except for very small houses, most American publishers entrust the presentation of a new book to their promotion department. The salesmen must be informed how to interest bookstores in 'the list,' and of course jacket copy and press releases must be designed and composed with the customer in mind. In the case of nine-tenths of the books I have translated, I have been asked to provide information about the contents, summaries of the 'story' and every possible angle and gimmick. Yet only on exception has such material been used, and in general jacket copy for European books is inadequate when it is not downright untrue. Yet for lack of well-defined contractual arrangements, the translator rarely has a say in the packaging of a book once his manuscript is in the copy-editor's hands, though he may be the last person to have read the book before it reaches the stands.

KEYS: French-English dictionaries most valuable to the translator are accurately described by Justin O'Brien in his article *From French to English* in the Harvard Press volume *On Translation.* Keys, unfortunately, are made only for particular locks, and no list of false cognates will keep a translator infallibly on the right track; if a French writer refers to Emerson's essay as 'Confiance-en-soi,' the translator must somehow know that what is meant is not 'Self-Confidence' but 'Self-Reliance.' Such knowledge (and without it, what forgiveness?) is a matter of experience and of reading, and therefore no translator can hope to avoid errors entirely. All he can do is improve.

LOW LIFE: It is more difficult to translate French texts dealing with pornographic subjects, metaphorical argot and low life than anything else. The French have developed a middle language somewhere between the smell of the sewer and the smell of the lamp, which in English is mostly unavailable. We have either the very coarse or the very clinical, and I do not see how we can produce an English version of a masterpiece like *Histoire d'O* until we work up a language as pure and precise–though as suggestive and colorful–as that of Pauline Réage, whose French, for all the scabrous horror of her subject, is among the finest of the century.

MAGAZINES: The free-lance professional translator is often asked to render articles for periodicals; here the problem is a little different from that of book-length translations. Time is of the essence, and since the pieces are generally short, pay scales are higher. Such work, however, is necessarily piecemeal, and must be wedged into spare time and loose space around the large items in a translator's schedule. Most magazine articles appear to require more editing on the part of the translator than he expects to be asked of him–certainly more than he would be permitted to perform in translating a book.

Newcomers: It would be churlish indeed, expressing so much dissatisfaction with the character and conditions of my trade, not to welcome to it anyone likely to change them for the better. The profession is not 'crowded,' as I was assured when I first contemplated giving up my job as a lexicographer to adopt and enter it; it is not crowded because even if you translate only one book for publication and turn it into sensitive English in the spirit of the original you belong to the rank of professional translators and will be with Saint Jerome as Keats wanted to be with the English poets; and even if you translate fifty books and your English is blurred by incomprehension you are a blundering amateur and Saint Jerome will only sick his lion on you.

Other translators: I have never had the opportunity of discussing my work with other translators. As I suggest in Articles of Faith, I believe I am unable to read French writing in translation fairly, and I suspect other translators of similar incapacities where I am concerned. Even so, however, I am curious about my confreres. Though I know a number of scholars, many editors and even one or two reviewers who have *done* translations, I do not know any of the men and women of my profession. I often wonder about them–do they have as paranoiac a sense of me as I of them? What would we have to say to each other at a party, not to mention a panel?

Professionalism: 'No one,' remarks Professor O'Brien, '*wants* to be a professional translator.' He means, of course, that no one wants the drudgery of having to accept almost any assignment. In America, however, circumstances are such that one can become a professional translator and still translate, almost without exception, only books one enjoys putting into English. My own experience has repeatedly impressed me with the good will of American publishers, their eagerness to publish foreign work if it has merit and the slightest chance of attracting a readership. Again and again I have been able to approach many editors with projects which have been welcomed, encouraged, even accepted: the translator in America, if he has a sense of timing and repertory, is in a good position to do just the sort of work he likes, provided his interests are not impossibly parochial or obscure. That his financial rewards will be always adequate is another matter, but we are discussing professionalism, not profiteering. *See* Do-It-Yourself.

QUALIFICATIONS: It is folly to ask for a perfect knowledge of both languages. What translator has even in one direction the consummate gifts Mr. Beckett and Mr. Nabokov, those exasperating geniuses, have in two? With the exception of these writers, who have the advantage—whatever *they* call it—of translating only their own work, I know no translator who, regularly translating French into English, can also translate English into French with the same degree of choice and charm. The standard equipment for translating into English, of course, is knowledge of French which I suspect many French teachers would call 'passive' or 'reading' and a knowledge of English necessarily active (creative); to *speak* French properly and easily, to be at home in France—both in Paris and the country—and to maintain a wide acquaintance with French literature as a developing organism are, indeed, recommendations of the highest order. But I do not think they are supreme qualifications. I should think (exposing myself completely) that it is more important, more valuable for the translator of French to be at home in English, to maintain the same wide acquaintance with his own literature that he keeps up with the French, and to develop a strong and lively sense of the period qualities of his own tongue. A model is often necessary, and one must have freedom to reject the first possibility. Taking the cue from my author himself, I confess to doing a lot of prowling among translations of classical historians before I found the right movement and manner to aim at in rendering de Gaulle's *Mémoires de Guerre:* nineteenth-century versions of Tacitus. Naturally such cue-taking can be carried too far. One author asked me to revise a translation I had made of his work, requesting that my treatment be 'more Shakespearean and at the same time more in accord with the laws of Greek tragedy.' I'm not sure my revision followed these lines, but it involved another three weeks work on a text already polished to the point of despair. No translation, of course, is ever finished; as Valéry said of poems, it can only be abandoned. My own training, aside from purely literary preparation, quite fortuitously happens to be lexicographical; for five years after college, graduate school and study in France I worked as an editor of American dictionaries, and I should imagine that the fact of passing the language word by word through my mind and hand some five or six times has been of considerable value in subsequent attempts to render French prose into English. Certainly more helpful than if I had been working on French lexicons.

RATES: In my experience, these vary widely: the standard minimum rate for most literary translations in America is ten dollars a thousand words. An experienced translator with a number of successful jobs to show for his efforts ('Mr. X has served his original faithfully.' 'Mrs. Y's English version is suggestive') can reasonably hope for twelve dollars a thousand words. Difficult books, special problems or books which must be translated quickly often bring the translator fifteen dollars a thousand words. (A typewritten manuscript of two hundred pages, at this rate, earns about

900 dollars. But this is tops.) For what he is paid, the translator is generally asked to submit a fair copy and a carbon at a more or less closely specified time, and also to read galley proofs when they come in from the printer. Though I have translated some thirty books and fifty articles, I have never been paid on a royalty basis (save in the case of a play), though this is partly because the books I have translated are 'difficult' and do not appeal—or have not appealed—to large audiences; in such cases, one prefers the bird in the hand. A note on 'swelling': an English translation, an experienced editor will tell you, runs about 20 per cent longer than the original French text. This is not, alas, imperceptible to the reader of merely the English version; as one critic helpfully pointed out, translators —myself on this occasion—take into English far too many *quites* and *rathers*, *all the sames*, *I tell you*'s and other expressions of qualification and dilution. The French contrive to *use* these adverbial terms, but for us they have an effete quality, a weakness and nonchalance that are the symbol of translatorese.

SECRETARIES: Aside from plays, which I find I need to translate aloud from the very first, a secretary is a luxury. Even if the speed with which work can be executed is greatly increased, the margin of profit, never a fat one, cannot generally endure such paring.

TITLES: My principal conflicts with a publisher or an editor above the level of wrangles over money or time concern titles. Three examples: *a*) Robbe-Grillet's novel *La Jalousie*, published as *Jealousy*, though scarcely a betrayal under its English title, attracted a few critical snipers, who pointed out that the French title was also a reference to the bamboo blinds through which the obsessed husband is constantly spying on his wife. I had submitted to the publisher the title *The Blind*, which I felt played on the same ambiguity between seeing and feeling, since for all his efforts the husband never saw anything certain between the slats of his blind. The publishers, however, felt that such a title would indicate a treatise on ophthalmology rather than a novel of passion to our American public. *b*) The publisher who asked me to translate Monique Lange's short, light novel of Parisian homosexual life, *Les Poisson-Chats,* had already paid for an attractive cover based on the title *The Kissing Fish.* Yet when I translated the book, such an expression was entirely improper, it seemed to me, either as a rendering of the French title or as a suggestive English phrase. I had called the little book *Anne & The Boys,* but to my horror found that the cover, the spring list and the announcement in *Publishers' Weekly* made my preferences in the matter entirely academic. *c*) Claude Simon's novel *Le Vent,* in its first French edition, included a long subtitle, *A Tentative Reconstruction of a Baroque Altarpiece,* in small print. In the second French edition, contemporary with my translation, the subtitle was the same size as the words *The Wind.* And in the third, which appeared in France when the American edition was in the bookstores, the former subtitle was the title and *The Wind* has been relegated to an 'identifying' spot on the book's spine. The American publisher felt that despite this progress in French, any such modifications in his edition were supererogatory, to say nothing of incomprehensible, and the book was resolutely titled *The Wind,* giving no hint of the principles of composition employed. In all three of these cases, the publishers' notions of the books' appropriate titles, at variance with the translator's, have resulted from an image of the book-buying public which is, to say the least, not flattering. But perhaps the translator occupies a position too high in the ivory tower for the exigencies of publishing; perhaps, indeed, the realities are sterner than he cares to admit. *See* Jackets.

UMBRAGE: As the tone of these notes may indicate, translation is an unkind profession. Though it is pleasant for an American translator to visit writers and editors in France, it would not be pleasant for him to encounter another translator there. I find I waver, in my attitude toward my work, between hoping to be ignored, unmentioned or dismissed as 'adequate' on the one hand, and gasping for suggestive insight that is at once complimentary and helpful, on the other. It is useful to remember that 'the art of translation is a subsidiary art, and derivative.'

VERSIONS: John Hollander, in the Harvard collection *On Translation,* has ingeniously called the O.E.D. to his support in pointing out that our frequent use of the word *version* as a 'special form or variant of something resting upon limited authority or embodying a particular point of view' indicates that we think of it as different from a translation: there is almost always something queer about a version of a text, though not about a translation. Thus I would say that though we generally suppose we prefer a translation, once we have it we discover we would rather have a version.

WRITERS: Relations with the writers has turned out, in my experience, to be the greatest single reward the profession of translating has to offer, including the money. I think that the pleasure of being praised for good work and of being paid for it would otherwise be cancelled out by the anxiety over censure and the inadequacy of just what one *is* paid. As it is, though, there is this great human advantage which I have been given so often, and which has become a central fact of my life, so that I can only be grateful to what might otherwise loom depressingly as a mug's game. When I began translating books, I had no ideas that encounters with their authors would become so rich an experience. The first author I ever met whose work I had translated was Monsieur François-Régis Bastide, author of *Les Adieux.* I discovered that it was easier for me to understand this man's mind than that of many of my friends: I had assimilated so many of its characteristic –and also so many of its exceptional–gestures. Subsequent visits to France have offered so many repetitions of this experience, and in such a diversity of modes, that I can scarcely praise enough the 'social' status of the translator –abroad. *See* Professionalism.

XYZ: Can a translation be better than the original? This is a hypocritical question I put here because I cannot think up any more letters. Since, as John Hollander says, no translation can ever be correct in quite the same way as an answer to a question like *Is it Tuesday?*, the first answer, if *better* means what Mr. Nabokov asks of a translation–lucid accuracy in the literal rendering of the author's words–is no. On the other hand, questions like *How do you feel?* have answers which seem to be correct in a very different sense, and it is to this class of questions that my XYZ question belongs, and therefore gets the answer: yes. The point is, whether better or not, it can only be better English than the original French, which is the same thing as asking whether Molière wrote better plays than Milton wrote poems.

E. ERNEST GOLDSTEIN

Copyright and Translation

E. ERNEST GOLDSTEIN, *Professor of Law at the University of Texas, has published, in addition to numerous articles in periodicals both here and abroad,* American Enterprise and Scandinavian Antitrust Law.

No matter how creative, deserving, or well-intentioned a translator may be in a contest with an author or copyright owner, he must come off—all things being equal—second-best under the copyright laws.

We are excluding from our considerations a translator commissioned by a publisher, who usually works under a license obtained by the publisher from the foreign-language copyright owner. Outside of problems of plagiarism and infringement related to copying someone else's translation, there are no serious legal problems for the commissioned translator.

Our concern here is with the free-lance translator who wishes to translate into English a book on speculation as, for example, a piece for a little magazine or a play for performance by an off-Broadway company. How can he ascertain the American copyright status of the foreign-language original? When there is no response to repeated letters asking for permission to translate, what decision should be made by this would-be translator? Fundamental to any suggested resolution of such questions is an understanding of the mechanics and objectives of our own copyright law.

Copyright is recognized by our Constitution and is embodied in a code of laws designed to protect authors by giving them certain exclusive rights in their work. The principal, exclusive right is the right to make copies of the work; other exclusive rights include: the rights to sell or distribute copies, to transform or revise the form of a work, to dramatize a work, and to record, subject to limitations. It should be noted that the right to translate is embodied in the right to revise, and an authorized translation is thus eligible for copyright protection in and of itself. An authorized translation is either one made under authority of the copyright owner or a translation of a work in the public domain.

We recognize in our law two distinct types of copyright: a common-law property right, and a statutory copyright. The common-law property right is a form of protection given to unpublished works, including the exclusive right to make copies, and it only terminates upon the obtaining of a statutory copyright or upon the publication, copyrighted or not, of the work.

Statutory copyright is given to both published and certain unpublished works and is for an initial term of twenty-eight years, with a possible renewal for a further twenty-eight years.[1] The time periods are of importance because in dealing with U. S. protection of works by foreign authors, it is American copyright terms, and not those of foreign countries, that are operative in determining the life of foreign-produced works in this country. On the other hand, a work by a foreign author first published abroad and in the public domain outside the United States would—with a few exceptions—not be protected here: if the period of protection, though it has expired in the country of publication, has not expired in the United

[1] However, the maximum term of copyright has for some cases been extended by a recent Act of Congress (P. L. 87-668, 87th Congress, Second Session, September, 1962). Under that Act, any renewal term of copyright that was scheduled to expire between September 19, 1962, and December 31, 1965, is automatically continued in force until December 31, 1965.

States or when the principles limiting the subject matter of copyright in that country are not applicable in the United States, then a work in the public domain outside the United States may be subject to protection in the United States.

Under American law, as distinguished from common practice in Western Europe, copyright validity of published works depends on publication with prescribed notice, so that publication without proper notice is an abandonment of the right to copyright. The proper notice must be placed upon the title page, or the page immediately following, in the case of a book. The three indispensable elements of the notice are the copyright symbol, the name of the copyright owner–i.e., the author or his assignee–and the year of publication. Both under the Universal Copyright Convention, which we discuss later, and under domestic law, the symbol © is acceptable. For purely domestic copyright purposes, either the word "Copyright" or the abbreviation "Copr." are also acceptable. For publications seeking protection under the Buenos Aires Convention, the further legend "All Rights Reserved," is essential.

In the case of unpublished works subject to statutory copyright, claims to copyright may be obtained by filing in the Copyright Office a proper application form, submitting a copy, and paying a registration fee of four dollars.[2] The term of copyright is for twenty-eight years, calculated from date of deposit of the manuscript, with a possible renewal for an additional twenty-eight years.

[2] Examples of unpublished works which may be copyrighted are dramas, lectures, music (lyrics to music); however, in the case of material classifiable as a book, periodical (or literary contributions to periodicals), registration cannot be made if the work is in unpublished form–this applies as well to translations of such works, but all such works may still enjoy common-law copyright.

After a published work has been copyrighted by publication with proper notice, its copyright may then be registered by filing a claim in the Copyright Office using the appropriate application form, sending along two copies of the work, and paying a filing or registration fee of four dollars. The registration is essential if one is to bring suit for infringement, but the protection of copyright also exists if one has only published with notice. Another advantage of registering is that a copyright can be renewed only provided it was originally registered. Though the law states that the registration of the claim and furnishing of copies are required only when demanded by the Copyright Office, it is advisable, for full protection and benefits, to register voluntarily promptly after publication. In the case of *ad interim* copyright, which applies to works published abroad in the English language either without a U. C. C. copyright notice or which were written by an American citizen or resident, registration of the work published abroad must be made within six months of publication to secure United States Copyright for an initial period of five years.

The right of a copyright owner to revise or transform includes the right to translation, and since the turn of the century, our laws grant a copyright to a translation whether it be of a work whose original is in the public domain or under license from the copyright owner. Thus, if a foreign copyright is protected in the United States, the right of translation is also protected.

Because a variation of facts may, in copyright law, often produce many permutations of results, our discussion here will be addressed only to the problems of the free-lance translator who wishes to translate into English a work by an author who is neither a citizen of the United States nor domiciled here. The translation, it will be assumed, is intended for publication in the United States.

At the outset, we leave out unpublished foreign-language works because we may assume that a translator would hardly be dealing with unpublished works without the consent of the author. We also exclude the foreign-language work of an American author first published abroad, which, being ineligible for protection under our law, is free to be translated without copyright inhibition.[3]

If a publication in a foreign language is protected under U. S. copyright, and if the would-be translator cannot obtain a license to translate from the owner of the copyright, then it is an infringement of the copyright to make and publish a translation, or to perform any U. S. copyrighted translations of dramas, or to render translations of U. S. copyrighted lyrics, if done for profit.

However, if a would-be translator determines that there is no copyright protection for the foreign-language work in the United States, then of course he is free to make his translation. Thus, if a work is first published in Russia, then all translators are free to make and publish as many translations as the market will bear, for we have no copyright relations with Russia and no protection is accorded works first published in that country.[4]

However, with most of the rest of the civilized world, we do have some sort of copyright protection arrangements on a reciprocal basis, and these arrangements are listed in the appendix to this chapter.

Possibly the best way to determine whether a foreign-language work is protected by copyright in this country is to look—inversely—at the various ways in which United

[3] However, in those rare instances when a work is manufactured in the United States but first published abroad, it is protected by United States copyright.

[4] Copyright in the United States could, however, apparently be secured by an author of a book first published in Russia if he is a citizen of a country with which the United States *does* have copyright relations and if the work carries a good copyright notice.

States copyright protection may be received by foreign authors.

If an alien author writing in a foreign language is domiciled in the United States and if he first publishes his work in a foreign language in this country with proper notice, then he has full protection against unauthorized publication in the United States.

The more common situation derives from our copyright relations with the "proclaimed countries"–i.e., countries with which the United States has special treaties–and from the operation of the Universal Copyright Convention. In both situations, foreign authors first publish abroad in a foreign language. The degree of protection that now obtains for such foreign works, including the protection of the foreign copyright owner's translation rights, is a reflection of the treatment extended to Americans in the countries whose publications or subjects are afforded reciprocal protection under our laws. An understanding of the development of this basis for copyright protection assists in any evaluation of the operation of the present provisions of law.

From the adoption of the first federal copyright statute in 1790 until the passage of the International Copyright Act of 1891, only the works of U. S. citizens and U. S. residents were protected under our copyright statutes. Some Western European nations, during this same period, provided foreign protection for the works of their authors by means of bilateral agreements. In 1886 many of the major nations of Western Europe signed the Berne Convention for the Protection of Literary and Artistic Works. The Berne Convention operates on the principle of national treatment, so that works originating in a member country are protected in another member country. We are not parties to the Berne Convention, which in its various forms had approximately fifty adherents.

By the Act of March 3, 1891, works of foreign authors were for the first time eligible for United States copyright protection. The controlling factor in determining eligibility was the nationality of the author. If the author were a citizen or subject of a state that gave American authors the same treatment as the state's own authors, then the major statutory requirement was met. A finding by the President that a country gives to American authors the same treatment as it gives to its own subjects—what is known as "national treatment"—then results in a proclamation of the eligibility of that country's subjects to copyright.

From 1891 to 1909 there were sixteen "proclaimed countries": Belgium, France, Great Britain, Switzerland, Germany, Italy, Denmark, Portugal, Spain, Chile, Mexico, Costa Rica, the Netherlands, Cuba, Norway, and Austria.

The nature of the presidential proclamation and its legal basis were somewhat changed by the Copyright Act of 1909, which serves as the principal base for the proclamations which are in effect today. Under the 1891 Act, there were two situations justifying a proclamation, that U. S. citizens got the "national treatment"—that is, the same treatment as citizens of the proclaimed country—or that the country was a party to an international copyright agreement to which we could adhere. The 1909 Act added a further basis for a proclamation, the giving of reciprocal copyright treatment to U. S. citizens. In other words, the foreign country indicated its willingness to give approximately the same protection to our citizens' copyrights as we gave its citizens' copyrights.

The sixteen original countries proclaimed under the 1891 Act were reproclaimed under the 1909 Act, and there are now almost forty "proclaimed countries."

An author, or the copyright holder if he is not the author, who has a copyright valid in a "proclaimed country" is eligible to register his work for copyright in the Copyright Office.

Indeed, for some time it was thought that publication without proper notice in the "proclaimed country" forfeited any right to registration of copyright in our country. However, by the decision in the Heim case (Heim v. Universal Pictures Co., Inc., 154 F.2d 480, 2d Cir. 1946), the rule was established that publication in a "proclaimed country" with such notice as was there sufficient was no bar to eligibility to copyright in this country, even if such original notice was insufficient by our domestic standards. This decision opened wide the doors of eligibility. In most foreign countries, particularly those which are members of the Berne Union, no notice is needed on a publication in order to insure copyright protection. As a result of the Heim decision, the Copyright Office accepted registrations where a foreign first publication did not contain a copyright notice that met domestic American standards.

Thus one cannot depend on the absence of copyright notice or date in a foreign-produced publication as being proof of no copyright protection in this country. Of course, anything which shows that the work was originally published more than fifty-six years ago (with the exception mentioned above, of those works on which the renewal copyright was extended to December 31, 1965) places the work in the public domain, making it fair game for any translator. This result obtains because the maximum duration of copyright in this country is an original term of twenty-eight years plus a renewal of another twenty-eight years. This is so even if the copyright in the "proclaimed country" still endures. On the other hand, any work in the public domain in the "proclaimed country" is usually in the public domain in this country.

Works published abroad less than fifty-six years ago and protected under a "proclaimed country's" copyright may in some cases not be eligible for copyright protection here.

Our copyright relations with Greece began in 1932 and provide an example. If a work was published by a Greek author for the first time in 1931 or earlier and protected under Greek law, it would not be eligible for protection in the United States and would be available to any translator and his publisher. Similar situations can be found in the Addendum list of copyright relations.

If, in checking a work, one finds that it was first published in a "proclaimed country" with acceptable notice and at a time covered by the proclamation, this is not in itself sufficient evidence that United States copyright protection has in fact been given to the work. There remains the question of registration of the copyright in the Copyright Office.

To determine whether or not there has been such a registration, one must search the records published in the Catalogue of Copyright Entries. This catalog is issued at frequent intervals (usually twice each year) by the Copyright Office and is available in many libraries. If a search is unavailing and if there are grounds to suspect the existence of a domestic copyright, the next step is to request the Copyright Office to make a search. This costs a minimum of three dollars.

If an original registration more than twenty-eight years old is found, then a search to determine the existence of a renewal copyright is in order. This too can be done either by a study of the Catalogue of Copyright Entries or by instituting a search at the Copyright Office in Washington.

When the Copyright Office makes a search to determine whether there has been a registration of copyright, it does not give an opinion as to the legal significance of the facts which it reports, nor does it search or compare copies of works to determine originality or similarity. When a search is requested, the Copyright Office should be given as much information as possible as to the nature of the work: whether it is a book, an article, or a pamphlet; its title; its author or authors; its possible copyright claimant; the best guess as to year of publication or deposit.

Until 1959 the Copyright Office, following the ruling in the Heim case, accepted for registration works first published abroad without full copyright notice. Subsequent regulations of the Copyright Office call for the use of an "adequate copyright notice" on works first published abroad. This would seem to require the use of the word "Copyright" or its abbreviation or the symbol © accompanied by the year of publication and the name of the copyright owner. Thus any work first published abroad after 1959 which lacks such a copyright notice would seem to be ineligible for copyright and thus available to any translator in this country and his publisher.

The second and now more important basis for copyright protection of foreign works derives from our treaty relationships, including several multilateral international agreements.

The Universal Copyright Convention, the latest and most effective of the international agreements, was ratified by the United States in 1954 and it became effective on September 16, 1955. Two other multilateral conventions to which we became parties prior to the Universal Copyright Convention are the Mexico City Convention of 1902, to which we adhered in 1908, and the Buenos Aires Convention of 1910, to which we adhered in 1914. It was intended, through the operation of these two earlier conventions, that we establish uniform copyright relations with a number of Latin American countries. However, no United States legislation was passed to implement the Latin American conventions, and their operation in the United States is therefore somewhat cloudy and in doubt. These two Latin American conventions have never really been used to any great extent, and there is little likelihood that they will be employed very much in the future. Now that we have the Universal Copyright Convention, there is little importance attached to the earlier agreements.

With the negotiation of the Universal Copyright Convention in 1947–52, the United States moves into a new era of international protection. There is now a possibility of almost universal protection by copyright, under minimum standards and under minimum conditions, designed to give authors or copyright holders highly desirable uniform rights. Since the signing of the convention, its subsequent ratification by the United States on December 6, 1954, and its becoming effective on November 16, 1955, more than forty countries have become parties. This, of course, means that there are more than fifty non-participants in the world, including the Soviet Union. However, the Universal Copyright Convention is a major step forward, and one can expect from time to time further accessions. The treaty, by its guarantee of increased protection to authors, obviously limits the freedom of translators to translate whatever they please.

Article V of the Universal Copyright Convention deals specifically with translations and provides the author with explicit protection of his right of translation. The article contemplates the possibility of domestic legislation that would set up a mechanism providing for compulsory licensing of translation in the event that within a seven-year period no translation is made. However, the United States has never enacted such legislation, and it is highly unlikely that we will have anything approaching compulsory licensing of translation in this country.[5]

The relevant section in Article V of the Universal Copy-

[5] The phrase "compulsory license" means that a state may enact legislation which would provide for the state's issuing a license to a translator (who would then be required to pay royalties, etc.) if a translation of a work protected under Universal Copyright Convention is not published within the state's borders after seven years of such copyright protection. Though we never have accepted "compulsory licensing" in this country (except in connection with the mechanical rights in music), it is common in the patent field in practically every Western European country.

right Convention states: "Copyright shall include the exclusive right of the author to make, publish, and authorize the making and publication of translations of works protected under this Convention."

This language thus creates four exclusive rights in the author: (1) the making of a translation, (2) the publication of a translation, (3) the authorization of the making of a translation, and (4) the authorization of the publication of a translation. This would seem to indicate that a privately made translation, not for publication, would be in theory an infringement of the exclusive right of translation. The enforcement of this right is another matter.

The criteria determining protection under the Universal Copyright Convention are not as limited as in the case of "proclaimed countries." Not only do nationals or citizens of a Universal Copyright Convention country receive protection in other "Convention countries" when they first publish in their home country, but also authors of other nationalities who first publish in a "Convention country" are, with one exception, protected. The exception applies in the United States, where a work written by a U. S. citizen in a "Convention country" does not by virtue of publication in that "Convention country" alone secure protection in the United States. Under U. S. law, copyright for such works can be obtained by *ad interim* registration.

The Universal Copyright Convention and the related implementing domestic legislation now make it easier for a foreign author who first publishes in a "Convention country" to obtain American copyright protection. Copyright is obtained on first publication if the work bears a notice of copyright in an appropriate place according to a formula which allows for less deviation than is allowed for purely domestic publication. The notice must contain the symbol ©, and there appears to be no room for substitutes such as the word "Copyright" or its abbreviation "Copr.," both of which have standing under U. S. domestic law. The symbol must be accompanied by the name of the author or copyright proprietor and the year date.

Works first published with proper Universal Copyright Convention notice automatically receive copyright under our law and are protected for twenty-eight years. Registration of this copyright in our Copyright Office and deposit of copies and of a catalog card are necessary only for perfection of the right to litigate against infringers. The deposits are not obligatory and copyright exists without such registration.

However, a renewal might require registration, and it is not an automatic result of publication with proper notice. Thus, beginning in 1983, it will be important for would-be translators to ascertain whether works subject to a 1955 Universal Copyright Convention Copyright have been renewed or abandoned. Initial prompt registration will facilitate a later renewal.

One obvious result of the Convention is that in a larger number of cases there is apparently no doubt as to the existence of a valid copyright if one can accept at face value the notice of copyright. It is relevant to note that copyright applies only to new and copyrightable materials in a work, so that a work which contains materials in the public domain along with new copyrighted materials might appear to the unwary as a totally protected work. No copyright is imposed on the work in the public domain, so that a would-be translator should inquire behind the notice. This is particularly necessary with compilations of short stories in which the only new and copyrightable material may be the illustrations or new introductory or analytical materials.

The Universal Copyright Convention came into effect in the United States September 16, 1955, but this does not mean that all works first published in "Convention countries" after that date and bearing a proper notice are accorded protection here. One must consult the chart appearing in the Appendix to learn the effective date for any given country.

Because of the multiplicity of routes to copyright protection for foreign works, there are many areas in which the law is presently not a little uncertain. Suppose, for example, that a work is published in one of the fifteen Latin American countries which are parties to the Buenos Aires Convention, using this Convention's form of notice for the protection of works, "All Rights Reserved," "*Derechos Preservados*," or similar Spanish-language equivalent. It is not clear whether such a work is protected without deposit and registration in the U. S. Copyright Office. Our statutes are not clear. Such a publication is, however, entitled to protection once the proper deposit and registration have been made and a would-be translator thus is again directed to the Catalogue of Copyright Entries.

The first step in any effort to determine the status of a work first published abroad is to ascertain the country of first publication. On this basis the applicable treaty, convention, or proclamation can be identified, and it is at that point that the citizenship of the author or the language of the original may prove important. The second step is to consult the Catalogue of Copyright Entries or institute a Copyright Office search.

Although the rules and procedures for ascertaining the copyright status of foreign published works may be thus simply stated, the practical application of the rules is a good deal more complicated. The varieties of situations and the possible areas of misunderstanding may be best illustrated by examples drawn from French publications.

Our copyright relations with France began on March 3, 1891, France being one of the first "proclaimed countries." Subsequently a further proclamation for France was made on July 1, 1909, and on January 14, 1956, France became a party to the Universal Copyright Convention. Thus any French work published less than fifty-six years ago is not automatically in the public domain. Its status depends on either copyright under the Universal Copyright Convention or copyright under the procedures applicable to "proclaimed countries."

By 1850 all twelve volumes of Chateaubriand's *Mémoires d'Outre-Tombe* had been published. As part of their Pléiade series in 1951, the French publisher Gallimard published a new edition with the following notice: "*Tous droits de reproduction, de traduction et d'adaptation réservés pour tous les pays y compris l'U.R.S.S.* © 1951, *Editions Gallimard.*" If one were to depend on the copyright notice alone, and if one were unaware of the actual history of the *Mémoires*, it would seem that this work of Chateaubriand's would be protected if it were promptly registered in the United States Copyright Office. The copyright, to the extent one may be effective in the United States, in fact applies only to that material which represents the contribution of the editors as distinguished from the original work by Chateaubriand. Thus anyone may translate Chateaubriand's *Mémoires d'Outre-Tombe* into English and be free of any infringement problem as long as the material translated was written by Chateaubriand.

The same reasoning would apply to the edition of Daudet's *Contes du Lundi*, which was published with the notice, "Copyright 1954 by Librairie Hachette." Obviously these pre-1907 short stories are not protected, and anyone can make use of them for translation in the United States as long as the translation is made from the public-domain version and not from any rewritten or simplified version.

It would be similarly proper to make a translation from the Livre de Poche editions of Zola's *Germinal* or *L'Assommoir*, despite the notice: "*Tous droits réservés by Fas-*

quelle, Editeur, Paris." The works are in the public domain.

The Livre de Poche edition of Frapié's *La Maternelle* bears the notice: "*Tous droits de traduction et de reproduction réservés pour tous pays y compris la Suède, la Norvège, la Danemark et les Pays Bas.*" The printing history indicates that this edition was printed in the fourth trimester of 1959. The Universal Copyright Convention notice requirements are not met. Research shows that Frapié died in 1949 and that *La Maternelle* was published prior to his death, prior to the effective date of the Universal Copyright Convention. The copyright status thus depends on compliance with the procedures applicable to "proclaimed countries."

Although it is probably true that most works of any importance now published in France bear the Universal Copyright Convention notice, there are at hand several examples of exceptions which would appear to be in the public domain in the United States as far as copyright is defined by the Convention. These works would also appear to be ineligible for copyright registration on the strength of France's status as a "proclaimed country," for the notice may not be "adequate" as presently required by the Copyright Office. Certainty as to copyright status of the following—and other—examples could only result from a study of the Catalogue of Copyright Entries and a search of the records of the Copyright Office.

A mystery story by Martin Meroy, entitled *Menuet pour l'Assassin,* was published by Presses Internationales in 1963, with a copyright notice reading: "*Copyright by Editions des Presses Internationales. Tous droits de reproduction, traduction, adaptation, réservés pour tous pays, y compris l'U.R.S.S.*" The year of publication appears at the end of the book in the legend concerning legal deposit under French law.

Similarly Jean-Paul Sartre's magazine, *Les Temps*

Modernes, November 1961 issue, contains a number of stories and articles that might well be translated. This issue's copyright notice reads: "*Tous droits de traduction et reproduction réservés pour tous pays.*" Chances are that, barring some informal agreement to the contrary, the material may be freely translated and published.

Translators, in common with authors, share many of the other aspects of protection of the copyright laws, for a translator may copyright his work and then is eligible to protect his exclusive rights.

However, this protection is not unlimited, as may be illustrated by a translation made from the public domain. If a translation is made of a work in the public domain and copyrighted, the copyright does not preclude other original translations of the same work being copyrighted. The mode of expression of ideas is the subject of protection, and if the second translation is an original effort and if it, as is more than likely, closely resembles the earlier translation, both are still protected equally under the law. The two-translations problem resembles the situation where two photographs of the Lincoln Memorial may both be copyrighted, though little difference is apparent to the naked eye. The original effort in each instance is what counts.

The translator can benefit greatly from the copyright laws whether he translates with express authorization or from the public domain. It is to the translator's advantage to recognize that the momentary frustration which the absence of a reply to a letter requesting permission to translate engenders is no excuse for a blatant disregard of the author's rights. The copyright laws on balance are the best available device for the protection of creative artists. Even though in some cases it may not profit to prosecute infringers, translators can render service by foregoing the temptation to exercise their skill illegally on someone else's creation.

ADDENDUM

By virtue of presidential proclamations, treaties, and conventions, the United States has established copyright relations with various other countries. This appendix is an attempt to present a complete and annotated list of those countries.

Proclamations by the President of the United States extending copyright protection, upon compliance with the provisions of the United States copyright law, to the works of foreign authors prior to July 1, 1909, were issued pursuant to section 13 of the Act of March 3, 1891 (26 Stat. 1106) and those issued subsequent to July 1, 1909, were issued under the provisions of sections 1(e) and 8(b) of the Act of March 4, 1909 (35 Stat. 1075) and as later amended. Section 8(b) was amended by the Act of December 18, 1919 (41 Stat. 368) and the Act of September 25, 1941 (55 Stat. 732). Those sections of the Act of March 4, 1909, as amended, became sections 1(e) and 9(b), respectively, of Title 17 of the United States Code when it was codified and enacted into positive law by the Act of July 30, 1947 (61 Stat. 652). A number of the proclamations were preceded or accompanied by exchanges of diplomatic notes which served as the basis for their issuance.

The period for compliance with the conditions and formalities prescribed by the copyright law was extended by proclamation with respect to certain works in the case of a number of countries because of the disruption or suspension of facilities essential for such compliance during World War I and World War II. In the case of World War I this period was extended by proclamations issued under the Act of December 18, 1919 (41 Stat. 368) to fifteen months after the proclamation of peace, as to works published after August 1, 1914, and before the proclamation of peace. In the case of World War II, this period was extended by proclamations issued under the Act of September 25, 1941 (55 Stat. 732) until such time as terminated or suspended, either by the terms of the proclamation itself or by the issuance of a subsequent proclamation. A number of the proclamations issued under the 1919 Act and all of the proclamations issued under the 1941 Act or section 9(b) of Title 17 of the United States Code refer to rights previously granted.

KEY TO SYMBOLS

Proclamations

P Proclamation issued pursuant to section 13 of the Act of March 3, 1891, Section 8(b) of the Act of March 4, 1909, and as amended, or Section 9(b) of Title 17 of the United States Code.

Pm Proclamation including mechanical reproduction rights for music under Section 1(e) of the United States copyright law.

Px Proclamation providing an extension of time under the Act of December 18, 1919, for compliance with the conditions and formalities prescribed by the United States copyright law.

Pmx Proclamation specifically including provisions similar to those contained in both "Pm" and "Px" proclamations.

Pxx Proclamation providing an extension of time under the Act of September 25, 1941, for compliance with the conditions and formalities prescribed by the United States copyright law.

Po Proclamation specifically issued for the purpose of terminating a proclamation issued under the Act of September 25, 1941.

Treaties and Conventions

BAC Buenos Aires Convention. Convention on literary and artistic copyright signed at the Fourth International Conference of American States at Buenos Aires August 11, 1910.

MCC Mexico City Convention. Convention on literary and artistic copyrights signed at the Second International Conference of American States at Mexico January 27, 1902.

UCC Universal Copyright Convention. Done at Geneva September 6, 1952.

C Bilateral convention.

Cm Bilateral convention including provisions covering mechanical reproduction rights for music.

Proclamations, Treaties, and Conventions Establishing Copyright Relations between The United States and Other Countries

Country	Document	Date of document	Date effective	Reference
Andorra	UCC	Sept. 6, 1952	Sept. 16, 1955	6 UST 2731
Argentina	Pm	Aug. 23, 1934	Aug. 23, 1934	49 Stat. 3413
	BAC	Aug. 11, 1910	Apr. 19, 1950	38 Stat. 1785
	UCC	Sept. 6, 1952	Feb. 13, 1958	6 UST 2731
Australia[1]	Pm	Apr. 3, 1918	Mar. 15, 1918	40 Stat. 1764
	Pxx[2]	Dec. 29, 1949	Dec. 29, 1949	64 Stat. A385
Austria[3]	P	Sept. 20, 1907	Sept. 20, 1907	35 Stat. 2155
	P	Apr. 9, 1910	July 1, 1909	36 Stat. 2685
	Px	May 25, 1922	May 25, 1922	42 Stat. 2273
	Pm	Mar. 11, 1925	Aug. 1, 1920	44 Stat. 2571
	UCC	Sept. 6, 1952	July 2, 1957	6 UST 2731
Belgium	P	July 1, 1891	July 1, 1891	27 Stat. 981
	P	Apr. 9, 1910	July 1, 1909	36 Stat. 2685
	Pm	June 14, 1911	July 1, 1909	37 Stat. 1688
	UCC	Sept. 6, 1952	Aug. 31, 1960	6 UST 2731

Bolivia	BAC	Aug. 11, 1910	May 15, 1914	38 Stat. 1785
Brazil	BAC	Aug. 11, 1910	Aug. 31, 1915	38 Stat. 1785
	Pm	Apr. 2, 1957	Apr. 2, 1957	22 F.R.2305
	UCC	Sept. 6, 1952	Jan. 13, 1960	6 UST 2731
Cambodia	UCC	Sept. 6, 1952	Sept. 16, 1955	6 UST 2731
Canada[1]	Pm	Dec. 27, 1923	Jan. 1, 1924	43 Stat. 1932
	UCC	Sept. 6, 1952	Aug. 10, 1962	6 UST 2731
Chile	P	May 25, 1896	May 25, 1896	29 Stat. 880
	P	Apr. 9, 1910	July 1, 1909	36 Stat. 2685
	Pm	Nov. 18, 1925	July 1, 1925	44 Stat. 2590
	BAC	Aug. 11, 1910	June 14, 1955	38 Stat. 1785
	UCC	Sept. 6, 1952	Sept. 16, 1955	6 UST 2731
China	T[4]	Oct. 8, 1903	Jan. 13, 1904	33 Stat. 2208
	T[4]	Nov. 4, 1946	Nov. 30, 1948	63 Stat. 1299
Colombia	BAC	Aug. 11, 1910	Dec. 23, 1936	38 Stat. 1785
Costa Rica	P	Oct. 19, 1899	Oct. 19, 1899	31 Stat. 1955
	P	Apr. 9, 1910	July 1, 1909	36 Stat. 2685
	MCC	Jan. 27, 1902	June 30, 1908	35 Stat. 1934
	BAC	Aug. 11, 1910	Nov. 30, 1916	38 Stat. 1785
	UCC	Sept. 6, 1952	Sept. 16, 1955	6 UST 2731

Proclamations, Treaties, and Conventions (Continued)

Country	*Document*	*Date of document*	*Date effective*	*Reference*
Cuba	P	Nov. 17, 1903	Nov. 17, 1903	33 Stat. 2324
	P	Apr. 9, 1910	July 1, 1909	36 Stat. 2685
	Pm	Nov. 27, 1911	May 29, 1911	37 Stat. 1721
	UCC	Sept. 6, 1952	June 15, 1957	6 UST 2731
Czechoslovakia	Pm	Apr. 27, 1927	Mar. 1, 1927	45 Stat. 2906
	UCC	Sept. 6, 1952	Jan. 6, 1960	6 UST 2731
Danzig	Pm	Apr. 7, 1934	Apr. 7, 1934	48 Stat. 1737
Denmark[5]	P	May 8, 1893	May 8, 1893	28 Stat. 1219
	P	Apr. 9, 1910	July 1, 1909	36 Stat. 2685
	Pmx	Dec. 9, 1920	Dec. 9, 1920	41 Stat. 1810
	Pxx	Feb. 4, 1952	Feb. 4, 1952	66 Stat. C20
	UCC	Sept. 6, 1952	Feb. 9, 1962	6 UST 2731
Dominican Republic	MCC	Jan. 27, 1902	June 30, 1908	35 Stat. 1934
	BAC	Aug. 11, 1910	Oct. 31, 1912	38 Stat. 1785
Ecuador	BAC	Aug. 11, 1910	Aug. 31, 1914	38 Stat. 1785
	UCC	Sept. 6, 1952	June 5, 1957	6 UST 2731
El Salvador	MCC	Jan. 27, 1902	June 30, 1908	35 Stat. 1934

Finland	Pm	Dec. 15, 1928	Jan. 1, 1929	45 Stat. 2980
	Pxx	Nov. 16, 1951	Nov. 16, 1951	66 Stat. C5
	UCC	Sept. 6, 1962	Apr. 16, 1963	6 UST 2731
France[6]	P	July 1, 1891	July 1, 1891	27 Stat. 981
	P	Apr. 9, 1910	July 1, 1909	36 Stat. 2685
	Pm	May 24, 1918	May 24, 1918	40 Stat. 1784
	Pxx	Mar. 27, 1947	Mar. 27, 1947	61 Stat. 1057
	Po	May 26, 1950	Dec. 29, 1950	64 Stat. A413
	UCC	Sept. 6, 1952	Jan. 14, 1956	6 UST 2731
Germany[3]	P	Apr. 15, 1892	Apr. 15, 1892	27 Stat. 1021
	P	Apr. 9, 1910	July 1, 1909	36 Stat. 2685
	Pm	Dec. 8, 1910	Dec. 8, 1910	36 Stat. 2761
	Px	May 25, 1922	May 25, 1922	42 Stat. 2271
Germany, Fed. Rep.	UCC	Sept. 6, 1952	Sept. 16, 1955	6 UST 2731
Ghana	UCC	Sept. 6, 1952	Aug. 22, 1962	6 UST 2731
Greece	Pm	Feb. 23, 1932	Mar. 1, 1932	47 Stat. 2502
Guatemala	MCC	Jan. 27, 1902	June 30, 1908	35 Stat. 1934
	BAC	Aug. 11, 1910	Mar. 28, 1913	38 Stat. 1785
Haiti	BAC	Aug. 11, 1910	Nov. 27, 1919	38 Stat. 1785
	UCC	Sept. 6, 1952	Sept. 16, 1955	6 UST 2731
Holy See	UCC	Sept. 6, 1952	Sept. 16, 1955	6 UST 2731

Proclamations, Treaties, and Conventions (Continued)

Country	*Document*	*Date of document*	*Date effective*	*Reference*
Honduras	MCC	Jan. 27, 1902	June 30, 1908	35 Stat. 1934
	BAC	Aug. 11, 1910	Apr. 27, 1914	38 Stat. 1785
Hungary[3]	Cm[7]	Jan. 30, 1912	Oct. 16, 1912	37 Stat. 1631
	Px	June 3, 1922	June 3, 1922	42 Stat. 2277
	T[8,9]	Feb. 10, 1947	Sept. 15, 1947	61 Stat. 2065
Iceland	UCC	Sept. 6, 1952	Dec. 18, 1956	6 UST 2731
India[1,10]	Pm	Oct. 21, 1954	Aug. 15, 1947	19 F.R. 6967
	UCC	Sept. 6, 1952	Jan. 21, 1958	6 UST 2731
Ireland[1]	Pm[11]	Sept. 28, 1929	Oct. 1, 1929	46 Stat. 3005
	UCC	Sept. 6, 1952	Jan. 20, 1959	6 UST 2731
Israel[12]	Pm	May 4, 1950	May 15, 1948	64 Stat. A402
	UCC	Dec. 16, 1952	Sept. 16, 1955	6 UST 2731
Italy	P[13]	Oct. 31, 1892	Oct. 31, 1892	27 Stat. 1043
	P	Apr. 9, 1910	July 1, 1909	36 Stat. 2685
	Pm[13]	May 1, 1915	May 1, 1915	39 Stat. 1725
	Px	June 3, 1922	June 3, 1922	42 Stat. 2276
	T[9,14]	Feb. 10, 1947	Sept. 15, 1947	61 Stat. 1245
	Pxx	Dec. 12, 1951	Dec. 12, 1951	66 Stat. C13
	UCC	Sept. 6, 1952	Jan. 24, 1957	6 UST 2731

Japan	C[15]	Nov. 10, 1905	May 10, 1906	34 Stat. 2890
	C[16]	May 19, 1908	Aug. 16, 1908	35 Stat. 2044
	T[17]	Sept. 8, 1951	Apr. 28, 1952	3 UST 3169
	Pm[18]	Nov. 10, 1953	Apr. 28, 1952	5 UST 118
	UCC	Jan. 3, 1953	Apr. 28, 1956	6 UST 2731
Korea	C[19]	May 19, 1908	Aug. 16, 1908	35 Stat. 2041
Laos	UCC	Sept. 6, 1952	Sept. 16, 1955	6 UST 2731
Lebanon	UCC	Sept. 6, 1952	Oct. 17, 1959	6 UST 2731
Liberia	UCC	Sept. 6, 1952	July 27, 1956	6 UST 2731
Liechtenstein	UCC	Sept. 6, 1952	Jan. 22, 1959	6 UST 2731
Luxembourg	P	June 29, 1910	June 29, 1910	36 Stat. 2716
	Pm	June 14, 1911	June 29, 1910	37 Stat. 1689
	UCC	Sept. 6, 1952	Oct. 15, 1955	6 UST 2731
Mexico	P	Feb. 27, 1896	Feb. 27, 1896	29 Stat. 877
	P	Apr. 9, 1910	July 1, 1909	36 Stat. 2685
	UCC	Sept. 6, 1952	May 12, 1957	6 UST 2731
Monaco	Pm	Oct. 15, 1952	Oct. 15, 1952	67 Stat. C16
	UCC	Sept. 6, 1952	Sept. 16, 1955	6 UST 2731
Netherlands and Possessions[20]	P	Nov. 20, 1899	Nov. 20, 1899	31 Stat. 1961
	P	Apr. 9, 1910	July 1, 1909	36 Stat. 2685
	Pm	Feb. 26, 1923	Oct. 2, 1922	42 Stat. 2297

PROCLAMATIONS, TREATIES, AND CONVENTIONS (Continued)

Country	*Document*	*Date of document*	*Date effective*	*Reference*
New Zealand[1]	Pm	Feb. 9, 1917	Dec. 1, 1916	39 Stat. 1815
	Px	May 25, 1922	May 25, 1922	42 Stat. 2274
	Pxx	Apr. 24, 1947	Apr. 24, 1947	61 Stat. 1065
	Po	May 26, 1950	Dec. 29, 1950	64 Stat. A414
Nicaragua	MCC	Jan. 27, 1902	June 30, 1908	35 Stat. 1934
	BAC	Aug. 11, 1910	Dec. 15, 1913	38 Stat. 1785
	UCC	Sept. 6, 1952	Aug. 16, 1961	6 UST 2731
Nigeria	UCC	Sept. 6, 1952	Feb. 14, 1962	6 UST 2731
Norway	P	July 1, 1905	July 1, 1905	34 Stat. 3111
	P	Apr. 9, 1910	July 1, 1909	36 Stat. 2685
	Pm	June 14, 1911	Sept. 9, 1910	37 Stat. 1687
	UCC	Sept. 6, 1952	Jan. 23, 1963	6 UST 2731
Pakistan	UCC	Sept. 6, 1952	Sept. 16, 1955	6 UST 2731
Palestine (excluding Trans-Jordan)	Pm	Sept. 29, 1933	Oct. 1, 1933	48 Stat. 1713
	Pxx[12]	Mar. 10, 1944	Mar. 10, 1944	58 Stat. 1129
	Po[12]	May 26, 1950	Dec. 29, 1950	64 Stat. A412
Panama	BAC	Aug. 11, 1910	Nov. 25, 1913	38 Stat. 1785
	UCC	Sept. 6, 1952	Oct. 17, 1962	6 UST 2731

Paraguay	BAC	Aug. 11, 1910	Sept. 20, 1917	38 Stat. 1785
	UCC	Sept. 6, 1952	March 11, 1962	6 UST 2731
Peru	BAC	Aug. 11, 1910	Apr. 30, 1920	38 Stat. 1785
Philippines	Pm	Oct. 21, 1948	Oct. 21, 1948	62 Stat. 1568
	UCC[21]	Sept. 6, 1952		6 UST 2731
Poland	Pm	Feb. 14, 1927	Feb. 16, 1927	44 Stat. 2634
Portugal	P	July 20, 1893	July 20, 1893	28 Stat. 1222
	P	Apr. 9, 1910	July 1, 1909	36 Stat. 2685
	UCC	Sept. 6, 1952	Dec. 25, 1956	6 UST 2731
Rumania	Pm[22]	May 14, 1928	May 14, 1928	45 Stat. 2949
	T[9,23]	Feb. 10, 1947	Sept. 15, 1947	61 Stat. 1757
Spain[5]	P[24]	July 10, 1895	July 10, 1895	29 Stat. 871
	P	Apr. 9, 1910	July 1, 1909	36 Stat. 2685
	Pm	Oct. 10, 1934	Oct. 10, 1934	49 Stat. 3420
	UCC	Sept. 6, 1952	Sept. 16, 1955	6 UST 2731
Sweden	P	May 26, 1911	June 1, 1911	37 Stat. 1682
	Pm	Feb. 27, 1920	Feb. 1, 1920	41 Stat. 1787
	UCC	Sept. 6, 1952	July 1, 1961	6 UST 2731
Switzerland	P	July 1, 1891	July 1, 1891	27 Stat. 981
	P	Apr. 9, 1910	July 1, 1909	36 Stat. 2685
	Pm	Nov. 22, 1924	July 1, 1923	43 Stat. 1976
	UCC	Sept. 6, 1952	Mar. 30, 1956	6 UST 2731

Proclamations, Treaties, and Conventions (Continued)

Country	Document	Date of document	Date effective	Reference
Thailand	T[25]	Dec. 16, 1920	Sept. 1, 1921	42 Stat. 1928
	T[25]	Nov. 13, 1937	Oct. 1, 1938	53 Stat. 1731
Tunisia	P	Oct. 4, 1912	Oct. 4, 1912	37 Stat. 1765
Union of South Africa[1]	Pm	June 26, 1924	July 1, 1924	43 Stat. 1957
United Kingdom	UCC	Sept. 6, 1952	Sept. 27, 1957	6 UST 2731
United Kingdom and Possessions[1]	P	July 1, 1891	July 1, 1891	27 Stat. 981
	P	Apr. 9, 1910	July 1, 1909	36 Stat. 2685
United Kingdom and the British Dominions, Colonies and Possessions with the exception of Canada, Australia, New Zealand, South Africa and Newfoundland[1]	Pm	Jan. 1, 1915	Jan. 1, 1915	38 Stat. 2044
	Pmx	Apr. 10, 1920	Feb. 2, 1920	41 Stat. 1790
United Kingdom, certain British Territories[1] and Palestine[12]	Pxx	Mar. 10, 1944	Mar. 10, 1944	58 Stat. 1129
	Po	May 26, 1950	Dec. 29, 1950	64 Stat. A412
Uruguay	BAC	Aug. 11, 1910	Dec. 17, 1919	38 Stat. 1785

References:

[1] The proclamations of July 1, 1891 and April 9, 1910 apply to "Great Britain and the British possessions", but the proclamations of January 1, 1915 and April 10, 1920 specifically except Australia, Canada, Newfoundland, New Zealand and the Union of South Africa. The proclamations of March 10, 1944 and May 26, 1950 enumerate the various British territories to which they apply, excluding the areas specifically excepted in the proclamations of 1915 and 1920. Proclamations establishing individual copyright relations with Australia, Canada, Ireland, New Zealand, Palestine, and the Union of South Africa are listed separately. (See also footnotes 2, 11, 12.) The proclamation of December 27, 1923 regarding Canada is considered as applying to Newfoundland at the present time.

The copyright proclamations of July 1, 1891, April 9, 1910, January 1, 1915, April 10, 1920, and March 10, 1944 regarding Great Britain and possessions each applied when issued to the areas now within the boundaries of Burma, Ceylon, India, and Pakistan. See footnote 10 with respect to India. No announcement has been made as to the application of the proclamations to Burma, Ceylon, and Pakistan since they acquired their new status.

[2] The proclamation of December 29, 1949 extends for one year from its date the period of time for compliance by citizens of Australia with the conditions and formalities prescribed by the copyright law of the United States.

[3] The United States entered into treaties restoring friendly relations with Austria, Germany, and Hungary at Vienna on August 24, 1921 (42 Stat. 1946; TS 659); at Berlin on August 25, 1921 (42 Stat. 1939; TS 658) and at Budapest on August 29, 1921 (42 Stat. 1951; TS 610), respectively. By virtue of these treaties the United States became entitled to the benefits of the provisions relative to copyright protection in the treaties of peace signed by Austria, Germany and Hungary at Saint-Germain-en-Laye on September 10, 1919, at Versailles on June 28, 1919, and at Trianon on June 4, 1920, respectively. (See also footnote 7.)

[4] The Treaty of Friendship, Commerce and Navigation (Art. IX) together with the Protocol (par. 5) signed at Nanking November 4, 1946, and the reservation and understandings in the ratification by the United States (TIAS 1871) govern present copyright relations between the United States and China. Although Article XXIX of this Treaty lists the earlier Treaty as to Commercial Relations signed at Shanghai October 8, 1903 (33 Stat. 2208, TS 430) as superseded by the 1946 Treaty, the

ratification by the United States provides in part that the 1946 Treaty is subject to the following reservation and understandings: "The Government of the United States of America does not accept Section 5 (c) of the Protocol relating to protection against translations of literary and artistic works, and with the understanding that United States interests in this respect will be interpreted in accordance with the provisions of the Treaty as to Commercial Relations signed at Shanghai, October 8, 1903, until further negotiations and agreement concerning translations are forthcoming."

[5] Treaties and Conventions containing provisions relative to copyright protection in territories ceded to the United States are not included in this table: for example, the Treaty of Peace with Spain signed at Paris December 10, 1898 (30 Stat. 1754; TS 343), Art. XIII (see also footnote 25); and the Convention with Denmark for the Cession to the United States of the Danish West Indies, signed at New York, August 4, 1916 (39 Stat. 1706; TS 629), Art. 9.

[6] The Department of State has made no announcement as to the application of the proclamations of July 1, 1891, April 9, 1910, May 24, 1918, and March 27, 1947 to Cambodia, Laos, and Viet-Nam.

[7] Copyright Convention signed at Budapest January 30, 1912 (TS 571). This Convention was continued in force following World War I by notice given by the United States on May 27, 1922 to Hungary in pursuance of Article 224 of the Treaty of Trianon concluded on June 4, 1920 (III Redmond 3539), to the benefits of which the United States became entitled by the Treaty of August 29, 1921 establishing friendly relations between the United States and Hungary (42 Stat. 1951; TS 660). The Convention of 1912 was kept in force or revived following World War II by notice given on March 9, 1948 by the United States to Hungary pursuant to Article 10 of the Treaty of Peace with Hungary (61 Stat. 2065; Department of State Bulletin March 21, 1948; p. 382).

[8] Treaty of Peace with Hungary (Annex IV A) dated at Paris February 10, 1947 (TIAS 1651).

[9] Except with respect to rights of third parties, the provisions relating to protection of copyright in the annexes to the Treaties of Peace with Hungary, Italy, and Rumania dated at Paris February 10, 1947, are bilateral in character. For example, the provisions of Annex IV A of the Treaty of Peace with Hungary relate, in general, to copyright relations between Hungary, on the one part, and each of the other ratifying or adhering States, on the other part. Those provisions do not pertain to copyright re-

lations between those other States, except for third party rights (see also footnotes 13 and 19). Annex IV of the Treaty of Peace with Bulgaria dated at Paris February 10, 1947 (61 Stat. 1915; TIAS 1650) contains similar provisions; however, there are no general copyright relations between the United States and Bulgaria.

[10] The proclamation of October 21, 1954 affirms the existence of copyright relations with India after August 15, 1947 (the effective date of the Indian Independence Act), as before that date (see footnote 1).

[11] The Department of State has determined that the entry into force on April 18, 1949 of the Republic of Ireland Act had no effect upon the proclamation of September 28, 1929 regarding the Irish Free State (Eire). Copyright relations with Ireland are therefore governed by that proclamation (see also footnote 1).

[12] The proclamations of March 10, 1944 and May 26, 1950 regarding Great Britain and possessions, also specifically refer to Palestine, excluding Trans-Jordan.

[13] The exchanges of notes between the United States and Italy, on the basis of which the proclamations of October 31, 1892 and May 1, 1915 were issued, were the subject of a note delivered on March 12, 1948 to the Italian Foreign Office by the American Embassy at Rome with respect to prewar bilateral treaties and other international agreements which the United States desired to keep in force or revive pursuant to Article 44 of the Treaty of Peace with Italy. The note stated in part "that the Government of the United States of America wishes to include the reciprocal copyright arrangement between the United States and Italy effected pursuant to the exchange of notes signed at Washington October 28, 1892 and the exchange of notes signed at Washington September 2, 1914, February 12, March 4 and March 11, 1915, among the prewar bilateral treaties and other international agreements with Italy which the United States desires to keep in force or revive. Accordingly, it is understood that the aforementioned arrangement will continue in force and that the Government of each country will extend to the nationals of the other country treatment as favorable with respect to copyright as was contemplated at the time the arrangement was entered into by the two countries". (Department of State Bulletin, April 4, 1948, p. 455.)

[14] Treaty of Peace with Italy (Annex XV A) dated at Paris January 10, 1947 (TIAS 1648).

[15] Copyright convention, signed at Tokyo November 10, 1905 (TS 450).

This convention is considered as having been abrogated on

April 22, 1953, pursuant to the provisions of Article 7 of the Treaty of Peace with Japan signed at San Francisco September 8, 1951 (TIAS 2490), since it was not included in the notification which was given on behalf of the United States Government to the Japanese Government on April 22, 1953, indicating the prewar bilateral treaties or conventions which the United States wished to continue in force or revive.

[16] Convention between the United States and Japan for reciprocal protection of inventions, designs, trademarks and copyrights in China and other countries where either contracting party may exercise extraterritorial jurisdiction, signed at Washington May 19, 1908 (TS 507).

This convention is considered as having been abrogated on April 22, 1953, pursuant to the provisions of Article 7 of the Treaty of Peace with Japan signed at San Francisco September 8, 1951 (TIAS 2490), since it was not included in the notification which was given on behalf of the United States Government to the Japanese Government on April 22, 1953, indicating the prewar bilateral treaties or conventions which the United States wished to continue in force or revive.

[17] Treaty of Peace with Japan (Articles 12, 14 and 15) signed at San Francisco September 8, 1951 (TIAS 2490). (See also footnotes 15, 16 and 19.)

[18] The proclamation of November 10, 1953 extends benefits under the copyright law for a period of four years from the coming into force of the Treaty of Peace with Japan (TIAS 2490). That period expired April 28, 1956.

[19] Copyright Convention with Japan for reciprocal protection in Korea of inventions, designs, trademarks and copyrights signed at Washington May 19, 1908 (TS 506).

This convention is considered as having been abrogated on April 22, 1953, pursuant to the provisions of Article 7 of the Treaty of Peace with Japan signed at San Francisco September 8, 1951 (TIAS 2490), since it was not included in the notification which was given on behalf of the United States Government to the Japanese Government on April 22, 1953, indicating the prewar bilateral treaties or conventions which the United States wished to continue in force or revive.

[20] The Department of State has made no announcement as to the application of the proclamations of November 20, 1899, April 9, 1910 and February 26, 1923 to Indonesia since it acquired its new status.

[21] An instrument of accession was deposited by the Philippine Government August 19, 1955. In a communication received by the State Department January 17, 1956, UNESCO stated that

by a note dated November 14, 1955, the Philippine Government informed the Director General that "the President of the . . . Philippines has directed the withdrawal of the . . . accession . . . to the Universal Copyright Convention prior to the date of November 19, 1955, at which time the Convention would become effective" for the Philippines. The Director General notified the Philippine Government that he "proposed to submit their communication to the States concerned, upon whom it is incumbent to declare what legal inference they intend to draw from it."

[22] In a note delivered February 26, 1948 to the Rumanian Minister for Foreign Affairs by the American Minister at Bucharest with respect to prewar bilateral treaties and other international agreements which the United States desired to keep in force or revive pursuant to Article 10 of the Treaty of Peace with Rumania (see footnotes 9 and 24), the following statement was made regarding the proclamation of May 14, 1928 and the exchange of notes on which it is based: "It shall be understood that the reciprocal copyright arrangement between the United States and Rumania effected pursuant to the exchange of notes signed at Bucharest May 13 and October 13, 1928 and at Washington May 12 and 19, 1928 and the proclamation issued May 14, 1928 by the President of the United States of America will continue in force." (Department of State Bulletin, March 14, 1948, p. 356).

[23] Treaty of Peace with Rumania, dated at Paris, February 10, 1947 (TIAS 1649).

[24] The proclamation of July 10, 1895 regarding Spain was based upon an arrangement between the United States and Spain effected by an exchange of notes signed at Washington July 6 and 15, 1895. An agreement restoring the arrangement of July 6 and 15, 1895 was effected by an exchange of notes signed at Madrid January 29 and November 18 and 26, 1902 (II Malloy 1710), following the Treaty of Peace between the United States and Spain signed at Paris December 10, 1898 (30 Stat. 1754; TS 343). The latter treaty also contains in Article XIII the following provisions: "The rights of property secured by copyrights and patents acquired by Spaniards in the Island of Cuba, and in Porto Rico, the Philippines and other ceded territories, at the time of the exchange of ratifications of this treaty, shall continue to be respected. Spanish scientific, literary and artistic works, not subversive of public order in the territories in question, shall continue to be admitted free of duty into such territories, for the period of ten years, to be reckoned from the date of the exchange of ratifications of this treaty."

[25] Treaty of friendship, commerce and navigation, protocol and exchanges of notes, signed at Bangkok November 13, 1937 (Art. 9 of the Treaty) (TS 940). This treaty replaces the treaty of friendship, commerce and navigation between the United States and Thailand signed at Washington December 16, 1920 (TS 655), Article XII of which contains provisions relating to copyright protection.

WERNER WINTER

Translation as Political Action

Translation can serve a variety of purposes: broadening of literary experience, enrichment of a culture, enrichment of an individual's life. But even more prominent would be the mere conveying of information.

Particularly fascinating is the comparatively neglected use of translation as a tool in political strategy.

Of course, we all are aware that translation helps to remove barriers between peoples, and is therefore an important instrument for international cooperation and well-being. Indeed, one might even claim that international understanding is a function of successful translation.

But to dwell on these matters would lead to a repetition of commonplaces, and I would prefer to draw attention to a case in which neither the content nor the quality of a translation matters, but the mere fact of translation itself.

The Ministry of Culture of the Soviet Union issues, for the use of librarians in the USSR, a weekly inventory of books just published or about to be published.[1] Among its features are statistical reports on book production in certain fields and these reports make fascinating reading.

We find, for instance, that in the Soviet Union, during the years 1918–58, works of Pushkin have appeared in 1,977 editions in 84 languages with a total of 89,266,000 copies. During the same period, Gogol was printed 793 times in 54 languages and in 33,500,000 copies; Gorki in

[1] This bulletin, *Novye knigi,* is a most welcome aid for anybody faced with the task of building up a Russian library, particularly in view of the organization of the Soviet publication and distribution system. In addition to the bibliographical data, the bulletin carries regularly a number of feature articles.

2,420 editions, 77 languages, and 91,918,000 copies. Of course, these figures are low compared with Stalin's astronomic total of 711,831,000 copies in 102 languages printed in 1918–59; but they compare very well with the figures reported for Marx and Engels (1918–59: 1991 editions, 70 languages, 72,862,000 copies) and provide striking testimony to the continuing strong interest of the reading public in the works of the great Russian heritage. To be sure, the figures are not the reflection of a free interplay of demand and supply; and yet the mere manifestation of the literature as an important factor on the Soviet scene is impressive.

Alongside Russian writers, authors from abroad provide a significant part of the Soviet reader's fare. A few figures for writers of two Western European countries will illustrate the point. Voltaire, 32 items, 7 languages, 1,657,000 copies; Balzac, 221 items, 17 languages, 11,905,000 copies; Anatole France, 177 items, 15 languages, 5,888,000 copies; Romain Rolland, 196 items, 21 languages, 7,316,000 copies; Goethe, 103 items, 12 languages, 2,000,000 copies; Schiller, 111 items, 18 languages, 1,829,000 copies; Jacob and Wilhelm Grimm, 209 items, 43 languages, 18,023,000 copies.

For American fiction, the figures for 1918–April 1959 show 2,699 works by 226 authors translated into 50 languages with a total of 87,900,000 copies; 53,300,000 copies were published after World War II. The six most-published authors are: Jack London, 20,300,000 copies; Mark Twain, 10,600,000; Theodore Dreiser, 9,100,000; Upton Sinclair, 4,200,000; J. F. Cooper, 4,100,000; O. Henry, 4,000,000 copies. The political slant is obvious, but it should be noted that Poe reaches 900,000 copies, Longfellow, 672,000, and Whitman, 300,000.

Similarly impressive figures are given for other major literatures. A strong concentration on nations of the Soviet orbit can be noted: Czechoslovakia, 72 authors, 464 items, 36 languages, 24,200,000 copies; Hungary, 45 authors, 457 items, 30 languages, 12,607,000 copies; Bulgaria, 47 authors, 263 items, 21 languages, 10,876,000 copies. The deliberate effort to introduce writers from 'fraternal nations' is clear if one compares the totals for Czechoslovakia and Bulgaria with the subtotals for the years 1946–58 and 1946–59 only: 21,077,000 and 10,597,000 copies represent 87.1% and 97.4% of the total output. Equally instructive are the figures available for Asian countries of the Communist camp. China, 1918–59: Total number of translations (of which 26,986,000 belong to *belles lettres*): 872 items, 36,000,000 copies; of these, 696 items with 32,744,000 copies appeared in the years 1950–59. Korea: Translations up to 1958: 100 items in 21 languages and 5,605,000 copies; of these, as many as 98 titles and 5,604,000 copies appeared during 1946–58. The totals for Vietnam and Mongolia are, as of 1959, 1,145,000 and 831,000 copies respectively.

Two things are remarkable in these figures. First, the concentration of publication efforts in the post-war years. Second, *belles lettres* outweigh every other type of publication by an overwhelming margin, and this is true of Western literature as well as that of the satellite countries. Only in the case of China do the figures for non-fictional writing exceed 10% of the total: here as many as 8,403,000 of the total of 36,000,000 are copies of socio-political works. This clearly indicates the status of Chinese contributions to the Communist ideology; works by Mao Tse Tung alone appeared in 2,631,000 copies. Apart from this exception, the importance of non-Soviet political writings, if measured by figures alone, can be considered marginal. Similarly low are the figures for non-political technical literature. To give an example, a total of 252,000 copies of technical treatises is listed as translated from Czech (against a figure of 24,200,000 in *belles lettres*, as pointed out above). The same predominance of fiction over non-fiction can be observed for American books: fiction makes up more than 90% of the total output. True, the figures for non-fiction remain impressive: socio-political writings, 159 items, 3,300,000 copies; science, 313 items, 2,600,000 copies; etc. (and of course, the potential public for technical writings is bound to be much smaller than for fiction so that the impact of small editions in medicine, agriculture, art, etc., can be considered to be relatively powerful.) Still, the much stronger preference for literature proper is worth attention.

Translations from Asian (and African) literatures are not limited to countries within the Soviet Union's own camp. Figures available for non-communist areas are equally impressive: India, 288 editions of 29 writers, translated into 28 languages and printed in 11,400,000 copies; Arab countries, 110 items, 27 languages, 4,100,000 copies; Iran, 72 items, 8 languages, 1,066,000 copies. Afghanistan, Indonesia, and Burma are represented with 514,000, 456,-000, and 110,000 copies respectively. The most remarkable point about these translations is their timing: the first works by Afghan, Indonesian, and Burmese writers began to appear in 1955. If one allows for a period of about two years for the translation and publication process, one arrives at the year 1953 as the probable time when these translation programs were initiated—i.e., immediately after Stalin's death when Soviet policy took on the more flexible, imaginative character which has affected international developments ever since.

We have, that is, a repetition of what happened with literature from the satellite countries in the years right after the war. When a certain area becomes a focal point of Soviet interest, the works of its writers become the object of concentrated translation efforts. The coverage is remarkably wide—and leftist leanings are by no means a prerequisite for an author to be translated, though of course preference is given to ideologically acceptable writers (at times, acceptability may derive just from the twist of a commentary attached to the work). Among the writers included are some of the great names in world literature; for example, among Iranian poets, Omar Khayyam has been issued in 137,000 copies, Saadi in 74,000, Hafiz in 111,000. Petöfi, a European writer, appeared in 671,000 copies.

It may be hazardous on the basis of the data available here to propose an explanation for what appears to be well-planned policy. Still, it would seem that these intensive translation efforts are extremely well-calculated propaganda moves. To take works of the literature of a nation and to make them available to members of another culture, is to take that nation's literature, that nation's culture, and that nation itself seriously. Such an effort, however ulterior its motives, is bound to impress the cultured strata of that country much more deeply than any attempt from an outside country to export its own literature. For the attitude of the taker will be interpreted as one of interest and respect, that of the giver as superiority and contempt. And it seems safe to assume that the long-ranged impact of these Soviet moves may be much more powerful than those efforts designed to tell people in Asia and Africa about America and the West in general—but to *tell* them only, without an attempt to listen in return.

And these apparent manifestations of far-sighted policy directed at the intellectual leaders are in line with the emphasis on oriental studies in the Soviet Union, the publication of original texts in representative editions useful to a scholar (e.g., Saadi's *Gulistan*, Firdousi's *Shahname*), the invitations extended to writers from Africa and Asia to meet in the USSR.

And this is only one side of the picture. Shrewd as the translation policy may seem when judged for its possible impact on nations outside the Soviet Union, it is equally well calculated as a move with respect to the inside. As can be seen from the data provided on these pages, translations are made regularly not into Russian only, but into virtually all other languages of the USSR as well (leaving out only extremely small ethnic groups with no written literature as of now). Thus, our sources inform us that the books taken from Burmese were translated into Russian, Georgian, and Turkmenian; those from Indonesian, into Russian, Tatar, Uzbek, and Adyg.

Consider this last case more closely. A translation into Adyg has little, if any, immediate practical value. Adyg is a language of the Caucasus, spoken by about 90,000 people —comparable, then, in relative importance on the overall Soviet scene to the language of a group like the Navahos in the United States. Until the time of the Revolution, Adyg was not used for writing at all (discounting here a few grammatical contributions by outside scholars); no figures concerning the total book production after the Revolution are available to me, but a closely related language, Abkhaz, spoken by about 59,000 people, may be taken as typical. Not employed as a literary language until the Revolution, Abkhaz has been used in books issued in a total of 2,600,000 copies by 1957; these works included translations from Pushkin, Tolstoy, Gorki, Rustaveli, Shevchenko, and others. Because of a special linguistic interest in Abkhaz, the book production appears to be somewhat higher in per capita output than for other small ethnic groups (Tadzhik, with about 1,000,000 speakers, is listed only with 7,000,000 copies, Ossetian, with 350,000 people, with 3,100,000 copies, etc.). But it can be used with confidence as an illustration of the Soviet policy of developing the local culture as a part of an overall, para-ethnic Soviet national structure and as a carrier for the many manifestations of Soviet indoctrination efforts.

We see that literary works from abroad are fitted into this cultural pattern alongside Russian, Ukrainian, Georgian classics. It is unlikely that criteria of formal or literary importance led to their inclusion; rather it would seem that works of Asian origin were thought to have a special appeal among non-European groups: an Asian writer and an Asian public would both feel honored by being made source and target of the translation process. The results of the policy, then, would be roughly the same outside and inside the Soviet Union. Conditions were created which gave Soviet efforts the appearance of genuine respect rather than colonialist paternalism and contempt. Works of literature proper were clearly best suited for this purpose, for the impression of good will and disinterested objectivity would have been much harder to convey if books of a tendentious or openly political nature had been chosen.

All in all, even if the observations and interpretations offered here are only approximately correct (and we need not be overly concerned with the ultimate reliability of the statistics), the situation sketched presents a major challenge to Western policy. It is a more subtle challenge than that offered by armaments or economic aid; but it is a challenge directed at the leaders of the countries of Africa and Asia, and therefore potentially of very great and lasting impact. This is hardly the place to discuss possible steps to be taken; and it may be enough merely to point out what attitudes must underlie any action that is to end in success. A vast realm of cultural riches is there for us to explore and to exploit; let it be done in a spirit of genuine curiosity, honest concern, and humble respect for ideas and forms different from our own, but equally human.

ROBERT FITZGERALD

Postscript to a Translation of The Odyssey

ROBERT FITZGERALD, *author of* In the Rose of Time, *has translated the short plays of Valéry and* Chronique *of St. John Perse, as well as the Theban plays of Sophocles. The following is a postscript which appeared in the Anchor edition of his translation of* The Odyssey (1963).

SOME DETAILS OF SCENE AND ACTION

I

The ship on which I sailed from Piraeus one summer night approached Odysseus' kingdom from the south in the early morning. Emerging on deck for the occasion, I saw a mile or so to the west the bright flank of a high island, broadside to the rising sun. This was Kephallenia, identified by tradition with Samê of *The Odyssey;* in fact the port where we presently put in is called Samê. Beyond it to the north and dead ahead rose another island mass, lying from northwest to southeast and therefore visible only on its western side, all shadow, a dark silhouette. This was Thiaki or Ithaka.

Now, one of the innumerable questions never quite settled by students of Homer is the intended meaning of these two lines, concerning Ithaka and neighboring islands, in Book IX of *The Odyssey* (lines 25 and 26):

αὐτὴ δὲ χθαμαλὴ πανυπερτάτη εἰν ἁλὶ κεῖται
πρὸς ζόφον, αἱ δὲ τ' ἄνευθε πρὸς ἠῶ τ' ἠέλιόν τε.

Uncertainties ramify handsomely in the first line, but let me confine myself here to the second, which literally means, or appears to mean, that Ithaka lies "toward the gloom, while the other islands lie apart toward the Dawn and the Sun." Long before my Ithakan landfall I knew that this line has been thought simply inaccurate. But when I saw the islands with my own eyes in the morning light I felt at once that I had discovered the image behind Homer's words. He, too, I felt sure, had looked ahead over a ship's bow at that hour and had seen those land masses, one sunny and one in gloom, just as I saw them. An overnight sail from Pylos would have brought him there at the right time.

This notion was, of course, highly exhilarating. I am sorry that further consideration has more or less deflated it. One trouble with it was that Homer (or Odysseus, the speaker in this passage) did not describe Ithaka as being itself shadowy or gloomy but as lying in a certain direction, "toward" the "gloom." If the contrast between Ithaka and Samê at sunrise had been in his mind, he could have put it more distinctly. Not that Homer is always lucid grammatically, but "toward the gloom" for "in gloom" is not his kind of vagueness. Then, too, the word ζόφος in Homer does not mean simply gloom; it means the gloom of one end of the world, one quarter of the compass, generally held by the ancients to be the west. ἤδη γὰρ φάος οἴχεθ' ὑπὸ ζόφον says Athena in Book III, 335, "The sun has gone down already under the gloom [of the west]," and Odysseus asks Elpênor in Book XI, 57, πῶς ἦλθες ὑπὸ ζόφον ἠερόεντα, "How did you come down under the cloudy gloom [of the world's end]?"

It would be excellent if these clear instances were also conclusive, and πρὸς ζόφον were to be translated "toward the west" or "toward the western gloom." But here precisely is the difficulty. Ithaka does not in fact lie "west" of the other islands in the group. Neither does Leukas, the more northerly island that some students have believed to be Homer's Ithaka. So far as Ithaka itself is concerned, the fact is that the northern horn of Kephallenia, across a channel a mile or so wide, reaches up along the length of the island to the west. How now?

Well, it must be recalled that Homer knew no other west than the direction of sunset, and in midsummer, in that latitude, the sun goes down at a spot on the horizon far north of true west. Whether the poet was an Ionian or an Athenian, he is unlikely to have visited the islands except in the sailing season. Homer's sunset quarter could have been roughly northwest by west. This very nearly solves the difficulty, but perhaps not quite. If we are still a few points off, so to speak, I am glad to say that recourse may be had to the later Greek geographer, Strabo.

According to Lord Rennell of Rodd, in the Annual of the British School in Athens, No. xxxiii, Session 1932–33, Strabo "entertained no doubt" that in the line I have quoted ζόφος "indicated the north, as the Sun does the south." That is to say, Strabo and Lord Rennell pass lightly over the antithesis between ζόφος and Dawn in that line of Homer in order to embrace the antithesis between ζόφος and the Sun, whose usual path in north latitudes passes south of the zenith. Most of Kephallenia does indeed lie to the south of Ithaka, and so does the island now called Zante, very likely the Zakynthos of *The Odyssey*. As for Doulikhion, Rennell and others rather desperately identify it with one of the small Ekhinades to the east.

Pondering this argument, I asked myself why each of the antitheses noted in the phrase should not be given equal value, or half of full value. Granted that Ithaka is "west" with respect to Doulikhion and "north" with respect to Zakynthos and Samê-Kephallenia, then πρὸς ζόφον could be briefly rendered "to the northwest," and the other islands πρὸς ἠῶ τ' ἠέλιόν τε could be said to "lie east and south." Here I left this question.

II

If you will do an hour or two of hard climbing on Ithaka you can reach the spinal ridge of the island and there, while you cool off, you can look across the blue channel to the west at the steep side of Samê a mile away. Close in to the other shore you will see a tiny islet known as Daskalion. This, with no great satisfaction, the commentators identify with Asteris, the small island behind which the suitors in their long boat lay in wait for Telémakhos at the end of Book IV. This identification in turn depends on another, that of a small round cove on the west side of Ithaka, somewhat north of the islet, as the harbor from which Telémakhos put out on his evening voyage. The longer I looked at this setting the more quarrelsome I felt with received opinion. It is true that at first glance all the requisites are there: the channel, the islet, the harbor. I am afraid, of course, that received opinion may be right. But on this point I have remained cranky and fond of my private reasons for dissent.

It appears that Polis Bay, as the round cove is tendentiously named, was once larger, and that it was a port of call in the classical period for Greek ships passing up the channel, outward bound for Italy. This fact of itself seems to me irrelevant if we are concerned to find the port of Ithaka at the time of the Trojan War, long before colonization or commerce with Italy, or even in Homer's time, late in the eighth century, when voyages to the western Mediterranean had just begun. The harbor described in *The Odyssey* serves, above all, ships that ply to and from Elis, the mainland of the Peloponnesus to the southeast, and Thesprotia, or Acarnania, to the east. It was from the southeast that my ship, the S. S. Miaoulis, arrived, and the Miaoulis put me ashore at Vathy on the deep harbor of the same name (it means "deep"). This is the longest and best sheltered of three bays opening southward off the wide Gulf of Molos, which runs inward from east to west and almost cuts Ithaka in two. Along the quay of Vathy in the evening I saw open caïques from the mainland unloading cattle in slings. From pasture land to the stony island, pastureless, the caïques had brought these cows to be slaughtered for Ithakan markets. Here was a ferry service exactly like the one alluded to in Book XX, 187, of *The Odyssey.* As the Gulf of Molos is the roadstead of Ithaka, Vathy is its natural harbor—or at least so it seems to the ferrymen, to the Greek steamship company, and to me.

But how could Vathy have been the port from which Telémakhos sailed, if on leaving it he would have had to issue eastward by the Gulf of Molos into the open sea, passing through no channel between Ithaka and Samê? This objection would be insuperable if Homer had been an Ithakan. Since he surely was not, but was a visitor like myself, I think it worth reporting that on the day after my arrival I had another visual revelation. From high ground on the north part of Ithaka I saw a small island, perfectly satisfying Homer's description of Asteris, that seemed to lie between Ithaka and Samê to the south. I said to my guide, "What island is that?" "Oh, that is Attako," he said. I looked at my map, which showed Attako lying in the sea to the east of Ithaka. "Are you sure?" said I. "Of course, I'm sure, I've been fishing there many times." No one would have guessed from the map that from the northeast height of Ithaka, looking south, you see this islet against the background of what appears to be another island mass but is in fact the southern part of Ithaka. What looks like a "channel" is the mouth of the Gulf of Molos.

My surmise is that Homer on his peregrination over Odysseus' island made mistakes like mine, that he confused the Gulf of Molos with the channel between Ithaka and Samê, and that his islet "Asteris" is the island Attako, not the tiny rock called Daskalion. Do not suppose that my theory lacks textual support. Attako has high ground from which the suitors could have kept their watch (XVI, 365); Daskalion has not. Moreover, to bear out my identification of Vathy with Telémakhos' harbor, I can refer to at least one detail of his embarkation. Athena is said to have moored his ship "at the harbor's edge," in Book II, 391 ἐπ' ἐσχατιῇ λιμένος, and once he had shoved off she sent him a following wind that took him out to sea. From what quarter blew this wind? From the west, for it is expressly called Ζέφυρος, the west wind, in II, 420–21. This is just the wind you would need astern if you wanted to put out from the mouth of Vathy Bay, but if you were putting out from Polis Bay it would blow you right back in.

It can be urged against me that the stern wind supplied by Athena lasted all night and took Telémakhos' ship all the way to Pylos. A steady wind from the west would have taken him not south to Pylos, but east, let us say, to Missolonghi. Perhaps, as I have myself argued that Homer's west lay in a more northerly quarter, his Zephyr also blew from that quarter and would serve a ship sailing from Polis Bay down the channel between Ithaka and Samê. I do not, of course, see why it could not have been the west wind at the start and have changed direction during the night, but in the end I compromised in deference to the established view. It is a northwest wind in my text. I may add that on my second evening at Vathy the wind freshened from that direction and, blowing over open water, made a fluttering and percussive effect in my eardrums—not entirely agreeable—like the noise of Homer's line for it:

ἀκραῆ Ζέφυρον, κελάδοντ' ἐπὶ οἴνοπα πόντον.

III

These notes may suggest some of the pleasures and complexities of going to see for yourself. I would be a fool to plume myself on my dip into those studies on ancient sites that have occupied good men and women for years. But I am forever grateful for my days on Ithaka as I am for other days, few but moving, in Athens and elsewhere in Greece. A rendering for the opening of Book III,

Ἠέλιος δ' ἀνόρουσε, λιπὼν περικαλλέα λίμνην

came into my head in the Saronic Gulf, and a week later at sunrise in Heraklion I found words for the next phrase, οὐρανὸν ἐς πολύχαλκον. By these and other keepsakes I am reminded that if I had never listened to the cicadas and drunk the resined wine I would have done the job differently, if I had done it at all. But most of it was what all writing is, a sedentary labor, or joy, sustained at a worktable. At one elbow, in this case, there were always those lines and parts of lines that have been pored over by so many for centuries. Of the puzzling ones I will give a few more examples, two at least of them notorious, with some account of the elucidation I think they demand. Multiply these cases by a thousand, and you will see what the preliminary or incidental work was like. As befits a dramatic poem, the first case is a tiny detail of action.

In Book XI Odysseus hears the shade of Agamémnon tell how Aigísthos and Klytaimnestra murdered him on his return from Troy, and with him his companions. They were all butchered, he says bitterly, like swine. I take it that he means what he says. The way you butcher a pig is by piercing or cutting his throat, and it does not seem unreasonable to imagine here, and to bear in mind elsewhere, that this is what happened to Agamémnon. He describes the banquet scene, the laden tables, and the floor fuming with blood where the victims lay. Then, in line 421, he says he heard a most piteous cry from his royal slave and mistress, Kassandra,

τὴν κτεῖνε Κλυταιμνήστρη δολόμητις
ἀμφ' ἐμοί, αὐτὰρ ἐγώ ποτὶ γαίῃ χεῖρας ἀείρων
βάλλον ἀποθνήσκων περὶ φασγάνῳ

and great difficulty has been found in grasping precisely what action this passage was meant to convey. Klytaimnestra was in the act of killing Kassandra, so much is clear, and Kassandra was close beside the fallen Agamémnon. But what does he say he himself was doing? Consider it word for word in the order in which it appears: "but I upon (or against) the ground lifting my hands / was throwing [them] while dying around the swordblade." Half the problem is to divide or punctuate this.

On one prevailing interpretation we should divide or punctuate after βάλλον and must therefore take ἀποθνήσκων περὶ φασγάνῳ to mean "dying around the swordblade," that is, with a blade left in his body. This is contrary to slaughtering procedure, but Professor W. B. Stanford in his annotated edition of *The Odyssey* tells us that there are many precedents for taking it so. He refers to four passages in *The Iliad* and to one in Sophocles' *Ajax*. With all respect I must say that none of these makes a good precedent for Stanford's reading, because in none of them does anyone die "around a swordblade" left in him by anyone else. Ajax has, of course, impaled himself on his own sword. Of the cases cited in *The Iliad*, one is concerned with an arrow and two with spears, weapons often left sticking in tenacious parts of the foe. It is otherwise with a sword; a sword in these poems was something a killer held onto if he could. The fourth case in *The Iliad* might be a better precedent, not for Stanford's notion of Agamémnon's wound but for mine (since it is an allusion to slaughtering), if the preposition used were not ἀμφὶ instead of περὶ. In short, the evidence is inconclusive.

Moreover, if you adopt this awkward reading, you are left with a clause that represents Agamémnon as lifting his hands and throwing them. With what purpose? Or perhaps I should ask, with what aim? Victor Bérard imagined that he meant to shield Kassandra. A. T. Murray, the Loeb translator, thought he tried to hit Klytaimnestra. Butcher and Lang, W. H. D. Rouse, and T. E. Lawrence accepted "let fall" as a translation of βάλλον: he lifted his hands and helplessly let them fall. Others, including Stanford, take ποτὶ γαίῃ as "against the ground" with βάλλον and suggest that he beat his hands against the ground to invoke vengeance from infernal powers.

I cannot myself hear the shade of the hero saying any of these things, except possibly what Murray has him say. But it is quite possible to punctuate the lines in another way, like this: "But I upon the ground, lifting my hands, was throwing them—while dying—around the swordblade." Or to put it in English, "As I lay on the ground I heaved up my hands and flung them with a dying effort around the swordblade." There is a scholion in which the lines are so understood, but the scholiast adds πρὸς ἐκσπάσαι τὸ ξίφος, "to pull out the sword"—no doubt in order to die more quickly. G. H. Palmer, one of the few translators to follow the scholiast, settled for "clutched" as a rendering for βάλλον. This was logical, since Palmer, like the Alexandrian and like Stanford, conceived the blade as embedded in Agamémnon. A man with a blade in his midriff would not "fling" his hands around it when all he had to do was, precisely, to clutch it. But βάλλον is stronger than "clutch," and the sword was not in Agamémnon, in any case. He would have had to heave up and fling his hands around the blade if the blade were a short distance away, within reach but still requiring an effort. This is where the sword of Klytaimnestra must have been while she slashed or poked at Kassandra. Therefore I prefer to think that as Klytaimnestra used the sword, Agamémnon, reckless of his hands, tried to get it away from her. Alone among modern translators, so far as I can discover, E. V. Rieu adopted this reading. It not only satisfies all the conditions, syntactical and verbal, but it makes all possible dramatic sense of the line.

IV

If you think of the poem as a play or a cinema—inevitable if not irresistible thoughts—you will find many problems for the set designer and the property man. There are two fine ones in the big closing scenes. How precisely are we to visualize the contest with Odysseus' hunting bow, announced by Penélopê in Book XIX and carried out in Book XXI? And in Book XXII what precisely is the layout of the great hall and adjoining passage by which the suitors, for the moment out of sight of Odysseus, are given throwing spears at a crucial point in the fight? The Greek is ambiguous or sketchy.

In XIX Penélopê tells her interesting new confidant of a sudden decision: next day her suitors will be challenged to perform an old feat of her husband's, and she will be the prize. It is a feat (line 573) with πελέκεας, axes,

τοὺς πελέκεας, τοὺς κεῖνος ἐνὶ μεγάροισιν ἑοῖσιν
ἵστασχ' ἑξείης, δρυόχους ὥς, δώδεκα πάντας.
στὰς δ' ὅ γε πολλὸν ἄνευθε διαρρίπτασκεν ὀϊστόν.

"those axes that he used to set up in his hall all twelve in line like a ship's ribs (or props), then he would take his stand far off and shoot an arrow through." The prize will go to that suitor who most easily strings her husband's bow and "shoots through all twelve axes." To this Odysseus replies in effect that tomorrow is not too soon; her husband will be there before any of the younger men can string the bow διοϊστεῦσαί τε σιδήρον "and shoot through the iron." It need not escape us that this phrase is rather an addition. We might imagine shooting through twelve axes if they were arranged in a line slightly staggered, leaving an interval of an inch or so for the arrow to pass. The alternative is to imagine apertures in the axeheads, and the phrase of Odysseus, repeated by Telémakhos in Book XXI, inclines us to that. He speaks with familiarity, not to mention his remarkable confidence. It is not the speech of a man still interested in concealing from his wife how well he knows her husband.

If the arrow is to pass "through the iron" and we interpret this to mean through apertures in the axeheads, then what apertures are meant? D. B. Monro in his edition of *The Odyssey*, Books XIII–XXIV, printed drawings of two perforated ancient axeheads, one from a Mycenean excavation, another from an early classical metope, and a third drawing of the very late classical *bipennis*, a double axe whose crescent blades form by their inner edges two circular openings, the one above the haft open and unobstructed. An arrow could pass through any one of these types of axeheads. With archaeological backing, then, we may imagine twelve pervious axes in alignment for the contest. Penélopê's phrase, "like a ship's ribs (or props)," in fact makes us see twelve axes stuck in the ground by their helves.

Oddly enough, there are quite serious objections to this reading. When we say "axe" we mean axehead and helve together. But it seems more likely that the word πέλεκυς to Penélopê meant "axehead" alone. In Book V when Kalypso gives Odysseus a πέλεκυς for cutting timber, she must complete the gift with a στειλειόν, or helve of olive wood (line 236). In all the references to the gauntlet Odysseus' arrow had to run, there is no allusion to a στειλειόν, though a closely related word appears. On the contrary, when Penélopê brings the bow back from the storeroom in XXI, 58, her maids bring along a basket full of iron and bronze "accessories of the contest," certainly axeheads without helves. Any normal axehead, then as now, had an aperture: it had the socket hole where a helve could be fitted. Is there positive evidence that this was the aperture in question? There is indeed.

When Odysseus finally makes his prize-winning shot in XXI, 420 sqq., we hear that

πελέκεων δ' οὐκ ἤμβροτε πάντων
πρώτης στειλειῆς, διὰ δ' ἀμπερὲς ἦλθε θύραζε.

"he didn't miss the πρώτης στειλειῆς of all the axeheads, and the arrow went clean through and out." Confusion about the word στειλειή appears to be ancient and inexhaustible; it was taken very early to mean "helve" or "haft"—that is, to be a synonym for στειλειόν—and translators in torment have tried to make sense of a shot that did not miss the first axe helve. But if Homer had meant that, if he had meant πρώτου στειλειοῦ, he could have said it. It is metrically equivalent and phonetically a little better. Professor Stanford thinks, and with excellent reason, that the difference in gender may be significant. He agrees with the twelfth century Archbishop of Thessalonica, Eustathius, that the feminine form, στειλειή, meant "socket" as στειλειόν meant "helve." What Homer intended to say was very simple: that Odysseus didn't miss his bull's eye, the first socket hole in the line of twelve.

It is a perfect conclusion, but it lets us in for other difficulties. If the axeheads were without helves, if each was turned so that its socket hole faced the archer, how were they set up and supported? In what respect was the line of axeheads comparable to "a ship's ribs (or props)"? The second question is easier to answer: the point of similarity could have been merely that in both cases there were equal intervals between one and another. As to the way of setting up the axeheads, all we have to go on are two lines and a half, XXI, 120 sqq., in which Telémakhos prepares the contest:

πρῶτον μὲν πελέκεας στῆσεν, διὰ τάφρον ὀρύξας
πᾶσι μίαν μακρήν, καὶ ἐπὶ στάθμην ἴθυνεν,
ἀμφὶ δὲ γαῖαν ἔναξε

Literally, "first he set up the axeheads, after digging a trench through for all, a single trench, a long one, and he trued [it or them] to the line, and he pressed earth on both sides." It is pertinent to remember that in Homer's "additive" style items are not always given in any particular order. That is, the pressing of the earth could have preceded or accompanied the truing, and we may understand that he trued the axeheads, not the trench. If we held the theory that axeheads fitted on helves were being set up, a trench would bed the helves, around which earth could then be pressed to hold them upright. I have given the evidence against that. On the other and better theory that axeheads alone were used, is there anything in the context to suggest how they were held up?

Well, a byproduct of a trench is a long pile of loose earth. If the loose earth beside the trench were "pressed" up in a narrow ridge, with peaks at equal distances, the axeheads could be stuck in these, one blade in the earth and one out, since the πέλεκυς was double-bladed. The verb νάσσω that appears here in the aorist active, ἔναξε, "pressed," had the sense "be piled" in the passive in later Greek. The very point of digging a trench could have been to supply enough earth for this purpose; if it had been a matter of embedding axe helves, they could have been planted in a line of holes like fence posts or fruit trees. It is a good deal to read into these lines, but I am willing to risk it because I see nothing else for it. Telémakhos made a bedding of earth for the axeblades and trued them ἐπὶ στάθμην, "to the line," by the wall builder's immemorial technique, a stretched cord. One more question: if set up in this way, could the axeheads have been high enough for the bowshot from the door? Odysseus made the bowshot while seated on his stool. He held the bow horizontally in the usual ancient style. If he shot from the hip just above knee level in a flat trajectory, the axeheads as I see them could have been at the right height.

V

If those passages needed unfolding, more unfolding still must be done to render with clarity the several lines beginning at 126 of Book XXII—a sketch for a ground plan or a stage set. Odysseus has been doing execution with his bow while Telémakhos has brought arms from the storeroom; now all the arrows are gone, and father and son and the two herdsmen arm themselves for combat with spears. The narrative continues:

ὀρσοθύρη δέ τις ἔσκεν ἐϋδμήτῳ ἐνὶ τοίχῳ.
ἀκρότατον δέ παρ' οὐδὸν ἐϋσταθέος μεγάροιο
ἦν ὁδὸς ἐς λαύρην, σανίδες δ' ἔχον εὖ ἀραρυῖαι.

"There was a certain ὀρσοθύρη in the well-built wall. And at the edge [or along the top] of the threshold of the hall there was an entry way into the passage, and well-fitted folding doors kept it closed." This is all baffling, and the editors have left it so. We wish to know what the ὀρσοθύρη was and in which wall it was located. We also wish to know what if anything the ὀρσοθύρη had to do with the passage, where the passage ran, and where precisely the "entry way" opened into it. These lines do not tell us. But we can learn some of the answers from the action that now takes place.

First, Odysseus tells the swineherd to stand over near the "entry way" and guard it, μία δ' οἴη γίγνετ' ἐφορμή, "for there was only one way in." Why guard it? Because it must be a possible exit for the suitors who have been under fire at the other end of the hall—the only possible exit, we gather, besides the main door where Odysseus and Telémakhos have taken their stand. Now one of the surviving suitors, Ageláos, says to the others,

"Ω φίλοι, οὐκ ἂν δή τις ἀν' ὀρσοθύρην ἀναβαίη
καὶ εἴποι λαοῖσι

"Friends, why doesn't someone climb up by the ὀρσοθύρη and tell the townsmen?" From this it is clear that by climbing through the ὀρσοθύρη you could get into the passage and out by the door where the swineherd has been posted. Out where? If ἀκροτατον δὲ παρ' οὐδὸν is taken to mean "along the top" of the threshold inside the main door, any man issuing at that point would run into the arms of Odysseus and company. It must mean "at the edge" of the threshold outside the entrance. If this were not the meaning, the swineherd would not have had to move to be in a position to guard the "entry way." His movement, incidentally, seems to have escaped notice by Ageláos, who has also failed to see that Odysseus has no more arrows. The goatherd, Melánthios, answers him:

> οὔ πως ἔστ', 'Αγέλαε διοτρεφές. ἄγχι γὰρ αἰνῶς
> αὐλῆς καλὰ θύρετρα καὶ ἀργαλέον στόμα λαύρης.
> καί χ' ἒις πάντας ἐρύκοι ἀνήρ, ὅς τ' ἄλκιμος εἰή.

"It can't be done. The fair door of the courtyard is terribly near [or the fair door is terribly near the courtyard] and the mouth of the passage is hard [to force]; one man alone if he were strong could hold off all of us." If the mouth of the passage is hard to force, it must be a narrow passage, narrow as a catwalk. Melánthios' remark that one strong man could hold it suggests that he has seen Odysseus order the swineherd outside. All this is fairly clear. But precisely what is "terribly near" to what? That is not so clear.

Monro and Stanford thought Melánthios meant that the gate into the courtyard from the road was near—near to Odysseus, or near to the exit from the passage. Since the gate is in fact on the other side of the courtyard, these editors thought it could be called "terribly near" only from the point of view of a man in fear of archery as he crossed the courtyard. I find this interpretation strange. A man thinking of making a run under fire would complain of how far the gate seemed, not how near. It may be irrelevant that there can be no more archery, anyway, for Odysseus is out of arrows; Melánthios, like Ageláos, may not have noticed this (neither Monro nor Stanford appears to have noticed it, either). But I doubt that αὐλῆς θύρετρα necessarily or even possibly means the gate from the road into the courtyard. The word θύραι has been used for this. Here is a different word whose proper meaning is certainly "door" and not "gate." It could mean the door from the passageway into the courtyard, and I think it does. To what or whom is that door terribly near? To Odysseus, who has already posted a guard there. On this interpretation these lines cohere.

Melánthios proposes to bring the suitors arms from the storeroom, and he climbs

ἐς θάλαμους 'Οδυσῆος ἀνὰ ῥῶγας μεγάροιο

"up the breaks of the hall and into the storeroom of Odysseus." The ῥῶγας or "breaks" have been thought to be steps, but steps are κλίμακες. A closer reading would be "fissures" or chinks in the wall, toe holds for a goatherd. Although it is not expressly mentioned at this point, there is no doubt that the aperture to which he climbs is the ὀρσοθύρη, and I should now note that etymologically this word almost certainly means a "raised door" or window. Since his destination is the storeroom, it follows not only that this window-opening gives on the passage by which Ageláos thought someone might get out, but that the passage itself leads to the storeroom at the back of the house. It is the same passage by which at the beginning of the slaughter Telémakhos ran to get arms for his father and friends. From the passage, through the window, Melánthios can hand out arms to the suitors.

Where is the ὀρσοθύρη? At the far end of the hall from the entrance, as stands to reason and as we learn explicitly later on in line 333 from the position of Phêmios, the harper, when the fight is over. It must be a window in one of the side walls, for two reasons. First, the passage that it lights and ventilates runs along the side of the hall from front to rear. Second, one of the side walls could have a recessed part like a shallow transept, not visible from the entrance. The context requires this. The ὀρσοθύρη and all that happens there are out of sight of Odysseus. The young men harried by his shooting would have huddled on the other side of any angle in the wall that offered shelter, and there the ὀρσοθύρη would have come to their attention. Odysseus may well have had this in mind when he ordered the passage guarded. But why didn't one of the suitors use the ὀρσοθύρη instead of letting the goatherd work for them? The question as framed almost answers itself: they were accustomed to service. There may be another reason, too. One of the scholia on the ὀρσοθύρη informs us that

ὑψηλοτέρα ἦν ἐφ' ᾗ ἦν ὀροῦσαι καὶ ἀναθορεῖν

"it was quite high; you had to make a jump to get up to it." Perhaps jumping for a hole in the wall was beneath the dignity of Akhaian gentlemen with flowing hair.

VI

Details like these may turn out to be self-consistent, but what of the poem as a whole? Does it hang together? Did a single composer hold it all in his mind? Whatever opinion we may hold on the famous Question, we may accept at least one modest principle: when proof to the contrary is lacking, any given passage should be interpreted in consonance with the rest. Take the eagles.

During the assembly scene in Book II, Zeus launches two eagles from a ridge, either τῷ δ' or τώ δ' according to the alternative readings. The Oxford editor, T. W. Allen, reasonably chose the first, meaning "for him," that is, for the last speaker, Telémakhos. The eagles are to be an omen for him. When in their gliding flight they reach a point over the center of the agora they wheel and beat their wings, and then we have two more alternative readings, ἐς δ' ἰδέτην πάντων κεφαλάς or ἐς δ' ἱκέτην πάντων κεφαλας, that is, either the pair "looked at the heads of all [below]" or they "came down on" all the heads. Again Allen chose the reading more charged with life and sense: "came down on." In the next clause, ὄσσοντο δ' ὀλέθρον, the verb has changed from the dual form, used when the pair of birds was the subject, to a plural form. Does this mean a change of subject? Not necessarily; Homer often uses plural verb forms for dual subjects; indeed he has already done so once in this passage, though not in this sentence. If it does mean a change of subject, then the "heads," or men in the crowd, are said to behold death or doom in the diving eagles; if it does not mean a change of subject, the diving eagles are said to make doom visible to the men, or in a word to menace them with doom. "Death was in their glare," as Murray ingeniously puts it, making perhaps the best of both alternatives. Perhaps, but wait. The next line presents us again with a dual form, this time in a middle participle. It goes:

δρυψαμένω δ' ὀνύχεσσι παρειὰς ἀμφί τε δειρὰς

"tearing, this pair, with talons, cheeks and all around necks (or throats)."

Now, the received interpretation of this, cited by Liddell & Scott and followed by Murray and practically everyone, takes the middle voice of the verb as reflexive here, meaning they tore *each other's* cheeks and throats. But first let me observe that the middle may or may not have this shade of meaning. It is the voice you would use in Greek if you wanted to say, "We cut ourselves a slice," and you would not be referring to a knife fight. Second, if the two eagles are a sign, what after all do they signify? What future event do they portend? The old augur Halithersês has no doubt, and neither have we: they stand for the return of Odysseus and the doom of the suitors. Why two eagles? In order that the sign, a sign for Telémakhos, may give him, or at any rate ourselves, to understand that he and Odysseus together will attack the suitors. The two eagles correspond to the two royal assailants. Why then should they assail one another? What would any intelligent augur make of that? No, no, surely; they assail the suitors, who have been arraigned by Telémakhos in the assembly, and if this were not the case there would be no point in their having "come down on the heads of all," for an eagle fight would have been as well or better conducted high in the air. A scholiast says, τὸ δὲ καταδρύψαι τὰς παρειὰς τὸν τῶν μνηστήρων ἐσήμανε φόνον, and *he* does not use the middle but the active voice: "that business of tearing the [suitors'] cheeks signified the suitors' violent death." We are to see the eagles' portent not merely "in their glare" but in their ripping talons.

Between Book II and Book XV no eagles fly, or at any rate no significant ones, but in Book XV, 160, as Telémakhos is taking leave of Menelaos and Helen, just as he is saying how fine it would be to meet his father on Ithaka so that he could tell him of their hospitality, ἐπέπτατο δεξιὸς ὄρνις, αἰετὸς ἀργὴν χῆνα φέρων "a bird, an eagle, flew up on the right, lugging a white goose." This portent is quickly interpreted by Helen. It means, she says, that just as the eagle flew from the wild mountain of his birth to pounce on the domestic bird, so Odysseus will appear out of the rough world of his wanderings to avenge the wrongs done him at home. Near the end of the same Book (525 sqq.) the motif is repeated. Again the omen appears as if in comment on a speech by Telémakhos, who has just been wondering aloud whether anything will prevent his mother's marriage to Eurýmakhos. This time the portentous bird is not an eagle, αἰετός, but a hawk, κίρκος, carrying a captured dove. And this time the interpretation is not given immediately; it is given to Penélopê in Book XVII (152 sqq.) by the diviner, Theoklýmenos, who tells her it meant that Odysseus had already landed on Ithaka. Again there is an interval of two Books, and in

XIX (535 sqq.) the motif comes to a kind of flowering when Penélopê recounts her "dream" to the beggar, who is Odysseus. This time there is a more exact correspondence between the terms of the equation; Penélopê was in a position to be exact. Upon the geese feeding at her house

> ἐλθὼν δ' ἐξ ὄρεος μέγας αἰετὸς ἀγκυλοχείλης
> πᾶσι κατ' αὐχένας ἧξε καὶ ἔκτανεν

"coming from the mountain a great eagle with crooked beak broke their necks and killed them all."

Thus in four passages the descent of Odysseus on the suitors has been foreboded or foreseen in strikes made by birds of prey. In three cases the attacking birds are eagles; once it is a hawk. The appearance of the motif twice in Book XVII and once again in Book XIX harks back to its introduction in Book II. It also anticipates the climax of the fight in Odysseus' hall in Book XXII. At that point Athena unfurls her storm cloud, the aegis, overhead, and the surviving suitors break and run like cattle stung by gadflies. Now (302) comes the simile:

> οἱ δ' ὥς τ' αἰγυπιοὶ γαμψώνυχες ἀγκυλοχεῖλαι
> ἐξ ὀρέων ἐλθόντες ἐπ' ὀρνίθεσσι θόρωσι, κτλ

"But the pursuers, like αἰγυπιοί with hooked talons and crooked beak issuing from the mountains to dive on flights of birds, etc." We had expected eagles, αἰετοί, or hawks, κίρκοι, but the word is αἰγυπιοί, and I am distressed to say that the usual translation of that is "vultures." Liddell & Scott give "vulture" for αἰγυπιός. But let us consider the case patiently. We have not met the word before in *The Odyssey*. Liddell & Scott and the Homeric lexicographer, Autenrieth, cite three occurrences in *The Iliad.* In Book VII, 59, when Athena and Apollo are represented as taking their seats on the oak of Zeus as Hektor challenges the Akhaians, ἑζέσθην ὄρνισιν ἐοικότες αἰγυπιοῖσι

"They perched like birds, like αἰγυπιοί." In Book XVII, 460, Automedon making chariot forays among the Trojans is likened to an αἰγυπιός among geese. Most interesting of all is the case in Book XVI, 428, when Patroklos and Sarpedon clash in battle—for here the first line of the simile is the very same line that we find repeated in *The Odyssey:*

οἱ δ' ὥς τ' αἰγυπιοὶ γαμψώνυχες ἀγκυλοχεῖλαι
πέτρῃ ἐφ' ὑψηλῇ μεγάλα κλάζοντε μάχωνται

"like αἰγυπιοί with hooked talons and crooked beak/on a high rock, crying loud, they fought."

Now, it seems to me that on the Homeric evidence there is something wrong with translating this word as "vulture." A vulture as we understand the term is a carrion bird rather than a hunting bird, and in every context of both *Iliad* and *Odyssey* where a vulture in our sense is clearly indicated Homer uses the word γύψ. In no instance, as we have seen, is αἰγυπιός used of a carrion bird; on the contrary, in two cases, one in *The Iliad* and one our climactic simile in *The Odyssey,* it is used of a hunting bird, and in one of the two remaining cases it supplies a simile for two gods at rest on a bough. If Homer had meant γύψ he could have used γύψ, a handy word and one he used often enough elsewhere. But he used another word, and used it because he unquestionably meant another thing. He meant a bird like a hawk or an eagle, a killer, a threat to geese, a hunter of small birds in general. He did not mean the stinking buzzard that feeds on corpses left by others.

In the first edition of my *Odyssey* I translated αἰγυπιοί in Book XXII as "eagles" to go with the eagle passages that lead up to it. I went too far. If the poet had wished to say "eagles" he could have used the word for eagles, αἰετοί. Instead, he lifted a line from *The Iliad,* as he often did, presumably because it would suit his purpose here. How, then, should αἰγυπιοί be rendered? Well, I see that John

Moore, in his recent excellent version of Sophocles' *Ajax*, (The Complete Greek Tragedies, ed. Lattimore & Grene, Chicago), encountering this problem in line 169,

μέγαν αἰγυπιὸν δ' ὑποδείσαντες, κτλ

translates

But fear of the huge falcon, etc.

possibly in view of considerations like those I have been expounding. In revising I have followed his example. I hope Homer would be better pleased. No doubt the four attackers in Book XXII are more justly likened to falcons than to eagles if, as I suspect, falcons more often hunt in company; the wild eagle, unless paired by Zeus, I imagine hunts alone.

SOME GENERAL CONSIDERATIONS

I

An artist in narrative as we know it will have been interested in his art through reading, and he will expect to be read. It is difficult for us to realize what it means that the man who made *The Odyssey* may never have read anything at all. Five or six centuries before his time, in the heroic age of his poem, there had been a Greek syllabary at Mykenai and elsewhere, apparently used mainly for keeping accounts and lists. A memory of this may have survived in a line of *The Iliad*, but the syllabary itself had long gone out of use, and the world of Homer was illiterate. During the eighth century B.C. the people of the Greek mainland and islands imported a Semitic alphabet and began using it, at least for brief inscriptions. If Homer lived to see this, he probably thought of it as a new magic or amusement, almost certainly not as the medium of his work. We can surmise that we owe our text of *Iliad* and *Odyssey* not to Homer but to the importunity of some technician who "took them down," as nowadays a man would do with a tape recorder. Even in the unlikely event that Homer himself wrote out versions of one or both poems, the fact would remain that he and his audience were not readers but auditors of stories in verse.

Dozens of these stories had been told, or sung, among Aegean people for generations before Homer, forming a tradition possibly as old as English literature is now. We may imagine small communities of a feudal sort whose gentry found in the recitation or performance of these tales all history, all theatre, and all that we think of as literary entertainment. The performers were no doubt sometimes amateurs, but more often as time went on they were professionals who spent a lifetime in a hard craft. Our poet came late and had had supremely gifted predecessors. He inherited a traditional art comparable in range and refinement to the art of the musical virtuoso in our day, but more creative and fluid, for in some degree it remained an art of improvisation.

Thirty years ago my teacher and friend Milman Parry showed how many Homeric lines were constructed out of metrical formulas, out of a vocabulary of metrical parts that with slight modification or none would serve in the context of various actions or descriptions. This vocabulary of phrases was like an Erector or Mecanno set for making verse as you went along. Parry and Albert Lord, who has continued his work, studied the similar technique of oral epic still practised in our day in Jugoslavia. Professor Lord's important book, *The Singer of Tales* (Harvard, 1960), is an account of their researches and conclusions, and it is indicated reading for anyone who wants to understand the kind of art that Homer practised. We appear to know more about this art than Plato did. It is a technique rather simply described: many formulas ready in the memory give the storyteller or singer a means of developing action and dialogue as the spirit moves him, with formulaic lines or passages to buoy him up when invention fails. A stringed instrument is indispensable. Meter is indispensable. What Lord calls the "phonological context," the alliterative and voweling pattern, to a certain extent determines invention.

I cannot refer to these studies without making one or two reservations. Parry thought Homer's vocabulary of formulas almost wholly traditional and conventional, but I could never see why originality in detail should be denied a poet to whom it was impossible to deny originality in the large—in conception and organization. I should suppose, too, that although his medium was suited to improvisation, it was no less suited to composition and rehearsal beforehand—an aspect of the matter rather slighted in Parry and Lord. Finally, while statements of the theory sometimes give us to understand that formulaic structure was all-pervasive in both *Iliad* and *Odyssey*, I have yet to see this proved. My own reading of both poems has left me with the impression that while there are many recurrences and reshapings, there are also many passages without echo or precedent—as we might infer from the fact that many Homeric words occur once and once only.

Our understanding of the Homeric poems, however, has been permanently altered and improved by Parry's work and Lord's, and the famous Homeric Question, the question of single or multiple authorship of *Iliad* and *Odyssey*, will never be the same again. There is little doubt now that from the singers before him Homer had learned not only a rich metrical language but a large repertory of themes. Old themes, like that of the return of heroes, he handled again with joyous elaboration and cunning. It is likely that his compositions, from the nature of the case, varied from one performance to another. No doubt a tale might be told either briefly and broadly or at length and with subtlety, depending on audience and occasion. There was no canonical version.

As Professor Lord puts it: "The theme is in reality protean; in the singer's mind it has many shapes, all the forms in which he has ever sung it, although his latest rendering of it will naturally be freshest in his mind . . . And the shapes that it has taken in the past have been suitable for the song of the moment. In a traditional poem, therefore, there is a pull in two directions: one is toward the song being sung and the other is toward the previous use of the same theme. The result is that characteristic of oral poetry which literary scholars have found hardest to understand and accept, namely, an occasional inconsistency, the famous nod of a Homer."

Our versions of *Iliad* and *Odyssey* must have originated in those versions that at the moment of dictation or recording the performer, whether Homer or a follower of Homer, happened to sing. He may have been more inspired on other occasions, but it is fair to assume that when it came to recording he did his best, and did well. Perhaps on this occasion he chose to record the "long songs" and to restore, so to speak, many cuts often made in performance. Neither poem as we have it could have been recorded at one sitting, and it is possible that long intervals elapsed between the recording of one part and that of another. Given the conditions, and given what Professor Lord calls the protean nature of the themes, we can no longer take inconsistencies in the poems as proof of multiple authorship.

Artist and writer know that any work, ancient or modern, even any masterwork, could easily have been very different from what it is. If you are curious about these matters, you can often see, in drafts and sketches, part at least of the sheaf or spectrum of possible forms of which the "final" version of a story or poem or picture represents a selection —not necessarily or invariably the best—or simply a terminus at which effort stopped. An element of the composite remains in all but the most perfect composition. Of this general truth the Homeric poems are special instances. It is not difficult to see in each poem traces of other stories, or of other versions in which the same stories were handled differently. For more than a century Homeric criticism devoted itself to spotting logical and linguistic discrepancies, discovering one or the other poem to be a "wretched patchwork," in the words of one eminent scholar. While I was engaged on this translation, Professor Denys Page's Bryn Mawr lectures, published as *The Homeric Odyssey* (Oxford, 1955), argued, or reargued, the case against "unity" with asperity and flourish. But many of his points were debater's points, and I doubt that Page realized all the implications of Parry's work or Lord's.

To sum up, *The Odyssey* could well have been composed by one singer, working with themes he had heard from others, in a medium developed by others; if single in one sense, the authorship was certainly multiple in another. There is no way of proving it single in any sense. An admirer, a son, an apprentice, a collaborator, may have contributed passages or sections—a final section perhaps, as many critics have thought—to the "long song" as we have it. But the contrary is also possible. The truth, I think, is that we are too remote in time and language to decide. These, roughly, are the considerations that ought to be present to our minds when we think of Homer. But it is not necessary to put the name in quotation marks.

II

A living voice in firelight or in the open air, a living presence bringing into life his great company of imagined persons, a master performer at his ease, touching the strings, disposing of many voices, many tones and tempos, tragedy, comedy, and glory, holding his auditors in the palm of his hand: was Homer all of this? We can only suppose that he was. If what we imagine is true, Homer must himself have been his poems, in a physical sense unequalled in the case of any poet since. Imagine *Henry IV* and *The Tempest* composed not for production by a company of actors but as solo performances by Shakespeare himself. Or imagine it in the case of either, not both. The notion is still astonishing, and it is difficult to believe it.

I learn from W. S. Merwin, in the introduction to his translations of *Spanish Ballads* (Anchor, 1961), that the wandering *juglares* of medieval Spain, who sang and recited the epic *cantares*, "might be accompanied in their performance by mimes, known as *remendadores*, and *cazarros*—a name which included clowns and most varieties of stunt man." Well, stunt men, or tumblers, are mentioned as performing along with a poet or singer at Meneláos' court in Book IV of *The Odyssey*. But no mimes assist any ἀοιδός in the Homeric poems. This of itself would not prove that Homer did his own impersonations. The ἀοιδός as Homer presented him was a figure of the heroic age, four or five centuries before his time. But so far as I know there is no evidence whatever that Homer himself, or the ἀοιδοί in his immediate tradition, or their successors, the rhapsodes, were accompanied by mimes or actors.

We have no perfect word for ἀοιδός, for the kind of artist Homer was. "Bard" was fairly exact but has become a joke. "Skald" takes us too far into druidical regions. "Minstrel" is better but still too slight, too trammeled with doublet and hose, and faintly raffish after Gilbert & Sullivan. The Italian compound word *cantastorie* is at least neutral and is a definition of sorts. Lord did well to adopt the English equivalent, "singer of tales." But I am not satisfied. The term does not do justice to the creative and inventive power of the ἀοιδός. It does not suggest his mimetic art. And there is a difficulty about "singer" as a term for the poet and performer of these things.

That the telling of a story, and the incidental acting of roles, should be called "singing"—this will strike us at first as affected or strange. We may indeed think of opera, disciplined and expressive opera like the *Orfeo* of Gluck, true lyric theatre as the Italians call it; but the orchestra and the stage, the whole convention, are alien to Homer. Perhaps it is enough to recall certain fine acting voices. As a child I sat aloft in the second balcony of an old theatre in Illinois while a traveling company played *Sancho Panza*, and I remember the beautiful voice of the late Otis Skinner rising effortless, malleable and pure, or falling to a crystalline whisper, far off there below, in unhurried declamation, while the whole theatre sat spellbound by that human instrument alone. There is no doubt that the master ἀοιδός had a gift like that, a trained voice of great expressive and melodic range.

By all accounts, too, the Homeric performer used a second instrument and depended on it: the κίθαρις, an affair of a few gut strings with some kind of resonator, possibly a tortoise shell, like the later lyre. It would be anachronistic to think of it as a guitar or lute, so I call it a "gittern harp" and sometimes refer to the performer as a harper. Homer describes him more than once as plucking or strumming an overture to a given tale or song, and he must have used the instrument not only for accompaniment but for pitch, and to fill pauses while he took thought for the next turn. No doubt the instrument marked rhythm, too.

We need not delude ourselves as to how far these generalities really take us. How in particular the voice, the metered verse, and the stringed instrument were related in these performances, and in the recital of poetry throughout antiquity, I do not well understand, and I do not think anyone does perfectly. In our own tradition the "music of verse" is one thing and "music" proper is another. A song is a song, not necessarily a poem. *The Peaceful Western Wind* and *Mistress Mine* indeed happen to be both, and I have heard Christopher Casson lean to a small Irish harp and sing *Oft in the Stilly Night* so attentively that it seemed twice the poem I had known before. But this is exceptional. Who would set to music the great lyrics of Yeats? Who could improve on Lear by scoring it? Here all is in the shape and movement of metered language. But we find the verse of Homer—and this is my point—as beautiful in itself as the verse of Yeats or Shakespeare. What we call a "musical arrangement" would disperse or confuse the effect of it. We can be sure, I think, that harp or κίθαρις played a very subdued part, however essential, in the original Homeric performance.

III

One of our first discoveries in reading Homer will be that he was a poet in our sense of the word, a man gifted at making verse. All the learning that we may later assemble, all we can know or guess of the artist as an improviser and entertainer, even our fugitive sense of him as the demiurge of a world transfigured, all this cannot supersede—indeed it is founded on—our pleasure in him line by line, the way we hear or read him. I will never forget how unexpectedly moved I was years ago when for the first time I heard Telémakhos in Book I speak of his father as

ἀνέρος οὗ δή που λεύκ' ὀστέα πύθεται ὄμβρῳ

Looking up, I said to myself, in effect, "Why, this really is poetry!" and I meant poetry as good as "Call for the robin redbreast and the wren." Many times afterward, in reading or translating Homer, I have again paused over a line or a pair of lines in recognition and homage.

Parry thought this incomparable medium, the formulaic hexameter, had been shaped through centuries of trial and error, a testing and refining process conducted on many occasions before generations of auditors, so that in the end only the fittest language survived and the virtuoso had at his command the best words in the best order for anything he cared to relate or invent. I used at first to feel that the recurrent epithets and formula lines were a mere convention and a bore. In time I realized that they were musical phrases, brief incantations, of which the miserable renderings gave little or no idea. These formulas entered the repertory not only because they were useful but because they were memorable, I mean because nobody who had once heard them could easily forget them; and that is true to this day.

Ἦμος δ' ἠριγένεια φάνη ῥοδοδάκτυλος Ἠώς

It is possible that by Homer's time even he could not have said precisely what the two epithets in this line meant —and there are a number of others of which the same is true—but the line had been kept for its fragrance, a fragrance of Dawn, inimitable and unsurpassable, no more boring in its recurrence than Dawn itself. Because there are hundreds of lines like this and more hundreds of half lines and phrases, the very medium of Homer is pervaded by lyric quality. The simplest phrases have it. Hear Hektor saying (*Iliad* VI, 264), "Don't offer me any sweet wine, dear Mother:"

Μή μοι οἶνον ἄειρε μελίφρονα πότνια μῆτερ

How could you render that? Consider the voweling, and consider how the first epithet, after the ghost of a pause, hovers between "wine" and "mother." There is, besides, a peculiar cleanliness and lightness of movement, as often in Homer, and there is something else that I call the cut or sculpture of words. It is easiest to be aware of this in the last two feet of certain hexameters: νόστον ἑταίρων and ἔνδον ἐόντων. These are rounded shapes.

I am not being what Professor Irving Babbitt used to call "fanciful." If you will make the effort to imagine this Greek as still virgin of any visual signs at all, associated with no letters, no Greek characters, no script, no print—as purely and simply expressive sound, you will be able to perceive it in the air, its true medium, and to hear how it shapes and tempers the air by virtue of stops and tones. I will quote two more lines, one for consonants, and one for vowels. The first is Aphroditê saying in *Iliad* V, 359, φίλε κασίγνητε κόμισαί τέ με δός τέ μοι ἵππους

in which we hear the light tongue of the goddess of love herself in three coquettish particles, τε... τε... τε... My second example is the first line sung by those temptresses of the sea, known to Homer as Seirênês, and it is a typical triumph of formulary art since it is a modified version of a line that occurs in *The Iliad* in quite a different context, and in the mouth of quite a different personage. Here it is, XII, 184:

Δεῦρ' ἄγ' ἰών, πολύαιν' Ὀδυσεῦ, μέγα κῦδος Ἀχαιῶν

There is a rhythm of anapests, and intricate rhyming: Δεῦ and σεῦ on the beat, λύ on the offbeat and κῦ on the beat, αιν' and αι on the beat, ῶν on the beat and ών on the offbeat, and ἄγ' turned round widdershins on μέγα: this is a conjuring kind of echolalia. But more: the crooning vowels are for low seductive voices, rising in mid-line with αιν' and then rising and opening with a savage shout in Ἀχαιῶν at the end.

You might call this sort of thing "phonetic wit"—though it may have come to the artist without calculation. Along with it, in Homer, there is a lot of verbal wit enjoyed for its own sake and also syntactical wit, a quality of style that Chapman and Pope could appreciate. Chiastic order is a favorite form, and *The Iliad* especially teems with it. Book IV, 125:

λίγξε βιός, νευρὴ δὲ μέγ' ἴαχεν, ἆλτο δ' ὀϊστός

I could go on indefinitely, but I should cut this short and say that we are not meant very often to stop and consider so curiously. The narrative pace does not encourage it. You can be a connoisseur of the single line if you like, but this is only the beginning of appreciation. Homer is lyric but rarely indulges the lyric, he keeps his surface alive but keeps it moving; the line is only the medium, as I began by calling it, and as such it is subordinate to practically everything else. It is subordinate in the first place to the passage, to the effect created by the placement of lines in succession. Continuous prose cannot achieve the switches and surprises that you get by playing on a regular meter, a measured base. Of these effects Homer, formulas and all, was a master. We have often heard how the movement of the hexameter line itself could be varied by pauses, lightened by dactyls, retarded by spondees; but we have heard less of what could happen in the movement from line to line and in the course of action or speeches. A change of pace, a change of mood, an ironic aside, a quick look into the past or into the distance—we find all these between one line and the next.

Homer's humor, too, in *The Iliad* rather grim or slapstick, in *The Odyssey* more subtly comic, often dawns on us at the unexpected swerve of a new line. In *Iliad* VIII there is a crash of lightning against the Akhaians and the best charioteers give way: Idómeneus retreats, Agamémnon retreats, big Aias and little Aias retreat, but Nestor? Nestor alone stood fast, we hear, and just as we begin to admire the veteran the next line says (81),

οὔ τι ἑκών, ἀλλ' ἵππος ἐτείρετο

"Not that he wanted to in the least, but one of his horses was disabled." In *Odyssey* IV, after Helen's story of how virtuously she kept Odysseus' secret when she had recognized him spying in Troy, Meneláos cannot refrain from a pointed story to keep the record straight. There is a march of hexameters extolling Odysseus' courage when he and the Akhaian captains were waiting in the wooden horse to bring death upon the Trojans. Then abruptly, in 274, ἦλθες ἔπειτα σὺ κεῖσε. The words make a trochee and two amphibrachs: "Who should come by there but *you* 1
then"—and he goes on to tell of the peril she put them all in by mimicking the voices of their wives. You can see this trick of the sudden change of movement and tone played

by Eurýmakhos in *Odyssey* I, 405, when after several lines of hearty assurance to Telémakhos he looks at him harder, ἀλλ' ἐθέλω σε, φέριστε, περὶ ξείνοιο ἐρέσθαι and the sneer becomes, yes, audible.

Another thing, more highly dramatic, is of course the calculated and gradated heightening of tone or energy throughout a longer passage. For a crescendo of passion, I suppose Akhilleus' great tirade in *Iliad* IX, 307 sqq., cannot be matched, but Odysseus, among his other gifts of gab, has a way of beginning mild and ending deadly. In XVIII there are two examples, a relatively brief one in his reply to Iros, 15 sqq., and a longer one to Eurýmakhos, 366 sqq.

Now all these that I have mentioned are tiny applications of a principle everywhere at work over the expanse of both poems. Narrative art lives as a river lives, first by grace of tributaries—in Homer by the continual refreshment of invention and unlooked-for turns—and second by the direction of flow. If in the line and passage the poems are interesting, as they are, heaven knows they are even more interesting, in the ways they take as their currents widen. Not that Homer is free of *longueurs:* Phoinix' tale of Meleagros in *Iliad* IX strikes me as windy, and in the slow movement of *The Odyssey* at least one of the digressions and retards—the pedigree of Theoklýmenos—was too much even for this virtuoso to bring off. He nods, and we nod with him. But almost always the attention of the audience is courted and held. The earliest critics noticed how Homer varied his effects: for an offhand example, Telémakhos arrives off Pylos by sea at dawn, arrives at Sparta by land at nightfall. The battle scenes in *The Iliad* are sometimes thought monotonous; in fact they are prodigiously inventive and differ one from another not only in general shape but in detail: time after time, it is true, a man falls and his armor clangs upon him, but either he or the man next to him has just been killed in an entirely new way. The formulas give the narrative musical consistency; the innovations keep it alive. The more it is the same, the more it changes. In the very use of the formulas themselves, remarkable effects are got by slight additions or modifications. Penélopê's visits to the banquet hall in *The Odyssey* are formulary: she appears with her maids, she draws her veil down and across her face, she speaks, she retires, weeps, and goes to sleep. The first time (I, 365) after she is gone the suitors make a din, they all swear they will have her; the second time (XVI, 413) she appears and retires as before but there is no din, no swearing; the third time (XVIII, 212) there is no din, but on her appearance (not on her withdrawal) a new line is added to the formula, telling us that the suitors' knees were weakened with lust for her; then comes the swearing line from Book I. Someone has called this trick of style "incremental repetition." It can be, as it is in this case, very powerful.

IV

A probable rate of Homeric performance was about five hundred lines an hour. So far as I know, nobody has gone very far with deductions from this fact. The first four books of *The Odyssey* are obviously a narrative and dramatic unit, so are the next four, and so are the next four. These are three successive waves of action, and each runs to about two thousand lines or about four hours of performance. There is no reason for not regarding this as the duration of a formal recital. If we look again at the second half of the poem we will see that these twelve Books, too, fall into three divisions of about the same length: XIII through XVI, XVII through XX, and XXI through XXIV. These six divisions could well be considered the true Books of *The Odyssey*, within which the traditional Books are like chapters or cantos. Please understand that I have no positive authority for this suggestion; it merely accords with units of probable performance and with the organization of the poem. I would not discard the traditional twenty-four sections, made by Alexandrians who were perhaps following a still earlier tradition.

My six divisions, at any rate, will help us to see the entire poem in outline. In the first performance (I through IV) the last is of course foreshadowed if not determined, Olympian decisions are taken, we are introduced on the scene to the situation that is to be remedied, the conflict to be decided, and we are prepared to meet the famous man who has it all to cope with. In the second (V–VIII) we find him in a distant setting and see him in action, facing other situations, other challenges, making his way back toward the big one that awaits him. In the third (IX–XII) he himself takes over the narration and interests us directly in his past adventures, as though he were now the poet before us. In the fourth or "slow movement" as I call it (XIII–XVI) we see him at last near to his home and battleground, gathering information, testing a likely helper, and reunited with his son. In the fifth (XVII–XX) he enters the scene itself, comes to grip with his situation, suffers it, and sizes up the persons involved in it at close hand. In the sixth (XXI–XXIV) he fights and wins, remedies and recomposes everything.

That is an outline in the most general terms. If I tried to follow and comment on the narrative in detail I would never finish. But there are a few matters. . . . One is this: the universe of *The Odyssey* is subject to moral law, and in the first few lines briefly, or amply in the first few hundred, we are informed of this law, of how it may be violated, and how badly, sooner or later, the offenders come off. The poet was not Plato, Augustine, or Immanuel Kant, and we need not bother to pick flaws in his thinking. He tells us that Odysseus' crew perished for their ἀτασθαλίῃσιν, and then Zeus remarks that Aigísthos in particular and mortals in general have aggravated their lot by the same misdemeanor. What is this misdemeanor? Presumption, impious and reckless: a folly of greed. It is more than taking what belongs to a vague "someone else" —for you are permitted some raids and wars of conquest; it is claiming and taking more than your share in your own commonwealth, without a decent respect for the views of heaven or the opinions of mankind. Wife-stealing and murder, usurpation and insolence: these are the crimes against private and public order that the Olympians meditate as the poem opens. Specific objects of meditation are two Akhaian kingdoms left masterless by the war. Mykênai succumbed, now Ithaka is threatened. The two casts of characters are paralleled, as they will be often again, openly or by implication, throughout the poem: Aigísthos and the suitors, Klytaimnéstra and Penélopê, Agamémnon and Odysseus, Orestês and Telémakhos. The present action will stand out more sharply by contrast with the dark action in Mykênai years before.

A very learned and close student of literature, Erich Auerbach, was led by the argument he was making at the time to assert that "the Homeric style knows only a foreground, only a uniformly illuminated, uniformly objective present." It would be better to remove the word "only" and to add that the Homeric style knows a constant background of retrospect and allusion to the past. It is so in *The Iliad,* and more so in *The Odyssey*. In fact, that past of which the events of *The Iliad* form a part stands everywhere behind the events of *The Odyssey*, the perspective in which *The Odyssey* takes place.

The relationship between the two poems is fascinating. Clearly, both are drawn from the same great fund of stories about the heroes of the expedition against Troy, both are composed in the same formulary tradition, and *The Odyssey* was second in order of composition. Besides a great many lines of *The Iliad* adapted or even playfully parodied in *The Odyssey,* there is one curious bit of evidence that I do not remember seeing noticed. The audience of *The Iliad* had to be kept straight at every point as to which of the two armies was being referred to, hence a great number of formula lines ending with the Greek for "Akhaians," a short syllable and two longs in any of the plural cases. These line endings were so convenient metrically that they were kept throughout *The Odyssey,* even in contexts where they were no longer functional, where it was unnecessary to distinguish Akhaians from anyone else. But no single incident or event of *The Iliad* is so much as referred to in *The Odyssey,* and this is so striking (there are also a few odd differences of vocabulary) that it has been possible to argue that the composer of *The Odyssey* did not even know *The Iliad.* We will be sensible to conclude that he not only knew but leaned on it familiarly; that he, like Odysseus, did not hold with twice-told tales; and that he wanted to complete and complement *The Iliad* by working into his background events that took place after the funeral of Hektor, the close of that poem.

Of these events, the fate of Agamémnon, as I have said, is from first to last the pattern of tragedy against which *The Odyssey* is played to a happy ending. In the successive appearances of the Mykênai theme, something is added each time—here is incremental repetition for you—until the climax in Book XI when Agamémnon himself tells his story. There is also a coda, in Book XXIV. But of course Mykênai is only a part of the background richly given in the first four Books and kept in view later, a background not only of depth in time but of the wide world beyond Ithaka. To make clearer the disorder of that realm there is first the order of Nestor's kingdom, where sacrifice and prayer are duly offered before meat (the suitors in Books I and II neither sacrifice nor pray) and then the splendor of Meneláos' court. In the discourse of the two great gentlemen there are echoes of battles long ago, and there are also images of other seas and lands far to the east and south. Most important of all, from one Book to another in the "Telemakheia" the figure of the absent Odysseus grows more vivid in what is said about him. We are being prepared for an entrance. We are even prepared thematically, in Meneláos' story of seafaring, of detention on an island, of the nymph Eidothea and the Ancient of the Sea, for the adventures of Odysseus.

V

The Odyssey is about a man who cared for his wife and wanted to rejoin her. In the resonance of this affection, and by way of setting it off, the poem touches on a vast diversity of relationships between men and women: love maternal and filial, love connubial and adulterous, seduction and concubinage, infatuation superhuman and human, chance encounters lyric and prosaic. There are many women, young and old, enchantresses and queens and serving maids. In the "society," as we say, of *The Odyssey*, women can be very distinguished: Athena is powerful in the highest circles, Arêtê holds equal power with her husband in Phaiakia, Helen has been re-established in the power of her beauty, which if I am not mistaken she makes Telémakhos feel. The honor roll of lovely dead ladies in Book XI is fully appropriate to this poem. Three of the principal adventures of Odysseus are with exquisite young women of great charm and spirit, and during each of these episodes the audience must wonder how he can possibly move on. He wants to regain his home and kingdom, it is true. But besides that, as Kalypso inquires, what is it about Penélopê that draws him homeward? Her distinction is often mentioned, but do we ever see it overwhelmingly demonstrated?

I believe we do, or should. The demonstration, however, is dramatic and has been missed by many people, though not by all, through a failure to grasp the nature of *The Odyssey* as performance. Let me again insist upon it. More than half of this poem is dialogue. We know that in the first centuries after the Homeric poems were written down, they were presented as performances by rhapsodes who had them by heart, and we know from the *Ion* of Plato that such performances could be histrionic, highly and effectively so. There must have existed among these professionals a tradition of interpretation, nuance, gesture, and "business" in general that may easily have descended from the ἀοιδοί, the inventors, from Homer himself. Into later and literary ages none of this survived. The French Homerist Victor Bérard noticed years ago that our text of *The Odyssey* often resembles an acting script. But no stage directions are included, and if we ask how to play any particular scene we find that there has been no Harley Granville-Barker of Homeric studies.

Well, let us at our leisure look into one situation and one big scene that will answer Kalypso's question.

The purpose of Odysseus, determining the action of the poem, is to get home and to prevail there. Once he lands on Ithaka his problem is a tactical one: how, with his son and two fieldhands, to take on more than one hundred able-bodied young men and kill them all. By the end of Book XVI he has thought his problem through to a certain point: Telémakhos is to precede him to the manor, he is able to follow as a beggar, and at a signal from him the young man is to remove all shields, helmets, and throwing spears from those racks in the banquet hall where, as we remember, they were located in Book I. To be exact, not all are to be removed; a few are to be put aside for use against the suitors. My first observation is that this is as far as Odysseus ever goes, by himself, in planning the final combat. He goes no farther in the course of Book XVII and Book XVIII, and as if to fix this in our minds the poet at the beginning of Book XIX has him repeat his previous instructions about removing the arms; in fact he and Telémakhos do the job together. (This repetition used to be thought an interpolation; the arms, at any rate, are removed.)

Let us now consider what *does* happen in Books XVII and XVIII. If I am right in dividing the poem into six performances, these Books with XIX and XX make up the fifth. Early in XVII Telémakhos leaves the swineherd's hut, goes home to the manor hall, and passes on to his mother the news given him by Meneláos at Sparta—that Odysseus is not dead but alive. The words are barely out of his mouth before his supercargo, the diviner, swears to Penélopê that her husband is not only alive but on the island at that very moment. Since the first piece of news is certainly authentic, the second—though it may seem fantastic—must at least quicken her interest in any stranger who appears. The only stranger about to appear is Odysseus in his rags. We may or may not recall Helen's boast of having recognized him through a similar disguise in a similar situation at Troy; if we do—and after all we heard the story only the other evening—our feeling of suspense may be heightened. Presently, strange to relate, Odysseus is in fact recognized just outside the manor. A dying old hunting dog who hasn't seen him for twenty years knows him by the sound of his voice.

Odysseus now enters the hall, begging, and one of the suitors banqueting there hits him with a footstool. Penélopê has heard the scene from her room. She orders the swineherd to fetch the beggar in case he has news of Odysseus, and the swineherd tells her the beggar does indeed have news, at least he has sworn that Odysseus is nearby on the mainland and will soon be home. "If Odysseus comes, he will repay the violence of the suitors," she says, using the future tense for that eventuality in the most hopeful speech she has yet made. At this point Telémakhos, downstairs in hall, sneezes, and Penélopê laughs at the good omen—the first time she has laughed in *The Odyssey*. She goes eagerly to the door, but Eumaios returns without the beggar, who wishes to put off a meeting until the young men have left the hall for the night. In spite of her impatience, the lady concedes that the stranger is right and is no fool.

Are we to suppose here, at the end of XVII, that it has even crossed her mind who the stranger might be? For the audience, this is already a very interesting question. The answer is, probably not—though it is clear how excited she has become.

In the next Book, XVIII, Penélopê feels impelled for reasons she cannot analyze to go downstairs among the suitors, to dazzle the young men with her beauty and to be solicitous of the beggar, who has come off well in a fist fight. She is now in the beggar's presence. Is it his presence that prompts her to a rather gratuitous speech, a speech with an air of being "to whom it may concern," recalling her husband's instructions when he left for the Trojan War? Her point is that she cannot hold out much longer against marriage with one of her suitors. She induces the young men to give her some gifts (to the amusement of Odysseus) and then withdraws until the evening is over and the suitors have left the place. We come to Book XIX. It is after dark. From the empty banquet hall Odysseus and his son remove the arms and put them back in a storeroom. Before they do this, however, Telémakhos has the old servant, Eurýkleia, temporarily lock all the maids in the women's quarters. Why? Because among these women there are a dozen mistresses and accomplices of the suitors, who are only waiting until the house is quiet to slip out and join their lovers in the town. We already know one of these girls, Melántho, mistress of Eurýmakhos. When Penélopê comes down to interview the beggar by firelight, this girl is with her, as the poet carefully makes us see. The whole interview is conducted in her presence. If she should suspect the identity of the beggar, Odysseus' tactical plan—to catch the suitors in hall without spears and trust to Athena—will miscarry, to say the least.

As the interview begins, Penélopê follows the usual formula and asks the stranger who he is. His reply is evasive, though it is moving if we remember that these are the first words he has spoken to her in twenty years. She proceeds to explain to him—to him, a stranger and vagabond—what her predicament is. She tells him of the famous feat of weaving and unweaving by which she had kept her suitors waiting for more than three years. It is as if she were justifying herself aloud for being, as she tells him she is now, at the end of her resources. Justifying herself to her husband? That is the fact, but it may still be something of which we are meant to be aware while she is not. In return for her confidence, Odysseus confides that he is a grandson of King Minos of Crete and that he once entertained Odysseus at Knossos. The lady weeps. She dries her eyes and asks him to prove it by recalling how Odysseus looked. He does so, very accurately, describing a brooch and tunic that Penélopê had given him. He adds, with a typical Odyssean touch, that the Cretan women had found him a fine sight in his tunic. The lady weeps a second time and remarks that *she* will never lay eyes on Odysseus again.

The beggar now contradicts her. He now ventures a speech that, taken along with all that has led up to it, looks like a serious effort to impart information. He not only repeats what he has already told the swineherd and the swineherd has relayed to her—that Odysseus is on the mainland and coming home—but he swears very solemnly that Odysseus will arrive (306)

τοῦδ' αὐτοῦ λυκάβαντος

"this very λυκάβας" and "between the waning and the new moon." Nobody can be sure what λυκάβας means, but it may well mean "the going of daylight" and the phrase could have the sense "before another day passes." As to the phrase about the new moon, there is very little doubt that this is precise. The next day, as we will hear in Book XX, is a feast day to Apollo, and that would be the festival of the new moon awaited in the evening. So he is telling her twice, cryptically and elliptically for the benefit of the maids in earshot, that her husband will be home tomorrow.

Now we, the audience, must suppose that this lady, who

has been represented often as extremely intelligent, will be asking herself with some urgency how the vagabond before her could possibly swear to anything so definite. She is controlled, as usual. She answers that if he were right he would soon know her love, but no, he can't be right. Odysseus cannot return. She offers him a footbath and he declines it unless there is an old maid-servant to give it to him. Penélopê says there is in fact an old woman who nursed Odysseus in infancy, and she tells Eurýkleia to bathe him. Here is an actor's line (358).

νίψον σοῖο ἄνακτος

"Bathe your master's—" the line begins, and a shiver runs through the audience. The next word, however, is not πόδες "feet" but ὁμήλικα "coeval" or "contemporary." (I think that Sophocles, for one, noted this feat of brinkmanship in a single line.) Now we have the well-known episode of the footbath during which Eurýkleia recognizes Odysseus by his scar, but he throttles her and keeps her quiet. This has been generally held to be the only recognition that takes place in Book XIX. At the climax when the old woman glances toward Penélopê as if to reveal Odysseus, the poet tells us that Athena has turned the lady's mind elsewhere so that she doesn't notice. Penélopê, in other words, is lost in thought, and we are aware of all that she has to think about. I find the outcome of her thinking very impressive.

When Penélopê speaks again, she tells the beggar that she has a dream for him to interpret—the dream of her pet geese killed by an eagle who professed to be Odysseus. In this there is a remarkable little confession that she had grown fond, in a way, of having the suitors about her, but there is more to it than that. When she says that on waking she saw the dream geese still there, what can she possibly mean except, "It is a dream to think that you can kill them; they are so many, they will survive and you will not."

This at any rate is what the beggar answers. He assures her that there is no other way to interpret the dream than as Odysseus, in the dream, has already done: the suitors will be killed. Assuming the presence of the unfaithful maid—or maids—he takes a serious risk here in order to make it clear to her that he is ready for battle. She now remarks that dreams are not to be counted on, but that she has one more thing to tell him: listen carefully. She has made up her mind that *tomorrow* will be the day of decision as to whom she will marry, and the decision will be reached through the test of the bow. In reply to this the beggar says in effect that that will be excellent and tomorrow will not be too soon.

I agree with the late Philip Whaley Harsh, of Stanford, that this is one of the most interesting recognition scenes ever devised. Part of my argument was anticipated by Professor Harsh in the *American Journal of Philology*, Vol. 71 (1950). It is possible—though I think barely possible—to read the scene in the previously accepted way as involving no more communication between the man and woman than is compatible with their respective roles of lady and beggar, the roles they stick to, though so precariously. On this reading all evidence of understanding between them is coincidence and irony. But that is simply not consistent with the situation as a whole—a situation built up for the audience in the course of this performance. During the day, before the evening, Penélopê has been told first that her husband is alive, second that he is on the island, and third that he is coming soon. She has been waiting for ten years with no such authentic news and no such startling expectations and had made the suitors wait for nearly four. Are we, the audience, to believe that she wouldn't wait a few days longer to see if her husband turns up? Is it conceivable that, instead of waiting, the woman so distinguished for tenacity would this very evening give up the waiting game and seriously propose to marry the next day? How could she come to this abrupt decision in the course of her evening scene with Odysseus unless she realized that the stranger before her was indeed her husband?

Why, in short, underrate the high and beautiful tension of the scene and the nerve, the magnificence of Penélopê? Not Kalypso, not Nausikaa, not Kirkê could have played this scene. Consider what she bestows on Odysseus. Up to now his plan of action, as I have noticed, has been fairly desperate. Now it is she, not he, who remembers the big hunting bow that has hung in an inner room since he left Ithaka. Archery against men who have no missiles is in fact the only practical way of beating the numerical odds. Penélopê supplies the weapon for the suitors' downfall, and she does so for that purpose and no other. At the opening of Book XXI when Athena sends her for the bow, the goddess is said to prompt her to this as "the contest and start of slaughter"—a phrase that goes naturally by the syntax with what is in Penélopê's mind. In the course of that Book it is Penélopê who insists at the crucial moment that the beggar be given a try at the bow; she all but literally places it in his hands. I conclude that for the last and greatest of Odysseus' feats of arms his wife is as responsible as he is. The reasons for his affection should now be clear.

VI

If in other Books, especially in XXIII, there are details inconsistent with the interpretation I have given, we may regard these as instances of what Professor Lord has called the varying "pulls" of previous versions. But I am not sure there are any real inconsistencies. There is a certain mystery, if you like, but so is there mystery in *Daisy Miller*. Harsh explained Penélopê's affected incredulity and hesitation in XXIII as due to emotional exhaustion (she had been terribly afraid that Odysseus couldn't do it) and to the need to collect herself before resuming a marriage interrupted for twenty years. Twenty years is no trifle. If you left home to take part in the Second World War, imagine yourself lost to view afterward and only now returning; or if your father went to the war, imagine it of him. One difference between Homer and many of his commentators is that Homer could imagine people in situations. Some commentators even call it an "inconsistency" that the shade of Amphímedon in Book XXIV credits Odysseus with having thought up the archery contest—as though Amphímedon could have known any better, or made any better assumption.

As I noted earlier, Book XXIV has often been regarded as a later addition to the poem. This is mainly because two early critics, Aristophanes and Aristarchus, are said to have called line 296 of XXIII the "goal" or "end" of *The Odyssey*. This line, on which Odysseus and Penélopê retire to bed, could have been the conclusion of an old-fashioned movie but not of a poem like this. It is true that there are also some linguistic grounds, but they do not appear to be probative. Even if they were, I could only say that in substance Book XXIV is fully "Homeric" and that whoever composed it knew what he was doing. The many references to Laërtês throughout the poem require Book XXIV; so do at least two previous allusions by Odysseus to the aftermath of the fight with the suitors. In this Book the comparison between Penélopê and Klytaimnéstra, recurrent throughout the poem, is rounded off by Agamémnon himself. But there is another artistic reason for Book XXIV, and a great one. If Homer's incidental purpose in *The Odyssey* was to complete and complement *The Iliad*, XXIV in effect completes both poems at once. The Akhaian antagonists of *The Iliad*, Agamémnon and Akhilleus, are here reconciled among the dead, and as *The Iliad* closed with Hektor's funeral, *The Odyssey* does not come to a close until the funeral of Akhilleus has been described.

A page or so more and I will have done with my reflections. I have named Professor Lord's book and Professor Harsh's article, each illuminating in its way. Two more books that I have valued are *Homer and the Monuments,* by H. L. Lorimer (Macmillan, London, 1950) and *The Poetry of Homer* by S. E. Bassett (University of California Press, 1938). Rhys Carpenter on *Folk Tale, Fiction and Saga in the Homeric Epics* (University of California Press, 1946) is full of interesting arguments. So, as I have said, is Denys Page's book on *The Odyssey,* though I read it rather as a brief than as a judgment. His later book, *History and the Homeric Iliad* (University of California Press, 1959) is more brilliant still. The most recent good annotated edition is W. B. Stanford's (Macmillan, London, 1947). D. B. Monro's annotated edition of Books XIII–XIV, with its long Appendix (Oxford, 1901), is a superb monument of scholarship and good sense in its time. I am indebted to it for my excision of lines 275–278 in Book I, an excision that obviates one of Page's chief criticisms. I like Monro's statement about the "Telemakheia": "It secures that gradual heightening of interest which is the chief secret of dramatic art." I also owe to Monro, and to J. D. Denniston's wonderful book, *The Greek Particles* (Oxford, 1954), confirmation of my sense that the colloquial entered into Homer's style in *The Odyssey.*

A word about "translation." *The Odyssey,* considered strictly as an aesthetic object, is to be appreciated only in Greek. It can no more be translated into English than rhododendron can be translated into dogwood. You must learn Greek if you want to experience Homer, just as you must go to the Acropolis and look at it if you want to experience the Parthenon. There is a sense, however, in which the Greek poem was itself a translation. It was a translation into Homer's metered language, into his narrative and dramatic style, of an action invented and elaborated in the imagination. This action and the personages involved in it were what mattered most to poet and audience.

It might be possible to translate, or retranslate, this action into our language. We may assume that Homer used all the Greek he knew, all the resources of the language available to him and amenable to his meter. Three or more Greek dialects and perhaps half a millennium of Greek hexameter poetry contributed to Homer's language; so did a wide spectrum of idiom from the hieratic to the colloquial. Anglo-Irish-American provides comparable linguistic and poetic resources, a spectrum of idiom comparably wide. If you can grasp the situation and action rendered by the Greek poem, every line of it, and by the living performer that it demands, and if you will not betray Homer with prose or poor verse, you may hope to make an equivalent that he himself would not disavow.

Why care about an old work in a dead language that no one reads, or at least no one of those who, glancing at their Rolex watches, guide us into the future? Well, I love the future myself and expect everything of it: better artists than Homer, better works of art than *The Odyssey*. The prospect of looking back at our planet from the moon seems to me to promise a marvelous enlargement of our views. But let us hold fast to what is good, hoping that if we do anything any good those who come after us will pay us the same compliment. If the world was given to us to explore and master, here is a tale, a play, a song about that endeavor long ago, by no means neglecting self-mastery, which in a sense is the whole point. Electronic brains may help us to use our heads but will not excuse us from that duty, and as to our hearts—cardiograms cannot diagnose what may be most ill about them, or confirm what may be best. The faithful woman and the versatile brave man, the wakeful intelligence open to inspiration or grace—these are still exemplary for our kind, as they always were and always will be. Nor do I suppose that the pleasure of hearing a story in words has quite gone out. Even movies and TV make use of words. *The Odyssey* at all events was made for your pleasure, in Homer's words and in mine.

Perugia, June 1962

Appendix

Cicero: *de optimo genere oratorum*, v, 13–14 (ca. 46 b.c.)

Since there was a great misunderstanding as to the nature of their oratory [Aeschines' and Demosthenes'], I thought I should undertake a work which would be useful to my students, though not necessarily to myself. That is, I translated the most famous speeches of the two most eloquent Attic orators, Aeschines and Demosthenes . . . And I did not translate them literally [*ut interpres*] but as an orator, preserving the same ideas and forms, or tropes as it were, in language consonant with our usage. In doing this, I did not think it necessary to translate word for word [*verbum pro verbo*], I preserved the general style and force of the language. For I did not believe it was my duty to count out words to the reader like coins, but rather to pay them out by weight as it were.

Horace: *Ars Poetica*, 128–135 (ca. 20 b.c.)

'It is difficult to develop everyday themes in an original way, and you would do better to present the *Iliad* in dramatic form than if you were the first to produce unknown materials never used before on stage. Material in the public domain will never become your private property if you do not waste your time going around in worn-out circles, and do not be a literal translator, faithfully rendering word for word [*nec verbo verbum curabis reddere/ fidus interpres*] from the Greek, and do not be merely an imitator thereby getting yourself into a hole from which either good conscience, or the laws of the work itself, will forbid you to climb out.'

(trans. by Norman J. DeWitt)

SAINT JEROME: Letter LVII (*de optimo genere interpretandi*) (A.D. 395)

. . . Terence has translated Menander; Plautus and Caecilius have translated the old comic poets. But do they stick at the literal words? Don't they rather try to preserve the beauty and style of their originals? What men like you call accuracy in translation, learned men call pedantry. It was men of that sort who were my teachers twenty years ago, and even then I was the victim of the same sort of mistake which is now ascribed to me, though I certainly never thought the charge would come from *you*. When I translated Eusebius' *Chronicle* into Latin, I made among other points in my preface the following observations: "It is difficult when one is following lines laid down by other men not at times to diverge from them; and it is difficult to retain in translation the particular verbal felicities of a foreign language. Every single word has its own individual meaning; it may be that I have no word with which to render it, and if I skirt it with a circumlocution, I must make a lengthy detour. Add to these difficulties the problems of tortuous transpositions, case-differences, variations in metaphor and, finally, the peculiar and, as I call it, *indigenous* quality of the language. If I translate word for word, the result sounds clumsy and absurd; if I am forced to change anything or to rearrange, it will look as though I had failed my duty as a translator." Then, after a long discussion which it would be tiresome to follow here, I added, "If anyone supposes that translation does not drastically affect stylistic beauty, let him render Homer word for word into Latin. No, I will go further and ask him to turn Homer into Latin prose.

And what will the result be? The syntax becomes ridiculous, and the most articulate poet who ever lived is turned into a stammerer."

My only purpose in quoting from my own writings is to establish that from my youth onwards, I have always aimed at translating sense, not words. But if my authority is insufficient, read and reflect on this brief preface from the biography of St. Antony:[1]

> A literal translation from one language to another obscures the sense; just as with grass, too lush a growth reduces the yield. So long as diction is subservient to cases and figures of speech, a literal translation must explain by tiresome circumlocution what a few words could otherwise make clear. This error I have tried to avoid in translating, at your request, the life of St. Antony; and though I am not always literal, I have been fully loyal to the sense. Let others clutch at syllables and words; for your part, look for the sense.

Time would fail me if I cited as witnesses all those who have translated according to the sense. For the present I need only mention the case of Hilary the Confessor, who translated a group of Homilies on Job and several Psalms from Greek into Latin. But he did not stick with the drowsiness of the letter, and chain himself with stale and vulgar literalism. Like a conqueror he led away captive into his own language the meaning of his originals . . .

Preface to the Book on the Sites and Names of Hebrew Places (A.D. 388)

. . . I have explained my method once for all in the preface to my translation of the *Chronicle,* where I said that I might be called at once a translator and a composer of a new work . . .

[1] The preface to Athanasius' life of Antony was written by Bishop Evagrius of Antioch.

Preface to the Books of Samuel and Kings (A.D. 391)

. . . Read, then, by Samuel and Kings; mine, I say, mine. For whatever by diligent translation and careful emendation we have mastered and made our own, is ours. And when you understand that of which you were ignorant before, either regard me as a translator, or, if you are ungrateful, a paraphraser, though I am not in the least aware of having diverged from the Hebrew original . . .
(trans. by William Arrowsmith)

ALEXANDER BARCLAY: The Argument, *The Ship of Fools* (1509)

'But concernynge the translacion of this Boke: I exhort ye reders to take no displesour for it is not translated word by worde accordinge to the verses of my actour. For I have but only drawen into our moder tunge, in rude language the sentences of the verses as nere as the parcyte of my wyt wyl suffer me, sometime addynge, sometyme detractinge and takinge away suche thinges as seemeth me [un]necessary and superflue.'

KING JAMES BIBLE: The Translators to the Reader (1611)

Translation it is that openeth the window, to let in the light; that breaketh the shell, that we may eat the kernel; that putteth aside the curtain, that we may look into the most holy place; that removeth the cover of the well, that we may come by the water, even as Jacob rolled away the stone from the mouth of the well, by which means the flocks of Laban were watered. Indeed without translation into the vulgar tongue, the unlearned are but like children at Jacob's well (which was deep) without a bucket or something to draw with or as that person mentioned by

Esau, to whom when a sealed book was delivered, with this motion, 'Read this, I pray thee,' he was fain to make this answer, 'I cannot, for it is sealed'. . . .

Another thing we think good to admonish thee of (gentle Reader) that we have not tied our selves to an uniformity of phrasing, or to an identity of words, as some peradventure would wish that we had done, because they observe, that some learned men somewhere, have been as exact as they could that way. Truly, that we might not vary from the sense of that which we had translated before, if the word signified the same in both places (for, there be some words that be not of the same sense every where) we were especially careful, and made a conscience, according to our duty. But that we should express the same notion in the same particular word; as for example, if we translate the Hebrew or Greek word once by 'purpose,' never to call it 'intent,' if one where 'journeying;' never 'travelling'; if one where 'think,' never 'suppose'; if one where 'pain,' never 'ache'; if one where 'joy,' never 'gladness'; etc. Thus to mince the matter, we thought to savour more of curiosity than wisdom, and that rather it would breed scorn in the atheist, than bring profit to the godly Reader. For is the kingdom of God become words or syllables? Why should we be in bondage to them if we may be free, use one precisely when we may use another no less fit, as commodiously? A godly Father in the primitive time showed himself greatly moved, that one of newfangledness called κράββατον σκίμπους, though the difference be little or none; another reporteth, that he was much abused for turning *cucurbita* (to which reading the people had been used) into *hedera*. Now if this happen in better times, and upon so small occasions, we might justly fear hard censure, if generally we should make verbal and unnecessary changings. We might also be charged (by scoffers) with some unequal dealing towards a great number of good English words. For as it is written of a certain great Philosopher, that he should say, that those logs were happy that were made images to be worshipped; for their fellows, as good as they, lay for blocks behind the fire: so if we should say, as it were, unto certain words, Stand up higher, have a place in the Bible always; and to others of like quality, Get ye hence, be banished for ever; we might be banished for ever; we might be taxed peradventure with S. James his words, namely, 'To be partial in our selves and judges of evil thoughts.' Add hereunto, that niceness in words was always counted the next step to trifling; and so was to be curious about names too: also that we cannot follow a better pattern for elocution than God himself; therefore he using divers words, in his holy writ, and indifferently for one thing in nature: we, if we will not be superstitious, may use the same liberty in our English versions out of Hebrew and Greek, for that copy or store that he hath given us. Lastly, we have on the one side avoided the scrupulosity of the Puritans, who leave the old Ecclesiastical words, and betake them to other, as when they put 'washing' for 'baptism,' and 'congregation' instead of 'church': as also on the other side we have shunned the obscurity of the Papists, in their 'azimes,' 'tunike,' 'holocausts,' 'praepuce,' 'pasche,' and a number of such like, whereof their late translation is full, and that of purpose to darken the sense, that since they must needs translate the Bible, yet by the language thereof, it may be kept from being understood. But we desire that the Scripture may speak like itself, as in the language of Canaan, that it may be understood even of the very vulgar.

CHAPMAN'S HOMER: The Preface to the Reader (1611)

How much I differ, and with what authoritie, let my impartiall and judiciall reader judge—alwaies conceiving how pedanticall and absurd an affectation it is in the interpretation of any Author (much more of Homer) to turn him word for word, when (according to Horace and other best lawgivers to translators) it is the part of every knowing and judiciall interpreter not to follow the number and order of words but the materiall things themselves, and sentences to weigh diligently, and to clothe and adorne them with words and such a stile and forme of Oration as are most apt for the language into which they are converted. If I have not turned him in any place falsly (as all other his interpreters have in many and most of his chiefe places); if I have not left behind me any of his sentence, elegancie, height, intention and invention; if in some few places (especially in my first edition, being done so long since and following the common tract) I be somthing paraphrasticall and faulty—is it justice in that poore fault (if they will needs have it so) to drowne all the rest of my labour? But there is a certaine envious Windsucker, that hovers up and downe, laboriously engrossing al the aire with his luxurious ambition and buzzing into every eare my detraction—affirming I turne Homer out of the Latine onely, etc.—that sets all his associates and the whole rabble of my maligners on their wings with him to beare about my empaire and poyson my reputation. One that, as he thinkes, whatsoever he gives to others he takes from himselfe, so whatsoever he takes from others he addes to himselfe . . .

Ben Jonson: *Timber, or Discoveries,* "The Art of Poetry" (1640)

The third requisite in our poet, or maker, is imitation: to be able to convert the substance or riches of another poet to his own use: to make choice of one excellent man above the rest, and so to follow him till he grow very he, or so like him as the copy may be mistaken for the principal—not as a creature that swallows what it takes in crude, raw, or undigested, but that feeds with an appetite, and hath a stomach to concoct, divide, and turn all into nourishment; not to imitate servilely, as Horace saith, and catch at vices for virtue, but to draw forth out of the best and choicest flowers with the bee, and turn all into honey . . .

ABRAHAM COWLEY: *Pindarique Odes*, Preface (1656)

If a Man should undertake to translate Pindar Word for Word, it would be thought that one Mad-man had translated another; as may appear, when he that understands not the Original, reads the verbal Traduction of him into Latin Prose, than which nothing seems more Raving. And sure, Rhyme, without the Addition of Wit, and the Spirit of Poetry (*quod nequeo monstrare, et sentio tantum*) would but make it ten times more distracted than it is in Prose. We must consider in Pindar the great Difference of Time betwixt his Age and ours, which changes, as in Pictures, at least the Colours of Poetry; the no less Difference betwixt the Religions and Customs of our Countries, and a thousand Particularities of Places, Persons, and Manners, which do but confusedly appear to our Eyes at so great a Distance. And lastly (which were enough alone for my Purpose) we must consider that our Ears are Strangers to the Musick of his Numbers, which sometimes (especially in Songs and Odes) almost without any thing else, makes an excellent Poet. For though the Grammarians and Criticks have labour'd to reduce his Verses into regular Feet and Measures (as they have also those of the Greek and Latin Comedies) yet in effect they are little better than Prose to our Ears. And I would gladly know what Applause our best Pieces of English Poesie could expect from a Frenchman or Italian, if converted faithfully, and Word for Word, into French or Italian Prose. And when we have considered all this, we must needs confess, that after all these Losses sustained by Pindar, all we can add to him by our Wit or Invention (not deserting still his Subject) is not like to make him a Richer Man than he was in his own Country. This is in some measure to be apply'd to all Translations; and the not observing of it, is the Cause that all which ever I yet saw are so much inferior to their Originals. The like happens too in Pictures, from the same Root of exact Imitation; which being a vile and unworthy kind of Servitude, is incapable of producing any thing good or noble. I have seen Originals both in Painting and Poesie, much more beautiful than their natural Objects; but I never saw a Copy better than the Original, which indeed cannot be otherwise; for Men resolving in no case to shoot beyond the Mark, it is a thousand to one if they shoot not short of it. It does not at all trouble me that the Grammarians perhaps will not suffer this libertine way of rendring foreign Authors, to be called Translation; for I am not so much enamour'd of the Name Translator, as not to wish rather to be Something Better, tho' it want yet a Name. I speak not so much all this, in Defence of my manner of Translating or Imitating (or what other Title they please) the two ensuing Odes of Pindar; for that would not deserve half these Words; as by this Occasien to rectifie the Opinion of divers Men upon this Matter. The Psalms of David, (which I believe to have been in their Original, to the Hebrews of his Time, though not to our Hebrews of Buxtorsius's making, the most exalted Pieces of Poesie) are a great Example of what I have said; all the Translators of which (even Mr. Sands himself; for in despight of popular Error, I will be bold not to except him) for this very Reason, that they have not sought to supply the lost Excellencies of another Language with new ones in their own; are so far from doing Honour, or at least justice to that Divine Poet, that methinks they revile him worse than Shimei. And Buchanan himself (though much the best of them all, and indeed a great Person) comes in my Opinion no less short of David, than his Country does of Judaea. Upon this ground, I have in these two Odes of Pindar, taken, left out, and added what I please; nor make it so much my Aim to let the Reader know precisely what he spoke, as what was his Way and Manner of speaking; which has not been yet (that I know of) introduced into English, though it be the noblest and highest kind of writing in Verse; and which might, perhaps, be put into the List of Pancirollus, among the lost Inventions of Antiquity.

Sir John Denham: Preface to *The Destruction of Troy* (1656)

There are so few Translations which deserve praise, that I scarce ever saw any which deserv'd pardon; those who travel in that kind, being for the most part so unhappy, as to rob others, without enriching themselves, pulling down the fame of good Authors, without raising their own: Neither hath any Author been more hardly dealt withal than this our Master; and the reason is evident, for, what is most excellent, is most inimitable; and if even the worst Authors are yet made worse by their Translators, how impossible is it not to do great injury to the best? And therefore I have not the vanity to think my Copy equal to the Original, nor (consequently) my self altogether guiltless of what I accuse others; but if I can do Virgil less injury than others have done, it will be, in some degree to do him right; and indeed, the hope of doing him more right, is the only scope of this Essay, by opening this new way of translating this Author, to those whom youth, leisure, and better fortune makes fitter for such undertakings.

I conceive it a vulgar error in translating Poets, to affect being *Fidus Interpres*; let that care be with them who deal in matters of Fact, or matters of Faith: but whosoever aims at it in Poetry, as he attempts what is not required, so he shall never perform what he attempts; for it is not his busines alone to translate Language into Language, but Poesie into Poesie; and Poesie is of so subtile a spirit, that in pouring out of one Language into another, it will all evaporate; and if a new spirit be not added in the transfusion, there will remain nothing but a *Caput mortuum*, there being certain Graces and Happinesses peculiar to every Language, which gives life and energy to the words; and whosoever offers at Verbal Translation, shall have the misfortune of that young Traveller, who lost his own language abroad, and brought home no other instead of it: for the grace of the Latine will be lost by being turned into English words; and the grace of the English, by being turned into the Latine Phrase. And as speech is the apparel of our thoughts, so are there certain Garbs and Modes of speaking, which vary with the times; the fashion of our clothes being not more subject to alteration, than that of our speech: and this I think Tacitus means, by that which he calls 'Sermonem temporis istius auribus accommodatum'; the delight of change being as due to the curiosity of the ear, as of the eye; and therefore if Virgil must needs speak English, it were fit he should speak not only as a man of this Nation, but as a man of this age; and if this disguise I have put upon him (I wish I could give it a better name) fit not naturally and easily on so grave a person, yet it may become him better than that Fools-Coat wherein the French and Italian have of late presented him; at least, I hope, it will not make him appear deformed, by making any part enormously bigger or less than the life, (I having made it my principal care to follow him, as he made it his to follow Nature in all his proportions). Neither have I any where offered such violence to his sense, as to make it seem mine, and not his. Where my expressions are not so full as his, either our Language, or my Art were defective (but I rather suspect my self); but where mine are fuller than his, they are but the impressions which the often reading of him, hath left upon my thoughts; so that if they are not his own Conceptions, they are at least the results of them; and if (being conscious of making him speak worse than he did almost in every line) I erre in endeavouring sometimes to make him speak better; I hope it will be judged an error on the right hand, and such an one as may deserve pardon, if not imitation.

JOHN DRYDEN: Preface to the Translation of Ovid's *Epistles* (1680)

All translation, I suppose, may be reduced to these three heads.

First, that of metaphrase, or turning an author word by word, and line by line, from one language into another. Thus, or near this manner, was Horace his *Art of Poetry* translated by Ben Johnson. The second way is that of paraphrase, or translation with latitude, where the author is kept in view by the translator, so as never to be lost, but his words are not so strictly followed as his sense; and that too is admitted to be amplified, but not altered. Such is Mr. Waller's translation of Virgil's Fourth *Aeneid*. The third way is that of imitation, where the translator (if he now has not lost that name) assumes the liberty, not only to vary from the words and sense, but to forsake them both as he sees occasion; and taking only some general hints from the original, to run division on the groundwork, as he pleases. Such is Mr. Cowley's practice in turning two Odes of Pindar, and one of Horace, into English.

Concerning the first of these methods, our master Horace has given us this caution:

> *Nec verbum verbo curabis reddere, fidus*
> *Interpres . . .*

> Nor word for word too faithfully translate;

as the Earl of Roscommon has excellently rendered it. Too

faithfully is, indeed, pedantically: 'tis a faith like that which proceeds from superstition, blind and zealous. Take it in the expression of Sir John Denham to Sir Richard Fanshaw, on his version of the *Pastor Fido*:

> That servile path thou nobly dost decline,
> Of tracing word by word, and line by line:
> A new and nobler way thou dost pursue,
> To make translations and translators too:
> They but preserve the ashes, thou the flame,
> True to his sense, but truer to his fame.

'Tis almost impossible to translate verbally, and well, at the same time; for the Latin (a most severe and compendious language) often expresses that in one word, which either the barbarity or the narrowness of modern tongues cannot supply in more. 'Tis frequent, also, that the conceit is couched in some expression, which will be lost in English:

> *Atque iidem venti vela fidemque ferent.*

What poet of our nation is so happy as to express this thought literally in English, and to strike wit, or almost sense, out of it?

In short, the verbal copier is encumbered with so many difficulties at once, that he can never disentangle himself from all. He is to consider, at the same time, the thought of his author, and his words, and to find out the counterpart to each in another language; and, besides this, he is to confine himself to the compass of numbers, and the slavery of rhyme. 'Tis much like dancing on ropes with fettered legs: a man may shun a fall by using caution; but the gracefulness of motion is not to be expected: and when we have said the best of it, 'tis but a foolish task; for no sober man would put himself into a danger for the applause of escaping without breaking his neck. We see Ben Johnson could not avoid obscurity in his literal translation of Horace, attempted in the same compass of lines: nay, Horace himself could scarce have done it to a Greek poet:

Brevis esse laboro, obscurus fio:

either perspicuity or gracefulness will frequently be wanting. Horace had indeed avoided both these rocks in his translation of the three first lines of Homer's *Odysseus,* which he has contracted into two:

Dic mihi musa virum captae post tempora Trojae,
Que mores huminum multorum vidit, et urbes.

Muse, speak the man, who, since the siege of Troy,
So many towns, such change of manners saw.
—Earl of Roscommon

But then the sufferings of Ulysses, which are a considerable part of that sentence, are omitted:—

ὃς νάλα πολλὰ πλάγχθη

The consideration of these difficulties, in a servile, literal translation, not long since made two of our famous wits, Sir John Denham and Mr. Cowley, to contrive another way of turning authors into our tongue, called, by the latter of them, imitation. As they were friends, I suppose they communicated their thoughts on this subject to each other; and therefore their reasons for it are little different, though the practice of one is much more moderate. I take imitation of an author, in their sense, to be an endeavour of a later poet to write like one who has written before him, on the same subject; that is, not to translate his words, or to be confined to his sense, but only to set him as a pattern, and to write, as he supposes that author would have done, had he lived in our age, and in our country. Yet I dare not say, that either of them have carried this libertine way of rendering authors (as Mr. Cowley calls it) so far as my definition reaches; for in the *Pindaric Odes,* the customs and ceremonies of ancient Greece are still preserved. But I know not what mischief may arise hereafter from the example of such an innovation, when writers of unequal parts to him shall imitate so bold an undertaking. To add and to diminish what we please, which is the way avowed by him, ought only to be granted to Mr. Cowley, and that too only in his translation of Pindar; because he alone was able to make him amends, by giving him better of his own, whenever he refused his author's thoughts. Pindar is generally known to be a dark writer, to want connection, (I mean as to our understanding), to soar out of sight, and leave his reader at a gaze. So wild and ungovernable a poet cannot be translated literally; his genius is too strong to bear a chain, and Samson-like he shakes it off. A genius so elevated and unconfined as Mr. Cowley's, was but necessary to make Pindar speak English, and that was to be performed by no other way than imitation. But if Virgil, or Ovid, or any regular intelligible authors, be thus used, 'tis no longer to be called their work, when neither the thoughts nor words are drawn from the original; but instead of them there is something new produced, which is almost the creation of another hand. By this way, 'tis true, somewhat that is excellent may be invented, perhaps more excellent than the first design; though Virgil must be still excepted, when that 'perhaps' takes place. Yet he who is inquisitive to know an author's thoughts will be disappointed in his expectation; and 'tis not always that a man will be contented to have a present made him, when he expects the payment of a debt. To state it fairly; imitation of an author is the most advantageous way for a translator to show himself, but the greatest wrong which can be done to the memory and reputation of the dead. Sir John Denham (who advised more liberty than he took himself) gives his reason for his innovation, in his admirable Preface before the translation of the Second *Aeneid:* 'Poetry is of so subtile a spirit, that, in pouring out of one language into another, it will all evaporate; and, if a new spirit be not added in the transfusion, there will remain nothing but a *caput mortuum.*' I confess this argument holds good against a literal translation; but who defends it? Imitation and verbal version are, in my opinion, the two extremes which ought to be avoided; and therefore, when I have proposed the mean betwixt them, it will be seen how far his argument will reach.

No man is capable of translating poetry, who, besides a genius to that art, is not a master both of his author's language, and of his own; nor must we understand the language only of the poet, but his particular turn of thoughts and expression, which are the characters that distinguish, and as it were individuate him from all other writers. When we are come thus far, 'tis time to look into ourselves, to conform our genius to his, to give his thought either the same turn, if our tongue will bear it, or, if not, to vary but the dress, not to alter or destroy the substance. The like care must be taken of the more outward ornaments, the words. When they appear (which is but seldom) literally graceful, it were an injury to the author that they should be changed. But since every language is so full of its own proprieties, that what is beautiful in one, if often barbarous, nay sometimes nonsense, in another, it would be unreasonable to limit a translator to the narrow compass of this author's words: 'tis enough if he choose out some expression which does not vitiate the sense. I suppose he may stretch his chain to such a latitude; but by innovation of thoughts, methinks he breaks it. By this means the spirit of an author may be transfused, and yet not lost: and thus 'tis plain, that the reason alleged by Sir John Denham has no farther force than to expression; for thought, if it be translated truly, cannot be lost in another language; but the words that convey it to our apprehension (which are the image and ornament of that thought,) may be so ill chosen, as to make it appear in an unhandsome dress, and rob it of its native lustre. There is, therefore, a liberty to be allowed for the expression; neither is it necessary that words and lines should be confined to the measure of their original. The sense of an author, generally speaking, is to be sacred and inviolable. If the fancy of Ovid be luxuriant, 'tis his character to be so; and if I retrench it, he is no longer Ovid. It will be replied, that he receives advantage by this lopping of superfluous branches; but I rejoin, that a translator has no such right. When a painter copies from the life, I suppose he has no privilege to alter features and lineaments, under pretence that his picture will look better: perhaps the face which he has drawn would be more exact, if the eyes or nose were altered; but 'tis his business to make it resemble the original. In two cases only there may a seeming difficulty arise; that is, if the thought be notoriously trivial or dishonest; but the same answer will serve for both, that then they ought not to be translated:

> . . . *Et quae*
> *Desperes tractata nitescere posse, relinquas.*

Thus I have ventured to give my opinion on this subject against the authority of two great men, but I hope without offence to either of their memories; for I both loved them living, and reverence them now they are dead. But if, after what I have urged, it be thought by better judges that the praise of a translation consists in adding new beauties to the piece, thereby to recompense the loss which it sustains by change of language, I shall be willing to be taught better, and to recant. In the meantime it seems to me that the true reason why we have so few versions which are tolerable, is not from the too close pursuing of the author's sense, but because there are so few who have all the talents which are requisite for translation, and that there is so little praise and so small encouragement for so considerable a part of learning.

John Dryden: Dedication of *The Aeneid* (1697)

I am also bound to tell your Lordship, in my own defense, that, from the beginning of the *First Georgic* to the end of the last *Aeneid*, I found the difficulty of translation growing on me in every succeeding book: for Virgil, above all poets, had a stock, which I may call almost inexhaustible, of figurative, elegant, and sounding words. I, who inherit but a small portion of his genius, and write in a language so much inferior to the Latin, have found it very painful to vary phrases, when the same sense returns upon me. Even he himself, whether out of necessity or choice, has often express'd the same thing in the same words, and often repeated two or three whole verses which he had us'd before. Words are not so easily coin'd as money; and yet we see that the credit not only of banks, but of exchequers, cracks, when little comes in and much goes out. Virgil call'd upon me in every line for some new word, and I paid so long, that I was almost bankrupt; so that the latter end must needs be more burdensome than the beginning or the middle; and, consequently, the *Twelfth Aeneid* cost me double the time of the *First* and *Second*. What had become of me, if Virgil had tax'd me with another book? I had certainly been reduc'd to pay the public in hammer'd money, for want of mill'd; that is, in the same old words which I had us'd before; and the receivers must have been forc'd to have taken anything, where there was so little to be had.

Besides this difficulty (with which I have struggled, and made a shift to pass it over) there is one remaining, which is insuperable to all translators. We are bound to our author's sense, tho' with the latitudes already mention'd; for I think it not so sacred, as that one *iota* must not be added or diminish'd, on pain of an *anathema*. But slaves we are, and labor on another's man plantation; we dress the vineyard, but the wine is the owner's: if the soil be sometimes barren, then we are sure of being scourg'd; if it be fruitful, and our care succeeds, we are not thank'd; for the proud reader will only say the poor drudge has done his duty. But this is nothing to what follows; for, being oblig'd to make his sense intelligible, we are forc'd to untune our own verses, that we may give his meaning to the reader. He who invents is master of his thoughts and words; he can turn and vary them as he pleases, till he renders them harmonious. But the wretched translator has no such privilege; for, being tied to the thoughts, he must make what music he can in the expression; and for this reason it cannot always be so sweet as that of the original . . .

Lay by Virgil, I beseech your Lordship, and all my better sort of judges, when you take up my version; and it will appear a passable beauty when the original Muse is absent. But, like Spenser's false Florimel made of snow, it melts and vanishes when the true one comes in sight. I will not excuse, but justify myself for one pretended crime, with which I am liable to be charg'd by false critics, not only in this translation, but in many of my original poems—that I Latinize too much. 'Tis true that, when I find an English word significant and sounding, I neither borrow from the Latin or any other language; but, when I want at home, I must seek abroad.

If sounding words are not of our growth and manufacture, who shall hinder me to import them from a foreign country? I carry not out the treasure of the nation, which is never to return; but what I bring from Italy, I spend in England: here it remains, and here it circulates; for, if the coin be good, it will pass from one hand to another. I trade both with the living and the dead, for the enrichment of our native language. We have enough in

England to supply our necessity; but, if we will have things of magnificence and splendor, we must get them by commerce. Poetry requires ornament; and that is not to be had from our old Teuton monosyllables: therefore, if I find any elegant word in a classic author, I propose it to be naturaliz'd, by using it myself; and, if the public approves of it, the bill passes. But every man cannot distinguish betwixt pedantry and poetry: every man, therefore, is not fit to innovate. Upon the whole matter, a poet must first be certain that the word he would introduce is beautiful in the Latin; and is to consider, in the next place, whether it will agree with the English idiom. After this, he ought to take the opinion of judicious friends, such as are learned in both languages; and, lastly, since no man is infallible, let him use this license very sparingly; for, if too many foreign words are pour'd in upon us, it looks as if they were design'd not to assist the natives, but to conquer them.

Alexander Pope: Preface to *The Iliad* (1715)

. . . It is the first grand duty of an interpreter to give his author entire and unmaimed; and for the rest, the diction and versification only are his proper province; since these must be his own, but the others he is to take as he finds them.

It should then be considered what methods may afford some equivalent in our language for the graces of these in the Greek. It is certain no literal translation can be just to an excellent original in a superior language: but it is a great mistake to imagine (as many have done) that a rash paraphrase can make amends for this general defect: which is no less in danger to lose the spirit of an ancient, by deviating into the modern manners of expression. If there be sometimes a darkness, there is often a light in antiquity, which nothing better preserves then a version almost literal. I know no liberties one ought to take, but those which are necessary for transfusing the spirit of the original, and supporting the poetical style of the translation: and I will venture to say there have not been more men misled in former times by a servile dull adherence to the letter, than have been deluded in ours by a chimerical insolent hope of raising and improving their author. It is not to be doubted that the *fire* of the poem is what a translator should principally regard, as it is most likely to expire in his managing: however, it is his safest way to be content with preserving this to his utmost in the whole, without endeavouring to be more than he finds his author is, in any particular place. It is a great secret in writing to know when to be plain, and when poetical and figurative; and it is what Homer will teach us, if we will but follow modestly in his footsteps.

SAMUEL JOHNSON: *Lives of the English Poets,* 'Dryden' (1779)

The affluence and comprehension of our language is very illustriously displayed in our poetical translations of Ancient Writers; a work which the French seem to relinquish in despair, and which we were long unable to perform with dexterity. Ben Jonson thought it necessary to copy Horace almost word by word; Feltham, his contemporary and adversary, considers it as indispensably requisite in a translation to give line for line. It is said that Sandys, whom Dryden calls the best versifier of the last age, has struggled hard to comprise every book of his English Metamorphoses in the same number of verses with the original. Holyday had nothing in view but to shew that he understood his author, with so little regard to the grandeur of his diction, or the volubility of his numbers, that his metres can hardly be called verses; they cannot be read without reluctance, nor will the labour always be rewarded by understanding them. Cowley saw that such *copyers* were a *servile race;* he asserted his liberty, and spread his wings so boldly that he left his authors. It was reserved for Dryden to fix the limits of poetical liberty, and give us just rules and examples of translation.

When languages are formed upon different principles, it is impossible that the same modes of expression should always be elegant in both. While they run on together, the closest translation may be considered as the best; but when they divaricate, each must take its natural course. Where correspondence cannot be obtained, it is necessary to be content with something equivalent. *Translation therefore,* says Dryden, *is not so loose as paraphrase, nor so close as metaphrase.*

All polished languages have different styles; the concise, the diffuse, the lofty, and the humble. In the proper choice of style consists the resemblance which Dryden principally exacts from the translator. He is to exhibit his author's thoughts in such a dress of diction as the author would have given them, had his language been English: rugged magnificence is not to be softened: hyperbolical ostentation is not to be repressed, nor sententious affectation to have its points blunted. A translator is to be like his author: it is not his business to excel him.

The reasonableness of these rules seems sufficient for their vindication; and the effects produced by observing them were so happy, that I know not whether they were ever opposed but by Sir Edward Sherburne, a man whose learning was greater than his powers of poetry; and who, being better qualified to give the meaning than the spirit of Seneca, has introduced his version of three tragedies by a defence of close translation. The authority of Horace, which the new translators cited in defence of their practice, he has, by a judicious explanation, taken fairly from them; but reason wants not Horace to support it.